MW01174313

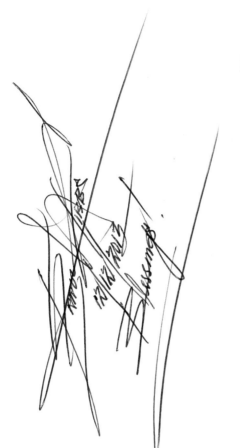

THOUGHTS TO ENLIGHTEN AND EMPOWER THE MIND

2001 QUESTIONS AND PHILOSOPHICAL THOUGHTS TO INSPIRE, ENLIGHTEN, AND EMPOWER OUR WORLD TO LIMITLESS HEIGHTS

THOUGHTS TO ENLIGHTEN AND EMPOWER THE MIND

2001 QUESTIONS AND PHILOSOPHICAL THOUGHTS TO INSPIRE, ENLIGHTEN, AND EMPOWER OUR WORLD TO LIMITLESS HEIGHTS

ERROL A. GIBBS
PHILIP A. GREY

authorHOUSE®

AuthorHouse™
1663 Liberty Drive
Suite 200
Bloomington, IN 47403
www.authorhouse.com
Phone: 1–800–839–8640

First published by AuthorHouse 12-23-2011

ISBN: 978-1-4567-4071-9 (sc)
ISBN: 978-1-4567-4070-2 (hc)
ISBN: 978-1-4567-4072-6 (e)

Library of Congress Control Number 2011902131

Printed in the United States of America

This book is printed on acid-free paper.

Cover design by: www.eCoverMakers.com
Edited by: www.catedit.com
Genre: Christianity, Religion/Inspiration/Enlightenment/Empowerment/
Philosophy (General)

We trust that you will read this book in its entirety, and send us your comments. Whether you live in the Occident or in the Orient, whether you are rich or poor, academic or lay person, religious or irreligious, we invite you to join us in making new history, not just for ourselves, but for future generations, as well.

Email: info@ffhdwritersinc.com
Website: www.ffhdwritersinc.com

DEDICATION

To our wives, Marjorie and Sandra: you were extraordinarily patient as we embarked on this journey that seemed never-ending. You have enabled us to overcome many challenges, as we have contemplated these *Thoughts to Enlighten and Empower the Mind.* Your vision and thoughtfulness have been our source of motivation in preparing this chronology of 2001 questions and philosophical thoughts. With gratitude, we now reveal them to our readers in the hope that they will cultivate a mind imbued with positive thoughts, peacefulness, and wholesome living.

—Errol and Philip

CONTENTS

FOUNDATION 3: SOCIAL FOUNDATION

FOUNDATION 4: INTELLECTUAL FOUNDATION

FOUNDATION 5: PHYSICAL FOUNDATION

APPENDIXES:

FOREWORD

We formulated *Thoughts to Enlighten and Empower the Mind* to present an alternate perspective from which to engage in discussion of human development in the modern era. This convenient text is a witness to the broad discourse in our research and discussion in the five–part text *Five Foundations of Human Development* (FFHD), and the companion text *Five Preeminent Foundations*. The reader understands through *"Reading by versus"* the basic premise of the text, which postulates that there is hope for a better world when we endeavor to enlighten, and empower our mind through a revolution of our thoughts. Thoughts inspire *feelings*, feelings inspire *actions*, and actions can have negative or positive ramifications.

It is a chronological listing of 2001 selected verses from FFHD; therefore it follows the same philosophical theme, with minor variations. However, excluded from this text are other vital elements of FFHD such as; over 1000 references to Biblical Scripture verses from the King James Version (KJV); the New King James Version (NKJV); and the New International Version (NIV); an extensive list of 47 graphics (37 figures (original) and 8 tables), cross–referenced over 250 times throughout the five foundations; approximately 35 tabular listings; approx. 115 footnotes and extensive citations by some of the world's prolific writers; and approximately 500 words research index.

We strive to present a balanced perspective informed by Western Christian thoughts, foundations, faith, and beliefs. We recognize and respect the works of other researchers based upon their religious, social, cultural, academic training, qualifications, observations, and life experiences. Likewise, we strive to render the utmost respect for the dignity, rights, difference opinions and experiential knowledge of every individual, regardless of circumstances or station in life. We are eternally gratified by people throughout the world who have journeyed with us, and have chosen to devote their lives to the pursuit of humane, peaceful and fulfilling lives, not just for themselves, but for all humanity as well.

We urge the reader not to dismiss these thoughts as "mere idealism." The unquenchable light of idealism lives within and underpins our hope for survival in the twenty–first century and in the new millennium. Whether the model is a rural farming village or the worldwide global village, the foundation of hope is crumbling. The scientist, the doctor, the lawyer, the engineer, the professor, the politician, the philosopher, and the ordinary person, feel a sense of hope and hopelessness. We must *all* engage in the global struggle to create a better world. This struggle requires a new *blueprint of hope* for our survival informed by these 2001 questions and philosophical thoughts.

PREFACE

Many great religious and philosophical thinkers, past and present have concluded that thoughts transform, and our innermost thoughts transcend out outwardly actions or reactions. Where do thoughts come from and why it is essential to think positive thoughts?" Thoughts are birthed in the mental realm and manifest in the physical realm. Our thoughts are the sum total of our experiences and circumstances, including, religious, racial, cultural, social, and economic. Our deeply contemplated thoughts determine our hopes dreams and aspirations. They motivate us to act or react to circumstances spontaneously or with pre –meditation.

Thoughts are the gatekeepers of the mind. Positive thoughts open gates for positive actions to blossom, conversely, negative thoughts opens gates for negative actions to blossom. Consequently, we have the capacity to direct our actions by our thoughts. The sum total of human knowledge teach that every action begins with a thought, and behind every thought there is a thinking being, and no physical action, reaction, or creation can precede the thought or the thinker. Neither can an action or object of creation come into being without a thinker?

It is for this reason that we believe that we (human beings) are capable of creating a better world, and making new history when we revolutionize the way we think. We present many of the critical enquires of our modern era in this anthology of revolutionary thoughts taken from our main body of work: *Five Foundations of Human Development* (FFHD) (Spiritual, Moral, Social, Intellectual, and Physical), and the companion text, *Five Preeminent Foundations*. These selected verses challenge conventional thinking regarding issues that have a significant impact on human existence. Some of these issues include, but are not limited to: Christianity, religion, hope, charity, peace, humility, leadership, authority, race, self–esteem, intelligence, education, militarism, capitalism, knowledge, capability, and health.

We strive to present a revolutionary response to problems and solution perspectives to some of the challenges of our modern era. Though our message relies extensively on references to Biblical Scripture, it is not a work exclusively for Christians. Our discourse recognizes the message of other world religions, researches, and revolutionaries in regard to their approach to solutions to the myriad of problems that confront us in the global village. We believe that it is only through a new and revolutionary way of thinking about human life, as one indivisible whole, with the need for unanimity, liberty, peace and justice we can revolutionize our mind, our sphere of influence and our world.

ACKNOWLEDGEMENTS

Note on historic biblical dates: Some historic Biblical dates are generally taken from the New King James Version. Copyright © 1982 by Thomas Nelson, Inc., Used by permission. All rights reserved. Some dates are taken from Reese, Edward; The Reese Chronological Bible, (King James Version) Minneapolis, Minnesota: Bethany House, 1977 Frank R. Klassen, Dating System, 1975. All dates are designated as approximate (approx.), due to variations in dates derived at by various other Biblical writings.

Special Acknowledgments and Citations

We acknowledge and express eternal gratitude to those who have granted us permission to include the copyrighted materials that we have cited in footnotes and in other citation formats. We are also thankful to other great writers (whom we have cited) of yesteryear and of the present, for their philosophical roadmaps to guide us in this modern age. Our work is only a minor contribution to the vast body of work penned by these notable philosophical giants. We stand on their shoulders as we take a 'panoramic view' of the twenty–first century and of the new millennium with hope and optimism for the future of our world.

We also thank family and friends who have accompanied us at various stages of this remarkable journey in our boundless search for higher knowledge, wisdom, and understanding of God; your influence has enabled the writing of *Thoughts to Enlighten and Empower the Mind.* Your academic insights, experiential knowledge, critiques, and comments have allowed us to present a message of hope and optimism. This book is a chronology of 2001 questions and philosophical thoughts taken from *Five Foundations of Human Development* (FFHD). It is a chronicle of our enduring faith, belief, and practice, nurtured by our transformation and progression from the thoughts of yesteryear to the enlightened thoughts of today. The message lives in us, and hope preserves.

THOUGHTS TO ENLIGHTEN AND EMPOWER THE MIND

2001 QUESTIONS AND PHILOSOPHICAL THOUGHTS TO INSPIRE, ENLIGHTEN, AND EMPOWER OUR WORLD TO LIMITLESS HEIGHTS

PART 1 FIVE PREEMINENT FOUNDATIONS

FOUNDATION 1: WHO IS GOD?
FOUNDATION 2: WHO IS JESUS CHRIST?
FOUNDATION 3: WHAT IS THE CHURCH?
FOUNDATION 4: WHAT IS THE HOLY BIBLE?
FOUNDATION 5: WHO IS A CHRISTIAN?

PREEMINENT FOUNDATION 1
—WHO IS GOD?

"God is spirit, and his worshipers must worship in spirit and in truth" John 4:24 (NIV). "God is our refuge and strength, an ever-present help in trouble" Psalm 46:1 (NIV). "God reigns over the nations; God is seated on his holy throne. The nobles and nations assemble as the people of God of Abraham, for the kings of the earth belong to God; he is greatly exalted."

Psalm 47:8-9 (NIV)

1) **Who is God?** Saint John (circa CE 27) tells us: "God is Spirit, and those who worship Him must worship in spirit and truth" (John 4:24 NKJV). God is not merely a Spirit; He is an infinite Spirit.

2) We can feel His spiritual presence within our spirit, but we do not know how to describe God in human terms, because His existence has no parallel in our physical existence.

3) There are countless definitions of God, just as there are countless definitions of religions and countless manifestations of God's presence.

4) To some, God is a mystery which continues to perplex the human intellect in our modern era. To the astute, God is an intellectual probability.

5) In defining God, it is essential to acknowledge God who has proven His mighty works, which He has chronicled in the inspired writings of the Holy Scriptures.

6) Biblical history confirms that nations which have violated the laws of God have suffered grave consequences, and failed to fulfill their promise (2 Chronicles 7:19-22).

7) God sacrificed the life of His Son Jesus Christ as the perfect example of suffering for righteousness to be the perfect example for humanity.

8) God has demonstrated His unique personal attributes through the life of His Son Jesus Christ, who manifested the heart of God by His love, joy, peace, patience (longsuffering), kindness, goodness, faithfulness, gentleness and self-control (Galatians 5:22).

9) The God of the Holy Bible is knowable. His Word transcends Christianity, which is a way of life, embodied in a corporate society or fellowship, centered on the worship of God.

10) God has revealed His presence to the world through His Son Jesus Christ of Nazareth, who lived as a humble human being for about thirty–three years in Palestine.

11) Jesus Christ's presence on earth also accentuated the wondrous works of God, through the Holy Spirit and thirty–seven miraculous acts penned by the writers of the synoptic gospels.

12) The Holy Spirit has character, a mind, and emotions. The Holy Spirit teaches. The Apostle Paul writing to the Corinthians counsels: "These things that we also speak, not in words which man's wisdom teaches but which the Holy Spirit teaches, comparing spiritual things with spiritual" (1 Corinthians 2:13 NKJV).

13) Through the revelation of the life and teachings of Jesus Christ, we are enlightened in our understanding of the Triune God (Reference: *Five Foundations of Human Development* (FFHD) —Figure 1: The Triune God (Godhead).

14) We should be no less mindful in the twenty–first century of God speaking to us through His Son Jesus Christ, who provides His followers access to His grace and manifestation through the Holy Spirit.

15) The first imperative of human existence is the realization of God's great gifts to humanity. His immutable law governs all life, and the law that governs all life is God.

16) God is omnipotent (all powerful), omnipresent (everywhere) and omniscient (all knowing). (Reference: *Five Foundations of Human Development* (FFHD) —Figure 3: The Greatness of God).

17) Can we live without a Godhead, Creator, and absolute authority of the universe that can bind all human civilization into a harmonious whole? Absolutely not!

18) God in His infinite wisdom gave the world Ten Commandments as the ultimate moral guide for humanity. The first four Commandments are directly concerned with religious belief and worship.

19) The spiritual presence of God in the world enables us to overcome our inclination to stray from His path. It helps us to understand and manage the conditions that cause hopelessness.

20) The search for God and the meaning of our existence has both defined and perplexed every civilization, from the earliest recorded nations to our modern society.

21) Our search for fulfillment in life is a search for our Spiritual connection with God through the Holy Spirit, and not a quest for fame, or fortune, or the other fleeting things which do not incorporate or further His purpose.

22) Diligent search for God means exercising conscious effort to find His purpose for our existence.

23) Our search is continual, and will always be continual, because we can never attain the fullness of God's purpose in this mortal body.

24) The turbulent twenty–first century presents the greatest challenge to our search, as humanity wanders farther away from our core religious beliefs.

25) God proves Himself to us every moment of our existence (Romans 1:20 NIV). His divine creation should inspire spiritual awareness in us.

26) The complexity and perfect balance of God's planetary system should be a constant reminder that God has revealed himself to us in a personal way on planet Earth.

27) The unanswered questions of the universe manifest God's creative power, but it is only His revelation and spiritual guidance that can ultimately aid us in our attempts to comprehend His creation.

28) Diverse religious beliefs have been present at every level of human civilization and most religions have a God or god that they worship.

29) Observe the challenges of our times. Many cry out to God to intervene and stop the decline of civilization. God *can* intervene, but He has instructed us in the solution to our problems.

30) Many profess the presence of God in their lives, yet there is a compulsion and an inherent weakness within us that separates us from His reservoir of spiritual power.

31) The most profound challenge in our lives is the exercise of the will, the conscious act of obedience or disobedience to God (Romans 12:2).

32) Without God's enlightenment, we sub consciously and even consciously resist His Spiritual manifestation and act in violation to His moral laws.

33) The natural mind of human beings is enmity to God (Romans 8:7–8), but this enmity is generally unintentional. An unrealized and passive hostility lives within our soul and subconscious mind.

34) The carnal mind sets up a barrier which blocks the source of God's power that enables us to do according to His will. When our will is not in conformity to God's will, we give into the tendency to do wrong to others and to ourselves.

35) Spiritual discernment allows us to comprehend human suffering and to have empathy for the suffering we cause or permit.

36) Spiritual discernment allow us to better understand and manage the circumstances of our birth, color, race, culture, family, ancestors, and other social and economic conditions, that previously had mastery over us.

37) God allows us to exercise free will and moral judgment (ethics, fairness, honesty and integrity), to choose to do according to His will, and experience His manifold blessings.

38) God promises us both spiritual and material rewards for our obedience. Our hope lies in God's manifold promises which He has kept from the beginning of the ages.

39) God reinstituted His "admonishment with promise" to children in the Old and New Testaments. "Honor your father and your mother, as the LORD your God has commanded you, so that you may live long and that it may go well with you in the land the LORD your God is giving you" (Deuteronomy 5:16 NIV) (Ephesians 6:1–3 NIV).

40) Whether we are rich or poor, strong or weak, educated or uneducated, and regardless of color, race, language, culture, or religion, God is just and merciful.

41) God's command is that we accept His grace and mercy and His offer of forgiveness with humility and contrition. This is His ultimate gift to humanity, but oftentimes we fail to comprehend His nature, His assurance of forgiveness, His love, and His promise of everlasting life (John 3:16).

42) The synoptic Gospel writer Matthew tells us that God promises to fulfill all of our needs when we seek Him and His righteousness as a first imperative of our existence.

43) God's promises require a change in the human condition and behavior. Every law, every command, every commandment, every statute, every covenant, every promise made in the Old and New Testaments calls us to hear, learn, observe, do, obey, seek, or humble ourselves before God.

44) The Proverbs of Solomon state: "When a man's *ways* are pleasing to the LORD, He makes even his enemies live at peace with him" (Proverbs 16:7 NIV). Is there a greater promise in these modern times for alleviating fear of man?

PREEMINENT FOUNDATION 2
—WHO IS JESUS CHRIST?

"He is the image of the invisible God, the firstborn over all creation. For by him all things were created: things in heaven and on earth, visible and invisible, whether thrones or powers or rulers or authorities; all things were created by him and for him. He is before all things, and in him all things hold together. And he is the head of the body, the church; he is the beginning and the firstborn from among the dead, so that in everything he might have the supremacy."

Colossians 1:15–18 (NIV)

45) **Who is Jesus Christ of Nazareth?** Was He God in the flesh or was He just a man? Jesus Christ is the Son of God and is God incarnate, born of the Virgin Mary.

46) Jesus (Y'shua, in Hebrew) means Jehovah is salvation. Christ (Christos, in Greek) means God's chosen one (or Mashiach, in Hebrew).

47) The synoptic gospel writers, Matthew and Luke state explicitly and unmistakably that Jesus came into the world through the miraculous work of God.

48) The Gospel teaches that Jesus Christ was conceived by the Holy Spirit and born of the Virgin Mary.

49) The writers of the synoptic gospels (Matthew, Mark and Luke) depict Jesus not as a hero of the times, but as a person of great humility, compassion, patience, sorrow, and hope for humanity.

50) The Old Testament (OT) prophecies proclaimed the coming of Jesus Christ. They spoke of His birth, life, ministry and events surrounding His life and death before He was born.

51) Jesus taught the simple gospel, and used simple reasoning and parables, relating His messages to everyday life to appeal to the hearts and minds of those to whom He spoke.

52) Jesus Christ did not carry with him the more mundane signals of authority – wealth, property, title or office. He neither commanded an army nor ruled any great empire.

53) Within three and one-half years of His ministry, Jesus left an indelible impression on the world that has had a transforming effect down through the ages to our present generation.

54) Jesus Christ's purpose for coming to earth was to fulfill God's ultimate purpose of salvation for us.

55) Jesus, without the formal education of the intellectual leaders of his era, surprised them with the depth of His wisdom and the breadth of His knowledge.

56) The needs of those who gathered together with Christ were paramount; He directed His gifts to the suffering of the common people rather than to gaining recognition on his own account.

57) The life and death of Jesus, and the teachings attributed to Him, have left a marked influence on the course of human history. His life and death continue to have an impact on our modern world.

58) Jesus' fundamental message was one of forgiveness and love for humanity. The rulers of His day knew that there was something uncommon about Him.

59) Jesus required personal sacrifice of His followers. He never promised them any material wealth or comfort to motivate them to give up everything to follow Him.

60) Jesus Christ's miraculous works, His compassion and empathy for the poor and the dispossessed, and His life sacrifice for humanity made Him the most important figure to have appeared in the history of the world.

61) In modern times, hundreds of millions of Christians on many continents profess belief in Jesus Christ, and follow His teachings.

62) Jesus has been an unfathomable figure throughout history. He exalted the poor, the blind, the weak and the shunned.

63) Our twenty-first century can be a century of hope for humanity, anchored upon the foundation of the two great commandments that can inspire and inform tens of thousands of human laws.

64) Christ's life on earth exemplified the two great commandments. In addition to being commandments from God, they are traditional Jewish teachings that Jesus affirmed and reinforced in the New Testament (NT).

65) Jesus lived a life completely yielded to God, a life of prayer and acknowledgment of God. His good works and absolute devotion to the will of God characterized his life.

66) The disciples were to emulate Jesus' devotion to the will of God in order to continue in Jesus' footsteps, if they were to take their place in God's plan to redeem the world.

67) Jesus prayed for His Father's Spiritual protection for His disciples, while they were in the world, because they had his great commission to fulfill.

68) Jesus prayed for all believers who would follow His teachings. He petitioned His Father in Heaven for the unity of all believers.

69) Jesus prayed that His disciples would glorify His Father in heaven, and that His Father would bestow His love upon them.

70) Followers of Jesus Christ can take comfort knowing that, 2000 years ago, Jesus recognized the potential growth of the Christian Church and its challenges down through the ages.

71) Christ's petition to His Father echoes His desire for unity among his followers. Christians should seek for ecumenical unity as well as unity within families, cultures, communities, nations and other facets of human relations.

72) Jesus' message was of love and hope, yet the secular authorities of the day arrested Jesus and put Him on trial. This Jewish teacher whose life, death and resurrection were reported by the evangelists is the basis of the Christian message of salvation.

73) Jesus not only assigned to His followers the responsibility of making disciples of people of all the nations, He promised to be with them always, to the end of the age (Matthew 28:20).

74) Jesus Christ also knew that after His departure from this earth we would be in need of a comforter (the "Holy Spirit"). He knew there would be times of difficulty in the lives of many that would require God's divine intervention through His Holy Spirit.

75) God, through His Son Jesus Christ, not only gave us access to the Holy Spirit for the manifestation of His truths, He empowered us.

76) The power derived from the Holy Spirit is for service, and to effectively carry out the Great Commission (Matthew 28:18–20).

77) The disciples dedicated their lives to Christ's purpose when it was revealed, and He gave them the Great Commission (Matthew 28:18–

20) (Reference: *Five Foundations of Human Development* (FFHD) — Figure 6: Jesus' Great Commission, His two Great Commandments, and His Great Reward).

78) Without the Holy Spirit, truth would be only what we are able to discern for ourselves, which is conditional upon human experience and limited by our own, mortal frame of reference.

79) Humanity can heal the pain and suffering that it inflicts upon itself by the simple application of the message Jesus gave to His disciples during His life on earth.

80) Jesus admonishes us to love our neighbor as ourselves. Jesus presented a message of love for one another as His central message to His followers.

81) The word neighbor is particularly important in Jesus' sermons, because Jesus refers to all of humanity.

82) Jesus helped His disciples to focus on a new worldview of love for one's neighbor. Essentially, this love for neighbor is critical for our survival, because it is the central message of peace.

83) Neighborly love can only come from faith and trust in God, and adherence to the message of His Son Jesus Christ.

84) Jesus Christ admonishes His followers in this New Testament (NT) message to live with the knowledge of His second coming. It is our hope of glory.

PREEMINENT FOUNDATION 3
—WHAT IS THE CHURCH?

"And I tell you that you are Peter, and on this rock I will build my church, and the gates of Hades will not overcome it" Matthew 16:18 (NIV). "[B]uilt on the foundation of the apostles and prophets, with Christ Jesus himself as chief cornerstone. In him the whole building is joined together and rises to become a holy temple in the Lord. And in him you too are being built together."

Ephesians 2:19–22 (NIV)

85) What is the Church? Is the Church a building set apart or consecrated for public worship, especially one of Christian worship?

86) When an individual thinks of a church, generally he or she thinks of a building or a place of worship. Two of the most famous and beautiful church structures in the world are the St. Peter's Basilica (built 1506–1626) and *Cathédrale Notre–Dame de Paris* (construction 1163–1345).

87) Each church era had its representative building generically called the church. The use of the word *church* in the Holy Bible, however, has a different meaning to believers.

88) The word *church* can be used to distinguish a local church or group of local churches, distinguished by name or groups of believers that follow the teachings of Jesus Christ.

89) The Church of the New Testament (NT) represents the Christian believers, people of God, followers of Christ who regularly congregate to worship God.

90) Throughout religious history and in our modern era, we have had a tendency to view each assembly, groups of ekklesia (Churches) or denominations as the Church or Churches. The Greek word ekklesia is translated as Church, or Churches in its plural form, ekklesiai.

91) The word *church* evokes the meaning of an assembly of Christians called out to a meeting or service in the name of Jesus Christ.

(Reference: *Five Foundations of Human Development* (FFHD) —Figure 7: The Church Invisible and Invisible with Jesus Christ as the Head).

92) In our present day, the word *church* may also refer to a denomination or para–church group. The important question is: What constitutes the church?

93) The church is a living entity that incorporates the immeasurable power of the Holy Spirit's sacrificial power, crucifixion power, resurrection power, transformation power, sanctification power, purification power, and unification power.

94) The church is a body which comprises believers spiritually bonded together by the blood of Jesus Christ. The Church in its perfect form is a flourishing union of its members with Christ as the head of the body.

95) Jesus Christ referred to the church in its universal context. Jesus Christ built His church to manifest His love, His peace, His hope, His mercy, His righteousness, and the triune unity: the unity among the Father, the Son, and the Holy Spirit.

96) Jesus Christ of Nazareth ushered in a new phase in God's plan for human salvation. This phase involves God's working through people ("the Church") who are transformed by the Holy Spirit.

97) The Church is a body ("invisible" and "visible") which comprises believers, spiritually bonded together by the blood of Jesus Christ. The *invisible* church is the body of true believers united by their living faith in Christ. The *visible* church consists of local congregations of faithful believers and overcomers (Revelation 2:11, 17, 26).

98) The work of the Church is not to condemn, but to bring light to the world. Jesus Christ prepared His disciples for three and one half years to be His messengers, and to be the foundation of the Church.

99) The church is a spiritual fellowship (*Koinonia* in Greek). The purpose of this fellowship is to demonstrate observable love and care for members of the body as well as others.

100) It is essential to understand that we make up both the invisible church, through spiritual connection with its Founder, Jesus Christ and the physical church, through the assembly of local believers.

101) The many challenges that face the Church today call into question the need for Christians to contemplate where we stand in relation to the oneness of the gospel of Jesus Christ.

102) The need for ecumenical understanding; and more importantly ecumenism has never been more paramount in our past history.

103) The twenty-first century church exists in the midst of great changes that are impacting the nature of our survival in the modern world.

104) The church has access to modern technological tools to propagate the gospel of the kingdom of God throughout the world. The digital electronic age has positively impacted the mission of today's mega-churches.

105) Many churches, other religious organizations, and non-governmental organizations (NGOs) engage in the monumental task of responding to constant waves of disasters and casualties, both natural and man-made.

106) The question facing the modern Church is whether these responses by the Churches and NGOs are permanent solutions to human problems.

107) The world is at a critical juncture in history, when the church needs to be visible and effective and to speak with one unified voice (Ephesians 2:14; Romans 15:5-7).

108) Church teachings must of necessity take a lead role in the building of a nation's spiritual equity.

109) The Church should also form part of a more comprehensive strategic framework to address the root causes of human problems. Our transformation is essential in order to carry out God's work for the ultimate benefit of humanity.

110) God is calling the church to engage in a new kind of ministry – one that requires us to "put on the full armor of God" (Ephesians 6:10-18).

111) The church needs to be at the forefront of the battlefield with new battle plans for the twenty-first century, because the clear evidence is that we are losing the wars on poverty, hunger, homelessness, drug abuse, genocide, and oppression.

112) We need to revert to the creed given to us by God, and we must have absolute faith in the leadership and authority of His Son Jesus Christ.

113) The church, both the *invisible* and the *visible*, must lead the battle for human survival with the power of God's agap`e love as the rallying cry.

114) Only by working to create a government informed by God's law, complemented by human laws, can we begin to implement permanent solutions to human problems.

115) The acknowledgment of God's sovereign authority over world nations is the first step toward solving our problems. Solutions to our problems require personal accountability on the part of world citizens.

116) World religions should use the great moral power inherent in their religions to urge their citizens and world governments to find peaceful solutions to our problems.

117) The history of human enterprise is littered with casualties of carnal wars, but the church is an army engaged in spiritual warfare.

118) God glorifies in the good work of the Church; therefore, Church members should play a vital role in the development of societies and nations. This role goes far beyond being a witness for Jesus Christ, and God's Word should extend to every human endeavor.

119) The Church must help world leaders to comprehend that the "natural intelligence" that we rely upon, drawn from our vast storehouse of human knowledge, is insufficient to direct our path.

120) The challenge of the church centuries ago was for its survival, both religious and physical. Its passage to the modern world is paved with the blood of Christian martyrs (Hebrews 11:36–40).

121) Over the centuries, the church has survived the Middle Ages, the persecutions of the Roman Empire, persecutions of saints, and martyrdom.

122) The ruins of the ancient Roman Forum lie silent, a scene of crumbling decay where emperors once ruled a mighty empire. The ancient temples of Jupiter and Venus are relics of past glory.

123) Christians in the modern era ought to be thankful for the great Constantine I. Many Christians venerate him as the most important emperor of Late Antiquity.

124) Constantine's legalization and support of Christianity and his foundation of a "New Rome" at Byzantium rank among the most momentous decisions ever made by a European ruler.

125) There is a need for the church to establish a New Mission Critical Direction (NMCD) for individuals and nations that seek the greater meaning and purpose of its existence.

126) During the last several decades, there has been a resurgence of the Apostles' doctrine and the sharing of the gospel of Jesus Christ.

127) Current generations are much more questioning than past generations. They also seek answers that are relevant and go beyond a purely scriptural response.

128) Church adherents should strive daily for a greater understanding of the rapid changes (moral, social, political, intellectual, and economic) that are taking place in the world.

129) The needs of individuals, societies, and nations are changing, but the church seems to maintain models that are generally unchanged, as our fast-paced materially driven life threatens the spiritual purpose of our existence.

130) A manifestation of the Spirit of God and renewed portrayal of His love throughout the world must reinvigorate the modern Church.

131) If the Church is to help to heal the world, it should immediately engage in a New Mission Critical Direction (NMCD), which is essentially an invigoration of the old mission.

132) The efforts of the Church, both *visible* and *invisible* will also create greater opportunities for peaceful relations among individuals and nations.

133) The modern Church and other world religions should emerge with a New Mission Critical Direction (NMCD) among our great religious seminaries and educational institutions.

134) Our mission should involve actively *engaging* the intellectual capacities of all, including, our great scientists, politicians, doctors, nurses, legal experts, engineers, philosophers, teachers, and students in the battle for human survival in the twenty-first century.

135) The battle for souls, however, does not only take place in our places of worship. The great battleground is also the corporate

boardrooms of the world, the manufacturing plants, the universities, colleges, schools, stadiums, hospitals, and our homes.

136) Prayer is central to our mission and is complemented by a blueprint to guide us. We must pray without ceasing for God's restraining power (2 Thessalonians 2:3–8); God's enabling power (1 Corinthians 10:13); and God's preserving power (Psalm 121:3–8).

137) Adherents to Christianity and other world religions believe that prayer changes circumstances; hence we call for prayer during personal and national calamities.

138) The Old Testament (OT) is a chronology of praying, seeking, asking and petitioning God for His mercies, guidance, blessings and protection in times of great calamities.

139) We can make a significant difference in our modern world when we go beyond prayer as an act of obedience or appeasement to our Sovereign God and make prayer the life–blood of our every human endeavor.

140) For centuries the church has of necessity focused on missionary work among those who suffer harm as a result of natural and man–made calamities.

141) We must continue our traditional missionary efforts, but there is a need for an additional mission that requires a new blueprint for the mission of the Church.

142) The formidable effort by human beings to solve our problems, have been centered on the symptoms, rather than on the root causes of human problems, which lie in the human spirit.

143) Our twenty–first century has not ushered in international peace and harmony nor has it achieved universal social and economic equity. What can the church do?

144) The church can boldly proclaim the words of Jeremiah, one of Judah's greatest prophets, who advises: O Lord, I know the way of man is not in himself; *It is* not in man who walks to direct his own steps (Jeremiah 10:23).

145) Have we sufficiently (visibly) placed our Christian scientists, engineers, politicians, psychologists, sociologists, doctors, lawyers, geologists, botanists, business professionals and other academics at the forefront of our religious and humanitarian struggles?

146) Fields of applied science and technology do not pose a threat to the sovereignty of the church. Discussions regarding the state of our world from this perspective ought to be critical issues for church dialogue.

147) Habitually, we lament the estrangement of our youth from religion and religious virtues. Some would assert that youth culture has negative effects and that we are 'losing our youths.'

148) We need to engage our youths as we develop "Integrity 500" institutions, organizations, and corporations where they will work.

149) There is much more to the existence of the modern church than is presently evident. Regardless of how one views the church in the modern world, it will continue to be one of the most influential institutions we have. Our greatest challenge should be to maintain its viability as a most powerful God–ordained institution.

150) We call upon the greatest minds to engineer solutions to our material problems. It would be spiritual neglect if we fail to call upon God's Spiritual intelligence to complement human intelligence to aid us in manifesting the spiritual purpose of our existence and to please Him, our Creator.

"But you, Daniel, close up and seal the words of the scroll until the time of the end. Many will go here and there to increase knowledge" Daniel 12:4 (NIV). "Behold I am coming soon! Blessed is he who keeps the words of the prophecy in this book. I, John, am the one who heard and saw these things. And when I had heard and seen them, I fell down to worship at the feet of the angel."

Revelation 22:7–8 (NIV)

151) **What is the Holy Bible?** The Holy Bible is the ultimate source of God's knowledge. It is the most extensively published and distributed book in history.

152) The Holy Bible is God's word. It has survived countless assaults down through the centuries, yet its power and influence in the world have been unfailing.

153) Approximately 83 million Bibles are distributed globally per year (*Gordon–Conwell Theological Seminary*) (2009). It is a book for the new adoption in Christ and for scholarly study. The Bible comes from the Greek word *biblos* (or *biblion*).

154) The main division of the Bible is between the Old Testament (OT) (Law, History, Poetry, and Prophecy), and the New Testament (NT) (Gospels, Acts, Epistles, and Revelation). The Bible is the Christian guide to the practice of Holiness.

155) The two Testaments complement each other. The Old Testament (OT) speaks to the various laws and covenants that God made with Moses (Wilderness Wandering Law Given 1446 B.C), and is about God dealing with man.

156) The New Testament (NT) speaks of grace and mercy through Jesus Christ the Son of God. The Bible also speaks to the church (followers of Christ), and to Christians.

157) The Bible is more than a seminary or scholarly study; it is a practical book for daily application and living. The Holy Bible is

God's Word - a gift of knowledge and revelation to humanity to guide us to all spiritual truths.

158) The Bible contains truths that enlighten, empower, and liberate us from our morbid fears. It is a collection of 66 Books, written by 40 authors over a period of approximately 1600 years.

159) Various non-Christian religions also have their sacred writings, such as the Torah, God's Word transcribed by Moses; these are the first five books of the Bible. Additionally, the Jewish Bible is essentially what is known as the Old Testament (OT).

160) No study of the Holy Bible can be effective without reference to both Old and New Testaments writings.

161) This sacred literature of the Jewish people has had a great effect on religions which came afterwards, notably Christianity and Islam.

162) God's Word in the Holy Bible brings a perspective to humanity that helps us to understand the spiritual nature of our existence, and the temporary nature of our present sufferings.

163) The Holy Bible is a book with a worldview that can provide the foundation for spiritual stability, and peace and security in our modern age of cynicism and uncertainty.

164) The Holy Bible considers every aspect of our Spiritual, moral, social, intellectual, and physical lives. It is concerned with competition in business, industry, and even athletics (2 Timothy 2:5).

165) The Holy Bible considers such practical matters as fairness in employment practices, equitable distribution of wealth and universal social justice.

166) God in His infinite wisdom instructed the inspired writers to pen a book that all who seek His divine knowledge would understand.

167) Every human being has access to God's divine knowledge through the words of the Holy Bible.

168) The Bible outlines the providential promises of God as a reward for those who live holy, faithful and righteous lives. Likewise, it gives warning of our self—condemnation as a result of disobedience to God's will.

15 BIBLICAL PERSPECTIVES
—PERSPECTIVE 1: A BOOK OF ABSOLUTES

169)   The Holy Bible establishes foundational principles essential to the betterment of society, nations, and the world. It guides us along paths of absolutes through a belief system that requires us to choose in whom or what we believe.

—PERSPECTIVE 2: A BOOK OF LIFE

170)   The Holy Bible contains life–saving prescriptions for a world that is beset with spiritual, moral, social, intellectual, and physical challenges. It gives life to those who meditate on the Word of God and who practice the principles taught by His Son Jesus Christ.

—PERSPECTIVE 3: A BOOK OF HOPE

171)   The Holy Bible provides us with hope for a better world. When many have sunk into the valley of deep despair, the Bible's powerful words reach down into the depths of the souls of human beings and provide a hope that surpasses the false hope of our material achievements.

—PERSPECTIVE 4: A BOOK OF LIGHT

172)   The Holy Bible is light for a world filled with ever–present darkness. The written Word illuminates the path for human beings as some blindly stumble through the dark corridors of fear and uncertainty.

—PERSPECTIVE 5: A BOOK OF KNOWLEDGE

173)   The Holy Bible instructs through Daniel, God's prophetic conduit to the Gentile and Jewish world, approximately two thousand years ago, "Knowledge will increase" (Daniel 12:4 NKJV) (circa 537 BCE). Our twenty–first century is testimony to Daniel's prophecy.

—PERSPECTIVE 6: A BOOK OF WISDOM

174)   The Holy Bible contains the rabbinical writings known to us as the Proverbs (*Sepher Hokhmah*, or "Book of Wisdom," in Hebrew). The wise King Solomon of Israel instructs: "The fear of the Lord *is* the beginning of wisdom, And the knowledge of the Holy One is understanding" (Proverbs 9:10 NKJV).

—PERSPECTIVE 7: A BOOK OF UNDERSTANDING

175)   The Holy Bible speaks to us, and we memorize the scripture verses, but committing words to memory does not constitute understanding. Understanding is the quality of having insight and good judgment in general matters, an insightful power of abstract thought and the ability to follow and implement an idea.

—PERSPECTIVE 8: A BOOK OF AUTHORITY

176)   The Holy Bible provides human beings with the perfect model of authority and leadership and gives specific instructions on how to exercise authority for the betterment of society, nations, and the world. "Jesus came and spoke to them, saying, 'All authority has been given to Me in heaven and on earth'" (Matthew 28:18–20 NKJV).

—PERSPECTIVE 9: A BOOK OF HUMILITY

177)   The Holy Bible teaches the virtues of humility and demonstrates the humility of the greatest human being to walk the earth in the person of Jesus Christ. It warns humanity of the evils of false pride, and of its destructive characteristics.

—PERSPECTIVE 10: A BOOK OF RESPONSIBILITY

178)   The Holy Bible contains the Apostle Paul's greatest work, in his 13 Epistles to the Romans. His writings establish standards of responsibility as the foundation for better "vertical relationships" with God (the Father) and His Son Jesus Christ, and better "horizontal relationships" with governing authorities and our neighbor.

—PERSPECTIVE 11: A BOOK OF PEACE

179)   The Holy Bible demonstrates the way of peace, and introduces us to our Peacemaker (Jesus Christ), yet we do not know the way of peace. After six thousand years of recorded history, and Jesus Christ's message of peace two thousand years ago, and the messages of other great prophets, we still grapple with the evils of war in our twenty-first century.

—PERSPECTIVE 12: A BOOK OF SPIRITUAL VALUES

180)   The Holy Bible provides its readers with a profound outlook on life and a set of spiritual values that brings human beings into spiritual union with each other. The Holy Bible counsels us that to

bear one another's burdens is an act of spiritual responsibility and is a portrayal of the "fruit of the Spirit" (Galatians 5:22).

—PERSPECTIVE 13: A BOOK OF SCIENTIFIC INSIGHTS

181) The Holy Bible is a book of scientific insights. The Bible provides guidance to human beings in every facet of human endeavor, including our scientific endeavors. The Bible makes known truths that science has confirmed empirically.

—PERSPECTIVE 14: A BOOK OF SACRED WRITINGS

182) Adherents of the Christian faith consider the Bible as a complete collection of books relevant to their faith. This collection of sacred writings is comprised of the Old Testament (OT) and the New Testament (NT). The Old Testament's sacred writings are essentially what is known as the Jewish Bible.

—PERSPECTIVE 15: A BOOK OF REVELATION

183) The Holy Bible is a Book of revelation. The final book of the Holy Bible provides a message that is both fundamental and enlightening. It promises that God will institute universal peace, prosperity, and cooperation over all of the earth immediately after the return of Jesus Christ and the beginning of the millennium.

184) The foregoing fifteen perspectives of God's Holy Bible provide insight into God's divine love for His creation; hence, He has provided us with His inspired Scriptures, which are the living Word. God's Word is alive and it gives life to those who seek it.

185) God's Word presents humanity with a historic perspective of things past, things present, and things to come, and that, with great accuracy.

186) The Holy Bible reveals: *Many will run to and fro, and knowledge will increase* (Daniel 12:4); *perilous times will come* (2 Timothy 3:1). Likewise, it comforts us: *Do not be afraid* (Matthew 28:10); *I am with you always* (Mathew 28:20); *because I live, you will live also* (John 14:19), *seek me and live* (Amos 5:4). God's Word was for yesterday; it is for today, and it will be forever.

PREEMINENT FOUNDATION 5
—WHO IS A CHRISTIAN?

"Everyone who believes that Jesus is the Christ is born of God, and everyone who loves the Father loves his child as well. This is how we know that we love the children of God: by loving God and carrying out his commands. This is the love of God: to obey his commands. And his commands are not burdensome, for everyone born of God overcomes the world? This is the victory that has overcome the world, even our faith."

1 John 5:1–5 (NIV)

187) **Who is a Christian?** A Christian is one who openly confesses his or her sins, seeks forgiveness, and commits to following the teachings of Jesus Christ.

188) A Christian is one who openly confesses his or her sins, seeks forgiveness, and commits to following the teachings of Jesus Christ. He or she is then transformed through the Holy Spirit, and by the grace of God, in whose grace rests our belief and repentance from our sins.

189) Repentance is the feeling and act in which one recognizes and strives to right a wrong or to gain forgiveness from the person, persons, or nation that he or she has consciously or sub–consciously wronged.

190) Repentance always includes an admission of guilt, a change of mind and action, and also includes: a solemn promise or resolve not to repeat the offense an attempt to make restitution for the wrong, or in some way to reverse the harmful effects of the wrong where possible.

191) When we openly repent of our sins and accept God's grace of forgiveness and transformation, we are born again into the family of God. This new birth is a spiritual birth; one does not necessarily experience a recognizable physical change.

192) Our physical birth introduces us as new persons within our physical families. Our spiritual birth introduces us into the spiritual family of God. We then strive daily for perfection in our new

knowledge in Christ, as our behavior towards our neighbor manifests God's will for our lives.

193)   A marked distinction exists between individuals who simply believe in God and those who have openly confessed their sins and who have consciously committed to live according to God's law and practice the teachings of Jesus Christ.

194)   This distinction also involves spiritual, moral, and social responsibilities, as we grow daily, both in our vertical relationship with God and in our horizontal relationship with our neighbor (Reference: *Five Foundations of Human Development* (FFHD) —Figure 11: Another Way to View the Cross–of–Christianity).

195)   The born again Christian seeks God's divine knowledge, wisdom, and understanding to enable his or her understanding of God's purpose for his or her life, and to grow in reverence and holiness before God and in humility before human beings.

196)   Merciful kindness governs the behavior of Christians. Christians believe in God the Father, the Creator of heaven and earth, and in Jesus Christ, the only begotten Son of God.

197)   Christians believe that Jesus Christ was born of the virgin Mary; they believe that He suffered under the Roman Senate, who accused Him of transgressing Roman law, and that He was tried and crucified.

198)   Christians believe, on the testimony of many contemporary witnesses that Christ died, was buried, and rose from the dead after three days (1 Corinthians 15:3–4).

199)   Christians believe that Christ's disciples saw Him on numerous occasions during the next forty days, before His ascension to His Father in Heaven.

200)   Christians believe that Jesus Christ sits at the right hand of God the Father, where He intercedes on behalf of the saints, and gives us access to God through the Holy Spirit.

201)   Christians also believe that Jesus Christ will come again to judge the living and the dead in His appearing and His kingdom.

202)   A practicing Christian embraces every opportunity to develop a mind like Christ and to think the way Jesus thought. This is the Christian ideal.

203) The true Christian life is one of learning, overcoming and growing toward a godlike character. In order to achieve this level of devotion, it is necessary to grow in knowledge of the character of God.

204) The Ten Commandments are an expression of God's law and His character; however it is not unusual for some devoted Christians to misunderstand that God sees all transgressions of His laws as equal.

205) Situational ethics and legal imperatives often inform our standards and measures, but God expects us to strive daily to keep every commandment, every precept, embrace every admonishment, and do good in the sight of all, so that the world will know that we are followers of Jesus Christ.

206) The challenge of being a Christian is to live our lives so that others will see the practical application of Christ's teachings, the message of the Sermon on the Mount, revealed through our lives.

207) The light of God that enables us to be the light of the world imbues us. Similar to the moon's reflection of the sun's light, as we relate to God and behold His glory, we reflect His Son's light.

208) Christians seek to follow the way of the life of Jesus Christ in every endeavor, every activity, every social situation, goal, and plan.

209) Christians seek God's way of life for humanity, His thoughts, and His will, so that our lives will bring glory to God and the name of Jesus Christ.

210) Christians are challenged daily to demonstrate, by their actions, their belief in the God they serve, and adhere to the Christian principles taught by our Lord and Savior Jesus Christ.

211) Daily challenges might place Christian beliefs and practices in contradictory positions to political and legal positions, but the wisdom of God is available to guide us.

212) Christians recognize the values of a world that operates on social, economic, religious, political, and legal imperatives as we strive to maintain a spiritual, moral, and social balance.

213) Even a devout Christian can find himself or herself in a challenging situating, as the imperatives of civic or corporate duty may come into conflict with the Christian response.

214) Despite the faith and desire of religious individuals to follow God's Word, we must recognize the great challenge to Christians,

and those of other faiths, who try to hold to their moral duties in an age of growing cynicism and secularism.

215) Western governments, given a sense of both moral and legal duty, have enacted human rights laws to provide legal recourse against those who promote or permit the violation of human rights.

216) A Christian life is the pursuit of a relationship with God through *(1)surrender; (2)sanctification; (3)separation; (4)sacrifice; (5)service,* and generally transformed living, which demonstrates love and service to our neighbor.

217) The above five key principles are complemented by the following seven daily practices: *(1)Fervent Daily Prayer and Fasting; (2)Daily Bible Reading and Study; (3)Practice of Peacefulness; (4)Practice of Righteousness; (5)Practice of Humility and Godly Worship; (6) Humanitarian Service; and (7)Evangelism.*

218) Our time for devotions and building of our spiritual assets often falls short of our own desire for self–elevation – spiritually. We must strive daily for some quiet time for contemplation on these seven (essential) daily practices.

219) On the surface, our spiritual and natural relationships seem like distinct relationships, on the one hand with God and on the other, with our neighbor.

220) Our natural relationship is encompassed within our Spiritual relationship, because the former is a function of our Spiritual relationship with God, who instructed us in our duty to our neighbor.

221) Spiritually speaking, we stand at the intersection of the two relationships. The obvious analogy is to the cross upon which Jesus Christ died to redeem us from our sins.

222) Christ became our perfect example of "suffering for righteousness sake" as he accepted the will of His Father and not His own will (Luke 22:42).

223) We have our "Vertical Relationship" with God because of the transformation Christ bestows on us through the Holy Spirit, because of our obedience to His Word and the exercise of spiritual disciplines.

224)   Our "Horizontal Relationship" with our NEIGHBORS intrinsically links to our "Vertical Relationship" with God through Jesus Christ.

225)   Most of us (Christian or non–Christian) try to live good lives that are peaceful and harmonious and to achieve the highest vertical relationship with God, and horizontal relationships with our neighbors.

226)   We can enhance our horizontal relationships when we practice them consistently with our vertical relationship practices.

227)   Christian conversion is a process that is similar to physical birth and development. It is a conscious change in the state of one's life, from our former conduct.

228)   Christian conversion may begin with an "altar call" when we take the first step towards the altar to publicly acknowledge our desire to seek a transformation (conversion) in our lives.

229)   The Holy Bible refers to this state as the "old man" and refers to our new state as the "new man," which God creates in us according to His righteousness and holiness.

230)   Our new state elevates us from good to righteous living with our neighbor. We seek daily cleansing from unrighteous conduct. We are sanctified — set apart — for holy and righteous living (sanctification is a fundamental and continuous spiritual experience).

231)   We seek restitution which involves remedies, such as diligently redressing and attempting to settle relational concerns or making amends or compensation for something lost, taken, or suffered.

232)   Similar to physical birth and development, Spiritual birth or Christian conversion is a process that is followed by certain practices, which enable healthy Spiritual growth.

233)   Christian conversion can manifest in many ways in one's life, such as acceptance, repentance, confession, rebirth, baptism, and a commitment to regular assembly with the body of Christ in order to grow in one's Christian maturity.

234)   The new convert knows that it is a most important decision that demands great seriousness; hence, the way in which he or she is initiated into the body of Christ is also critical.

235) Christian conversion requires belief in salvation through Jesus Christ. We accept that Jesus Christ has died in our place and is able to reconcile us to God.

236) The new convert confirms his or her decision of being a practicing Christian by observing the rite of water baptism. Baptism, however, is an *event*, but conversion (transformation) involves a *process*.

237) Christian conversion means that we are now kinder to one another, tenderhearted, forgiving of one another, just as God in Christ also forgives us. Can we be true Christians and not reflect the life of Christ in our daily lives?

238) Self–righteousness may inspire resentment and anti–Christian sentiment. True righteousness consists not of boasting (see, I do the right thing), but of doing the right thing regardless of who watches, and especially if none watch.

239) **Patrick Henry (1736–1799).** "It cannot be emphasized too strongly or too often that this great nation was founded, not by religionists, but by Christians; not on religions, but on the Gospel of Jesus Christ. For this very reason peoples of other faiths have been afforded asylum, prosperity, and freedom of worship here." — **Patrick Henry** First and sixth post-colonial Governor of Virginia http://www.quotedb.com/authors/patrick–henry

WHAT IS CHRISTIANITY? /CHRISTIANITY VERSUS RELIGION

240) Christianity is a practice. It is a way of life. Christians are saved by grace, live by faith, and will be judged by works (Matthew 25:34–40) (Reference: *Five Foundations of Human Development* (FFHD) — Figure 14: Christianity: A Way of Life and Judgment).

241) What is the difference between Christianity and religion? Christianity espouses God seeking man, through the advent of and redemption by Jesus Christ. Religion is a human construct, created within a framework of traditions, customs, and practices.

242) Through most religions, human beings continually seek to find God or reach Him by human effort. Under the New Testament (NT) dispensation, Christians reach God through the anointing of the Holy Spirit.

243) Christianity is the Christian way to God, and it is one of the great religions of the world, including Islam, Hinduism, Buddhism,

Sikhism, Judaism, Baha'i, Jainism, and Shinto (to name a few) as ways of life and practice to their adherents.

244) We note the influence and ancient knowledge that religions bring to the table of civilization. We are especially mindful of Judaism, one of the oldest religious traditions.

245) How do the vast number of denominations, non–denominational groups, parachurch groups of Christianity, and other world religions serve humanity?

246) Are all the denominations of Christianity the same? How did the denominations of Christianity come into being? Can the great diversity among the denominations of Christianity lead to misunderstanding in a world of differing religious beliefs?

247) The unity of Christianity experienced great divisions resulting in the formation of the Eastern and Western Churches in the tenth century. Further division of the Western Church occurred during the Protestant Reformation of the sixteenth century.

248) Despite the loss of singularity of the Church, it has survived – fragmented into numerous denominations, each certain that *its* particular doctrines and practices are *most* faithful to the will of God.

249) A Christian is a practitioner of the Christian faith, set apart from other religions by virtue of our Savior Jesus Christ, who, on the testimony of many contemporary witnesses, rose from the dead and ascended to God the Father in heaven.

250) The origin of many of the world's other religions, to a great extent, is common to geographic location, nationality, race, culture, and class. Some visibly cross some of the boundaries listed above.

251) Christianity crosses all geographic boundaries, and boundaries of nationality, race, culture, and class. Western nations have greater visibility as nations that are underpinned by Christianity.

252) Christianity is a universal religion. It has a central message that embraces all of humanity; hence, its influence throughout the world, and the response to the Great Commission of Jesus Christ to preach the gospel throughout the world.

253) Christianity has assumed an important role in the formation of Western constitutions, our governments, our societies and our lives.

254) Divergent doctrines have challenged the unity of Christianity throughout the ages to the present.

255) In our modern societies many question and even challenge the relevance of Christianity, and its orthodox beliefs, in a growing, multi–religious and multi–cultural world, but can societies survive without religion?

256) Except for atheists and agnostics, most individuals are born into some form of religion, be it one of the major religions of the world, a minor religion, or a tribal variety.

257) This birth into religion is the first step toward religious affiliation and toward the acknowledgement of one's God or god.

258) From tribal cultures to Eastern and Western cultures, some form of religious initiation takes place in the life of a child, even before the child begins to understand the meaning of religion.

259) Within Christianity, divergence has been extreme. Each denomination has a framework of doctrines, beliefs, practices, and customs that differs from the others.

260) The history of divergent Christian denominations began with the schism between the Western and Eastern Churches, and the emphasis on the Bible and its publication in the fifteenth century.

261) Western Christian denominations would not have been possible without the Protestant Reformation of the sixteenth century.

262) The move toward religious autonomy in the sixteenth century led to the formation of numerous sects and non–denominational groups that have steered their own congregations in various directions, based upon differing doctrinal understandings.

263) New and emerging debates tug at the unity of Christianity; the rights (and status) of the unborn, same–sex marriage, the build–up of armaments, military defense, terrorism, discipline of children, ordination of women, prayer in schools, capital punishment, and separation of church and State.

264) Denominational disagreements lead to divisions within, and among Christian denominations and the lay community. They also present a great challenge to the unity of the Church.

265) Political and religious bifurcation is problematic for nations, because governments and religious organizations take distinctly

different paths as they attempt to achieve similar goals for the creation of orderly societies.

266) Some individuals, as they reflect on the role that religion has played in genocide, wars, suffering, and injustices throughout history to the present day, have become skeptical of religion altogether.

267) The proliferation of splinter religions, the appeals of the faithful for direct intervention in purely human matters (with the predictable lack of result) and the violent assertion of the rightness of individual religions undermines the essential role of religion and dilutes and distorts God's true message to us.

268) Observation seems to indicate that the impact and sustainability of spirituality ebbs with each passing decade while, on the other hand, human knowledge grows exponentially (Reference: *Five Foundations of Human Development* (FFHD) —Figure 16: Decline in Spiritual Progress versus Exponential Growth in Material Progress in the World).

269) Many question the relevance of religion in a world that needs religion. What is the purpose of religion, and why is it central to the lives of human beings, if it does not lead us to the realization of the spiritual purpose of our existence?

270) Is love not more powerful than religion? Does the power of love not underpin religion? Practical religion must manifest itself in examples of love, joy, peace, longsuffering (patience), kindness, goodness, faithfulness, gentleness and self–control.

271) Practical religion helps us to recognize the needs of others; to embrace every opportunity to serve others; and to help our fellow travelers in their journey through life, so that they too may radiate the spiritual counsel that comes from above.

272) The practice of true religion is living in the radiant light of God. This is what religions must strive for, because it broadens the base of our relationship with others and give true meaning to the state of being religious.

273) How do we explain human suffering, the misery that results from slavery, apartheid, genocide, wars, colonization, and exploitation of our neighbors, historically, in the name of religion and the spread of God's Word?

274) Why do individuals and nations kill each other in the name of race, culture, and religion? The answer may lie in the fundamental differences in our various religious perspectives.

275) The practice of modern Christianity demands a constant awareness of what is taking place in the world and a godly perspective from which we interpret world situations.

276) We must be mindful that the indelible mark left on the world by New Testament (NT) Christians came with great sacrifice.

277) Many Christians have sacrificed their lives in order to preserve the Christian heritage by remaining faithful to the principles of the teachings of Jesus Christ.

278) Some adherents to Christianity and other world religions share a common belief in capital punishment, while others strictly follow the teachings of Jesus Christ, underpinned by God's grace and mercy in our New Testament (NT) dispensation.

279) The practice of Christianity should inspire Christians to demonstrate the love of God, and follow His guidance above all other imperatives.

280) We must allow God's guidance to permeate every decision that we make, and not allow our color, race, language, culture, religion, education, or politics to divide us.

281) The right to life of the unborn is probably one of the most divisive religious issues of the twenty-first century, but where does Scripture stand on this issue that divides individuals and denominations of Christians equally?

282) The three stages of life are given to us in God's Word (premortal; mortal, and immortal), and should be the cornerstone of our teachings regarding human life and the value of human life. To do otherwise would be to deny the precious Word of God.

283) The Holy Bible does not make any differentiation between the born or unborn. God's Word speaks to the sanctity of each stage of life, the preservation of which is our moral responsibility.

284) One might argue that the unborn cannot protect themselves. Likewise, one can argue that the weak and powerless are relatively incapable of protecting themselves as well.

285) This knowledge should lead us to demonstrate the same care for all human lives, unborn as well as lives wracked by poverty, disease, famine, war, and other avoidable human disasters.

286) God's Word teaches that God transforms our bodies from mortal to immortal in order for us to inherit His promise of eternal life (John 3:16).

287) There is a great need for a broader understanding of God's perspective regarding human life, and the preservation of *all* life.

288) We must, as followers of Christ, adopt God's view of life and reject any intentional or inadvertent differentiation of human life that is contrary to the teachings of Jesus Christ.

289) Over the centuries, human beings have dominated and killed each other for no other reason than social differences, God's choice of human distinctions, or the coveting of material wealth. Are these acts not contrary to the teachings of religion and Christianity? Are these acts not contrary to the sanctity of life?

290) It behooves us to move to a new paradigm regarding human life, which takes into consideration our three stages of life: premortal, mortal and immortal life (Reference: *Five Foundations of Human Development* (FFHD) —Figure 12: The Three Stages of Human Life).

291) Billions around the world follow some form of religion, but how can any observer reconcile acts of genocide, wars, slavery, exploitation, and greed, manifested concurrent with growth in world religions?

292) Why is the world not a kinder, gentler, more forgiving and compassionate place? Astonishingly, moral codes of ethics underpin most, if not all world religions.

293) The true adherents to the principles and practices of religion hold civilization together from disintegrating into unimaginable human disaster.

294) True adherents of religion come from every religion, from every race, from every culture, from every nationality, and from every faith; but why has religion been the catalyst for great violence, and intolerance in the world?

295) We have made a virtue of tolerance. The idea seems noble, but what is tolerance? It is inaction, acceptance, and permission. The concept is entirely passive yet has somehow been glorified as a positive, laudable course of conduct.

296) Tolerance is not the answer to human development; that answer lies in positive change, the shaping of our lives and our interactions to conform to God's will.

297) Tolerance is not the message of Christ, nor any of the great prophets. Should religions not lead by example, and in doing so, obey the ultimate stricture; to love one another as God loves us?

298) Exactly how did religion get on this highway of intolerance with few exits to the road of tolerance? The reality is that religion should strive to prevent intolerance. Tolerance fills the vacuum when intolerance is absent.

299) Christianity, and other world religions rightfully preach and teach tolerance, yet we are both victims and perpetrators of intolerance even in the twenty–first century.

300) We must revise our concept of tolerance from a praiseworthy undertaking to a spiritual imperative, nothing more than obedience to God's Word, in order to have any effect on human behavior.

301) Tolerance by itself makes no great demands on us; all it requires is for us to do nothing. Tolerance, by itself, does not deserve any reward.

302) Distinctions of belief and practice go to the heart of Christianity. God knows the hearts of human beings. He is aware of those who are sincere, religious, and tolerant, because He knows His own.

THOUGHTS TO ENLIGHTEN AND EMPOWER THE MIND

2001 QUESTIONS AND PHILOSOPHICAL THOUGHTS TO INSPIRE, ENLIGHTEN, AND EMPOWER OUR WORLD TO LIMITLESS HEIGHTS

SF

PART 2
FIVE FOUNDATIONS OF HUMAN DEVELOPMENT (FFHD)
—FOUNDATION 1
SPIRITUAL FOUNDATION

1.1. LOVE (CARING)
1.2. FAITH (ASSURANCE)
1.3 HOPE (EXPECTATION)
1.4. CHARITY (AID)
1.5. PEACE (HARMONY)
1.6. HUMILITY (SERVANT-HOOD)
1.7. PATIENCE (LONGSUFFERING)

FOUNDATION 1
SPIRITUAL FOUNDATION
—1.1. LOVE (CARING)

"Love must be sincere. Hate what is evil; cling to
what is good. Be devoted to one another in
brotherly love. Honor one another above
yourselves. Never be lacking in zeal, but keep your
spiritual fervor, serving the Lord. Be joyful in
hope, patient in affliction, faithful in prayer. Share
with God's people who are in need. Practice
hospitality."

Romans 12:9–13 (NIV)

303) **What is love?** Love is the most powerful force in the universe.
Love (*agap`e*) begins with God, and when we allow His love to flow
in us and from within us, it provides the spiritual bond that holds
humanity together.

304) In the entire body of inspired scriptural writings, John 3:16 is
probably the most universally inclusive passage written. It is the
ultimate gift of God to humanity.

305) The love of God for humanity, which is manifest in His Son Jesus
Christ, and symbolizes His love of the church, is called *agap`e* in the
original Greek text.

306) God's gift of love for us should be the ultimate guide towards our
higher spiritual purpose" and it should direct all of our activities
based upon self–sacrificing love for one another.

307) Ancient Greek writers made a distinction among various other
forms of love, such as *philia*, which refers to a special relationship
between husbands and wives or between close associates.

308) The characteristics of these relationships are the focus of the
intimate bond between two individuals who share their lives and
experiences.

309) The Greek writers refer to *storg`e* as a form of love that is displayed
between family members, such as the bond between parents and
children and brothers and sisters.

310) The Greek writers refer to *eros*, a form of love that is passionate and sexual in nature. Intense sexual desire motivates and sometimes underpins this form of love.

311) This expression of emotionless love distracts us from our first imperative of God's love for each other.

312) Our materially driven lifestyles seem to reduce our expressions of love to love for materialism.

313) The love that we exhibit for objects can lead to many forms of aggression and violence when the object of our veneration is threatened or taken away.

314) Our material possessions often are valued above human health, life, safety, and goodwill toward others.

315) God's love helps us to broaden our perspective of love to include all of humanity.

316) Unlike human love, God's love for His creation is absolute and unconditional. His love for humanity reflects His grace and mercy toward us.

317) God's love, manifested within us, breaks down barriers of intolerance between human beings regardless of color, race, class, culture, nationality, or religion.

318) God's love is not the natural quality of love within us that we exhibit, but it is the love of God that is essentially spiritual.

319) God's love makes our life include more of others, and brings us closer to the realization of the spiritual purpose of our existence.

320) God's love also heightens our capacity for empathy for others, and brings us closer to the realization of the spiritual purpose of our existence.

321) The Apostle Paul expresses the all–encompassing, timeless, and abiding nature of God's love for us.

322) What is it that causes us to question God's abiding love for His creation, and depend on human intellect alone?

323) Is it because our scientific minds demand mathematical and scientific validation for every human condition?

324) Is it because we cannot experiment on love in scientific laboratories? How can we demonstrate and validate the power of God's abiding love in us?

325) We can know that God's love is working in us and through us when we voluntarily enter the great battlefield of races, cultures, and religions and champion the causes of the poor, the aged, the hungry, the dispossessed, and the disenfranchised.

326) It is only within these environments that God's incomprehensible love manifests its greatest patience with us, and we see its capacity to transform human lives, to overcome fear, and to inspire care and compassion.

327) Love knows the temptation of transgression and, when others transgress against us, God's love directs us to one response – to forgive.

328) The ultimate expression and transforming form of love is expressed when one displays forgiveness and mercy to others, rather than seeks revenge.

329) Forgiveness and mercy portray great character and strength, and they open doors of reciprocal returns. These responses are the only true validation of God's love.

330) When God's love radiates in our hearts, the universality of humanity becomes a reality, and we begin to experience the same love for humanity as we do for ourselves.

331) God is faithful and just when we show love and compassion for others, yet there is an instinct within us to return hate for hate, aggression for aggression, which escalates to further fear and aggression.

332) We seek freedom from fear and aggression, yet all we need to achieve this is to emulate God's abiding love, which is the ultimate path of freedom. It is the perfect method to set up barriers of self–defense against any form of aggression.

333) In order to accomplish this capacity of love, we must renounce all forms of hatred and pursue a life of godliness, righteousness, and love for one another.

334) This form of love penetrates into every sphere of human existence, and removes any inclination towards fear, hate, and aggression.

335) As human beings, we must first understand the limitations of natural love in order to appreciate the need for God's love to permeate our lives.

336) Natural love is the love which we, human beings, are capable of, according to our nature.

337) Human beings by nature, are not capable of loving that which they do not understand; without a focus for emotion (be it an ideal, a person, an object), there is no natural love.

338) When we acknowledge that we can never understand the vastness, the perfection, and the order of God's creation, we at the same time acknowledge that our love can never equal His love for us.

339) Natural love today connotes an unreasoning passion or affection, often a transient one, as occurs during a period of infatuation among teenagers or adults.

340) The nature and intensity of this form of love lacks a spiritual foundation. Natural love is fleeting and based upon physical attributes.

341) This popularized idea of love (into and out of which people expect to regularly fall) today erodes our ability to even comprehend that God's love is immeasurably greater, all encompassing, and enduring.

342) Natural love is no more than an expression of what is in fact a strong affection. Although we are not capable of love such as God's, we improve ourselves in striving to be capable, and we increase our own capacity to love in a meaningful way.

343) Some marriages endure all of their many hardships; these are the people who honor their promise to maintain the bond of love.

344) Successful marriages are the ones in which the couples consider that the love in question, to make a true marriage, is more than natural love.

345) It is the supernatural love of God which sustains the union of His people. National statistics show marriage breakdown and the reasons for the breakdown, but the true cause of marriage breakdown is our failure to nurture God's love (*agap`e*).

346) God's love is the bond that guarantees marriage stability. As God has promised never to "leave or forsake us," so we must promise never to leave or forsake our wives or husbands.

347) The true achievement of love between human beings is when the light of the love of God shines from within us, but too often our love manifests in the physical as opposed to the spiritual realm.

348) Our material lives cause us to associate the meaning of love with a specific object, person, or idea. On occasion we give expensive gifts to others as an expression of our love.

349) An implied relationship between material gifts and expressions of love begins at birth with gifts for the newborn, and it extends through old age and bereavement.

350) The love of God is a free gift to humanity which is eternal and the value of which is incalculable.

351) The imperatives of God's love are the all–inclusive hope for humanity. God's love flows through us to others and motivates us to return good for evil. His love for us is in the spiritual realm, part of our vertical relationship.

352) God's love embraces all of humanity, but how can we know when His love abides in us? We know we have God's divine love in us when His love compels us to demonstrate love for others from within the human heart.

353) Our love for others is demonstrated by our actions in the natural realm through our horizontal relationships.

354) The nature of our outward behavior, reflected in our relationships is the measure of God's love in us and through us.

355) Our love for humanity should extend to all, from the highly sophisticated to the simplest and poorest individuals.

356) The geography of our birth, our race, our language, our culture, our religion, and our family members and friends often influences whom we extend our love to.

357) We joyfully extend our love to those with whom we are familiar, often with the expectation or assurance of their love in return, but the Holy Scriptures counsel us to love our neighbor as ourselves.

358) An intimate knowledge and understanding of the meaning of God's commandment is essential for neighborly love to flourish.

359) Without God's love operating within and through us, our fallible nature overwhelms us and keeps us awake to the selfish motivations of the flesh with which we often identify ourselves.

360) Without this divine understanding of God's love, we remain confined to a narrow sphere of selfish living and we merely exist, if we can exist at all.

361) Who is our neighbor? The word no longer has geographic limitations. Without such an understanding, we can only love in the natural, human sense of the word.

362) The imperatives of neighborly love are the all–inclusive love for neighbor. Jesus emphasized to His disciples that loving God and loving one's neighbor is an expression of God's love in us.

363) If we are followers of the teachings of Jesus Christ, then we have an obligation to love our neighbor. There is no second option, no alternative, no moral defense, and there is simply no excuse.

364) To love is to be living in the light of God. To hate is to be living in the darkness of the prince of darkness. Darkness and light are two absolutes representing the opposites of good and evil in the world.

365) The lack of God's love for our neighbor can translate into catastrophic events in the world, such as *World War I (1914–1918)*, and *World War II (1939–1945)*.

366) Ironically, in our modern day we spend billions of dollars to purchase gifts in an attempt to demonstrate love for each other, while we drain the world's human, material, and financial resources in military conflicts.

367) Rather than build our hopes on love, we have built our hopes for a better world upon peace treaties. Peace treaties can only be effective when underpinned by God's love, because the imperfect nature of man is otherwise the sole architect.

368) Many unsolvable problems faced by individuals and nations are rooted in our history of aggression (neighbor against neighbor) because of race, culture, nationality, religion, political ideology, and the breaking of pledges, contracts, bonds, and agreements.

369) Jesus Christ gave His life to set us free from our bondage of aggression and to usher in the New Testament (NT) era of love for neighbor. Love for God and neighbor defines the ethical and spiritual springs of human life.

370) We discount love's ability to heal the world of the evils of violence, genocide, and wars, which simply repeat themselves. We are not yet aware that when history repeats itself, the price grows, exponentially.

371) Imagine the world's deficit financing of the trillions of dollars extrapolated over the past century in pursuit of peace.

372) Imagine the cost in human lives, human energy and infrastructure, and the human genius that could otherwise be directed to creating a better world when we embrace the power of God's love, and reject the love of power.

373) Love is the ultimate path to peace (harmony), yet we have always sought peace through war and through subjugation.

374) God foresaw before time the threats to our personal, family, and national and international security as the biggest threats to our peace and harmony in the twenty–first century.

375) The centuries of civil wars among nations demonstrate the need for God's overwhelming love to prevail as a first imperative for their growth and stability.

376) Jesus demonstrates, through His words, the love that we should have for one another. Jesus is saying to us that we should make every effort to embrace others who are not of our color, race, language, culture, class or religion.

377) Essentially, we must call upon the power of God's love as the first response to our differences in social, economic, and political worldviews.

378) If we in the West fail to recognize the power of God's love to elevate human relations in the international community, it will be impossible to present God and His Son Jesus Christ as our ambassadors of peace to nations of other faiths.

379) Have we ever considered that our love for humanity is an antidote to the enormous human suffering and breakdown that is taking place in nations throughout the world?

380) We should strive daily for every human action to be a manifestation of the love of God and our love for humanity. It is the only true measure of hope for a world that seeks peace and harmony.

381) Principles of love for humanity underpin the philosophies of the great world religions and add force to the exercise of love.

382) It is essential for world religions to cross the great divide and expand our neighborhood love to others, regardless of geography of origin, nationality, race, culture or religion.

383) God's love is not simply the absence of intolerance among religions. The eternal God speaks not of religious tolerance, or passivity, but of love.

384) No can claim God's love if it is confined to a narrow sphere of love for its own.

385) Religious tolerance is akin to political correctness in our twenty-first century lexicon of religious appeasement, and it does not conform to the demands of true religion.

386) The world thinks of peace as the opposite of war, but the undeniable fact is that love, not peace, is the opposite of war.

387) The undeniable fact is that human beings cannot give nor bring about peace, because peace is an attribute of God, not of human beings.

388) God commands, absolutely, and without the boundaries that we establish to justify our narrow sphere of love.

389) Love for humanity underpins the teachings of major world religions, yet the practice of universal love for all of humanity still seems to be the greatest challenge to us in the modern age.

390) The Apostle Paul placed great emphasis on love because he knew that love is the most powerful attribute that comes from God. It has preeminence over the other spiritual gifts.

391) Love is the greatest gift because it is the foundation for all other Christian qualities and religious virtues. Love transcends all other human virtues.

392) Without love, all other human virtues are of no effect. Christian love transcends hope, trust, faith, forgiveness, compassion, and patience.

393) Love is above all and love conquers all. All things will come to an end, except God's love, because God's love extends beyond our mortal life to immortality (John 3:16).

FOUNDATION 2
SPIRITUAL FOUNDATION
—1.2. FAITH (ASSURANCE)

"Consequently, faith comes from hearing the
message, and the message is heard through the
word of Christ. But I ask: Did they not hear? Of
course they did: 'Their voice has gone into all the
earth, their words to the end of the world.' "
Romans 10:17–18 (NIV) "[W]e have gained access
by faith into this grace in which we now stand.
And we rejoice in the hope."

Romans 5:2 (NIV)

394) **What is faith?** Can human beings live without faith? Faith in
Jesus Christ is the only condition God requires for salvation.

395) Faith is not only a confession of one's belief in Jesus Christ, it is an
activity that manifests itself in the human heart, and requires faith
action.

396) The importance of faith in Jesus Christ is that it must be not only
for the moment but a continuing attitude of faithfulness.

397) Faith is not an intellectual exercise or one of religious astuteness.
The Word of God reminds us to have faith in Jesus Christ our
Savior, forty times in the Bible.

398) Faith in God requires belief and trust (Matthew 4:19). Faith
requires repentance and sorrow (2 Corinthians 7:10). Faith requires
obedience and sacrifice (John 14:15).

399) With faith in God we can accomplish much and overcome great
personal, national, and international challenges.

400) The Holy Bible sets the foundation principles upon which to base
our faith.

401) Faith helps us to comprehend the Word of God. Faithful servants
in the Bible provide examples of the practice of faith, through which
we can increase our faith.

402) Essentially, the Word of God is teaching us that victorious
Christian living must incorporate faith, belief, and practice

(Reference: *Five Foundations of Human Development* (FFHD) —Figure 13: The Keys of Victorious Christian Living).

403)   The Old and New Testament (NT) writers provide faith perspectives to strengthen our faith in the modern age. Following is a listing of *7 Faith Perspectives* for our edification.

SEVEN FAITH PERSPECTIVES
— (NT) PERSPECTIVE 1: OBEDIENCE

404)   The Bible teaches: By faith Abraham obeyed when he was called to go out of the place which he would *afterward* receive as an inheritance. And he went out, not knowing where he was going (Hebrews 11:8–10).

— (NT) PERSPECTIVE 2: SACRIFICE

405)   The Bible counsels: By faith Abel offered to God a more excellent sacrifice than Cain, through which he obtained witness that he was righteous, God testifying of his gifts; and through it he, being dead, still speaks" (Hebrews 11:4).

— (OT) PERSPECTIVE 3: GODLY FEAR

406)   The Bible advises: By faith Noah, being divinely warned of things not yet seen, moved with godly fear, prepared an ark for the saving of his household, by which he condemned the world and became heir of the righteousness which is according to faith (Hebrews 11:7).

— (OT) PERSPECTIVE 4: COURAGE

407)   The Bible assures: God protects the faithful and the innocent. For instance: He saved Daniel in the Lion's den. God protected Daniel's three friends in the fiery furnace of King Nebuchadnezzar (Daniel 3:25).

— (NT) PERSPECTIVE 5: SUFFERING

408)   The Bible counsels: Though we have faith, it will never be a guarantee that we will not suffer; neither is suffering necessarily the mark of the unfaithful. God have provided something better for us, that they should not be made perfect apart from us (Hebrews 11:36–40).

— (NT) PERSPECTIVE 6: SEEKING GOD

409)   The Bible teaches: By faith Enoch was translated so that he did not see death, 'and was not found, because God had translated him'; for

before his translation he had this testimony, that He pleased God (Hebrews 11:5–6).

— (NT) PERSPECTIVE 7: WALKING IN FAITH

410) The Bible counsels: For we walk by faith, not by sight (2 Corinthians 5:7). The pursuit of materialism seems to characterize our modern civilization, and it permeates the very fabric of our beings, our minds, our families, our societies, our cultures, and our nations.

411) The preceding seven perspectives of Old and New Testament (NT) faith establish the precedent for our faith in the turbulent twenty-first century, but fear often paralyzes the depressed and discouraged in this world.

412) None of us are immune to personal problems that bring on depression and cause us to lose faith in God's guidance as we face the challenges of the modern era.

413) Where is our faith, and in what or whom do we place our faith? We place faith in things seen (the physical) rather than in things unseen (the spiritual).

414) We place faith in pastors, priests, lawyers, doctors and stockbrokers. We place faith in modern education, in national lotteries, and in various political systems of government.

415) We place faith in modern medicine and in its capacity to find cures for uncontrolled and preventable illnesses.

416) We place faith in science and technology, in artificial intelligence, in longevity through science, as well as to genetically engineer our foods, plants, and even our bodies.

417) Regardless of the fleeting moment of our sojourn in this world, we have traded faith in an unseen God for faith in what we can see.

418) We also risk trading in eternity for a fleeting moment on earth. Our human minds are more trained to comprehend things that we can rationalize, measure, and analyze scientifically.

419) Our fast-paced contemporary lifestyles demand instant solutions to our problems, but in contrast, faith in God requires patience as we wait on Him for the answers to our problems in His own time.

420) Our faith in God is steadfast when we are uncertain that our medical doctors can cure us from illnesses, even terminal illnesses.

421) When we are reasonably certain that our medical doctors can cure our ailment, we may place faith in medical professionals first, and God may not seem necessary in such circumstances.

422) If our surgeon advises that all medical options have been exhausted, we may belatedly turn our attention to faith in God with fear and trembling. Faith in our surgeons through God is legitimate faith, since He uses any human being to manifest His purpose in our lives.

423) Will God respond to our call after we have exhausted all other options? Certainly! We often forget that His ways are not our ways, neither are His thoughts our thoughts.

424) God is attentive to our suffering, but suffering may increase, because we may be outside of His will for our lives.

425) We must always be mindful of our standing in God and of His will for our lives; therefore, even in suffering we must not lose faith in Him.

426) Pain and suffering alert us to His presence, but we often neglect our great opportunity to communicate with Him through our suffering.

427) God wants us to be mindful of His presence in every situation, not only to seek His help when we experience suffering or great disappointment, but also to give thanks when life is in our favor.

428) God speaks to the wealthy for He knows that they can afford the best of the material world, and they may neglect His presence and the need to have faith in Him.

429) Faith in great wealth may distract some of the wealthy from their dependence upon God.

430) God wants the wealthy as well as the destitute in His kingdom, but to enter the kingdom of God all must seek to do His will.

431) We expect God to supply our needs or wants because we have professed faith in Him.

432) When things do not go our way, we often question our faith, and God's faithfulness.

433) We petition God for a response to our needs or wants, in our timing, not being mindful that He has set before us a path that guarantees His provisions.

434) Rarely do we consider that the greatest thing we can put our minds to is the faith that God has ordained a purpose for our lives.

435) More often than not, we are oblivious to the fact that we are being tested, as God patiently awaits our response to His preconditions.

436) The Bible is illustrative of leaders who put their trust in God in times of great national crisis.

437) Faith in God is only the beginning; our works are an extension of our faith. James, in his Epistle, counsels: For as the body without the spirit is dead, so faith without works is dead also (James 2:26).

438) The exercise of faith is essential, but it is not sufficient to pray for material and physical needs or for victory over personal and national calamities. God knows our needs.

439) How would we conduct ourselves in suffering if it were to come upon us suddenly? Would faith diminish? Would we maintain faith in God?

440) The most poignant answer to these questions is in the writings in the Old Testament (OT) book of Job. The trials of Job and the dramatic conclusion of his experience in suffering are some of the greatest demonstrations of faith and patience recorded in biblical history.

441) God often uses His sovereignty to test us and to teach us patience. Job confesses his lack of understanding of God's purpose for his suffering, but rather than lose faith in God.

442) In order to derive a better understanding of our suffering, we need to focus on God (the Savior) rather than on our suffering. Yet, we focus on the circumstances of our suffering and often forget that it may be God's way of testing our faith.

443) The ancient Mayan, Toltec, Aztec, and Natchez civilizations made great sacrifices to appease and honor their gods. The greater the catastrophe they encountered, the more they exercised faith in their god(s), and made sacrifices for appeasement.

444) Christians also believe that there are intrinsic links between a nation's spiritual standing in God and catastrophic events.

445) Perhaps the most important question is: What would it take to elevate our faith in God to a more enduring and absolute faith?

446) The faith, belief, hope, and practice of Christians have been tested in every era, down to our twenty-first century, but the enlightenment of our era has had a great influence on our thinking.

447) Unlike the unyielding faith of Old Testament (OT) era, today we look for technological solutions as a first response to calamities.

448) God expects unquestioning faith from His believers, undiluted by human intellect and scientific reasoning, even in the light of technological advancements of the twenty-first century.

449) Job, Shadrach, Meshach, and Abed-Nego, Abraham, Moses, Noah and the Apostles all demonstrated this faith. This is the faith of the Old and New Testament (NT) saints.

450) It was the faith that saved Daniel *in* the Lion's den, not *from* the lion's den (Daniel 6:22). It saved Shadrach, Meshach, and Abed-Nego *in* the burning fiery furnace, not *from* the fiery furnace (Daniel 3:25). Paul and Silas were saved *in* the Philippi prison, not *from* going to the Philippi prison in the first place (Acts 16:26).

451) God's people must continue to persevere in faith and righteous acts towards each other, consistently practicing our beliefs and extending uncompromising love to each other.

452) Jesus Christ declares: "I say to you if you have faith as a mustard seed, you will say to the mountain, 'move from here to there,' and it will move; and nothing will be impossible for you" (Matthew 17:20 NKJV).

453) There are many mountains that we need to move in our modern age, such as world conflict, world hunger, world disasters (natural and man-made), religious division, and divisions among religions.

FOUNDATION 1
SPIRITUAL FOUNDATION
—1.3. HOPE (EXPECTATION)

"Praise be to the God and Father of our Lord Jesus
Christ! In his great mercy he has given us new
birth into a living hope through the resurrection
of Jesus Christ from the dead, and into an
inheritance that cannot perish, spoil or fade –
kept in heaven for you, who through faith are
shielded by God's power until the coming."

1 Peter 1:3–5 (NIV)

454) **What is hope?** Hope is the expectation of something to come in the future, something desired, seen or unseen.

455) The Holy Bible teaches: For we were saved in this hope, but hope that is seen is not hope; for why does one still hope for what he sees? But if we hope for what we do not see, *then* we eagerly wait for *it* with perseverance (Romans 8:24–25).

456) We place hope in our own capabilities, in others, and in God. Biblical hope consists of assurance in the heart, and confidence in God regarding events to come, because God's promise and revelation predicates this hope.

457) Hope begins with God, and hopelessness begins with our living apart from Him, choosing rather to rely upon human intellect as a guide to hope.

458) Any notion of hope that relies upon the human intellect alone as its capable guide is restricted to a narrow sphere of our material and our temporary existence.

459) C. S. Lewis (1898–1963): "Hope is one of the theological virtues. This means that a continual looking forward to the eternal world is not (as some modern people think) a form of escapism or wishful thinking, but one of the things a Christian is meant to do." (C. S. Lewis, *Mere Christianity*: New York, New York: Copyright ©1943, 1945, 1953 by Mcmillian Publishing Company, a division of Mcmillian, Inc., p. 118).

460) To have hope in God is to have one's faith solidly rooted in His Son, our Lord and Savior, Jesus Christ, and to have a confident trust in God (Psalms 33:21–22).

461) Many individuals vacillate between conditions of hope and hopelessness, even though some live in nations with great wealth.

462) These two prevailing human conditions are a reflection of a world divided between the developed and underdeveloped nations.

463) Many view hope for the future through their own and their nation's abundance. Their hope is rooted in the abundance of material things they possess and in the potential to acquire more things that will supposedly bring greater hope and happiness.

464) Let us briefly examine the word *happiness* for a moment. No one will deny that all of us seek happiness. Some of us may only experience fleeting moments of happiness although we may search for this elusive state all of our lives.

465) Interestingly, the Holy Bible does not mention the word happiness. How could this be? God wants us to achieve the higher state of joy.

466) Millions of individuals in underdeveloped nations rely on other individuals, their governments, NGOs, and the international community to provide occasional rays of hope.

467) What are we hoping for, and how can we attain it? Is the demand, the search, based upon one's single–mindedness, one's inclinations, one's maturity, or one's spiritual nature? We must answer these important questions in order for hope to become a meaningful and purposeful search.

468) Human survival is the eternal search for hope, but hope must encompass the desire for the survival of all of God's creation and not be merely a façade of hope in material possessions.

469) Nations of the world are in search of hope. Arguably, 80% of the world's population lives in differing conditions of hope and hopelessness in a daily act of survival.

470) Arguably, 20% of the world's population (which includes many of us in the West); things hoped for are generally within reach.

471) Basic human needs, such as medical care, nutritious meals, clean water, and adequate housing are out of reach for most of the world's inhabitants.

472) These inadequacies have a profound effect on the development of children in underdeveloped and developing nations.

473) In every level of society someone hopes for something. Individuals and nations hope to make great discoveries in modern medicine, succeed in space exploration, or win the most medals in Olympic competitions. Parents hope that their children will achieve success in scholastic and athletic competitions.

474) Leaders throughout the world hope to build better nations and a better world community.

475) Nations hope to achieve parity or dominance in international business and commerce, and they hope for victory in military conflicts with their neighbors. These great achievements bring prominence to nations, but do they constitute hope for all the peoples of a nation?

476) Could we say that winning and achieving are the wellsprings of hope for humanity?

477) Why do nations rise and fall throughout history in undulating states of hope and hopelessness? Why do we have to live on the brink of hopelessness?

478) Nations of other faiths, beliefs, and practices that subscribe to God or god(s) have the same responsibilities to honor the sanctity of their beliefs in promoting international hope, peace and harmony.

479) It is also essential for us to understand that when 80% of eighty percent of the world's population is socially, economically, and technically in trouble, then one hundred percent of the planet is in trouble.

480) Hope for building, and sustaining great civilizations lies in the spiritual realm, and not in the material, realm.

481) There is a plurality regarding the hope of humanity, because boundless hope lies in the minds and hearts of all citizens and nations.

482) Each being of God's creation has a creative responsibility to do something to further hope for the survival of humanity.

483) Hope is the aggregate desire of all people. There are no boundaries to hopelessness. Hope is not about me, but about us.

484) Real and lasting hope for the good of the many must take precedence over the hope for the good of the few.

485) No nation can reach the apex of true spirituality (exhibiting the fruits of the Spirit) when segments of its populations exist in various stages of hopelessness.

486) History has shown that the downfall of ancient civilizations is attributable to their great leaders isolating and insulating themselves from the hopelessness of the masses.

487) Autocratic leaders of the past failed to comprehend the intrinsic moral cord that links their survival to the hope of the masses.

488) Autocratic leaders of the past failed to comprehend that hopefulness; the rewards of labor; sharing of the fruits of production, and a healthy ecosystem are all part of the survival equation.

489) History did not guide the actions of many ancient leaders. What will be our legacy? Will we now make use of the six thousand years of lessons from history to guide us into the twenty–first century?

490) We are desperately in search of hope, but our search is generally, though unintentionally, one–dimensional and individualistic.

491) Our hope is for advancement of ourselves, our families, and the groups with which we identify in the areas of race, culture, language, class, nationality, and religion.

492) The hope of humanity must of necessity take on universal dimensions, and not be restricted to individuals, families, groups, societies or nations.

493) A universality of hope must spring from the spirit within us in an unquenchable desire to strive to lift individuals and nations to the same level of hope we hold for ourselves.

494) Hope for human survival rests on five principals: *(1) worship of God; (2) service to humanity; (3) care for family; (4) obedience to authority; and (5) management of creation.* These five principles, though revolutionary, embody Gods' threefold spiritual purpose for our existence (Reference: *Five Foundations of Human Development* (FFHD) —Figure 2: God's Threefold Spiritual Purpose for our Existence).

495) During Old Testament (OT) times, nations hoped and prayed to God for victory in battle, and God reassured those whom He had chosen.

496) Incongruously, in our twenty–first century, nations appeal to the God of the Old Testament (OT) to guide us to victory in territorial, religious, cultural, economic, and political wars.

497) God points us in the twenty–first century to the message of His Son Jesus Christ, which is a message of hope.

498) Our Lord and Savior bled and died on the cross to redeem us to a new paradigm of hope.

499) Jesus Christ placed before humanity a different and better hope that elevates the lives of the nations' citizens to conditions of hopefulness.

500) Hope is not accomplished by the gathering of an abundance of material wealth.

501) Hopefulness begins with an understanding of the causes and effects of hopelessness and the fear that results from a hopeless state of being.

502) God knew that individuals, societies, and nations, when left to human judgment, would reach dual states of hopelessness (eighty percent) and hopefulness (twenty percent), despite great material wealth.

503) Millions are destined for starvation. Pollution and overpopulation are emerging global challenges. Where can we go from here? Who will lead us?

504) Whom can we look to for national and international leadership and hope to face new and emerging problems in the new millennium?

505) God perspective of hope is different from ours. He has witnessed over the centuries and is still witnessing how we engineer hopelessness of the weak, either inadvertently or by design.

506) God listens to, but rejects, our rationalization for the state of the poor in society. He observes the widening economic gap between individuals and between nations.

507) God records how the big take advantage of the small; the strong take advantage of the weak; the educated take advantage of the uneducated; and how the defenseless lack the capacity to defend themselves physically, economically, and intellectually.

508) God is mindful of our compulsions to gain economic advantage as opposed to looking out for the interest of others as a first imperative of our existence.

509) Arguably, the world economy leaves behind eighty percent of its inhabitants, as twenty percent of its inhabitants reap the greater benefits of God's creation.

510) Our Holy Father (God) sees us as we perpetrate or permit (either by intent or by our silence) various forms of exploitation of human beings, as acts of self–preservation.

511) Whether the model is a rural farming village or the worldwide global village, the foundation of hope is crumbling.

512) Many religious and non–religious people cry out, "Can God not intervene and change the conditions of our world?" "Where is God?" We ask. Yet, we never ask where God is when we are enjoying the pleasures of life.

513) Must we always blame God for the things that we wrongfully engineer, yet take the credit when things are going well for us? Can you see the incongruity of our reasoning?

514) Some religious and non–religious people entertain the thought that the state of the world is either God's fault, or at least that He should fix world problems. Perhaps more relevant enquiries would be: Who engineered the problems that we now demand God to fix?

515) What benefit is it for God to free us of the consequences of our decisions, when we act contrary to His Word? On the surface, one might say that God is guilty, but it is pointless to blame God when we stubbornly resist His guidance and go it alone.

516) Some human beings have made a conscious choice to conduct their affairs contrary to the divine will of God, and He allows it for a time, but God is forgiving. God allows human beings to exercise their *will* as free moral agents, but He has not left us without His (ever–present) divine guidance.

517) God did not leave us alone to hopelessly engineer our destiny in His vast and complex universe. He ordained human governments to promote the general welfare of the community (Reference: *Five Foundations of Human Development* (FFHD) —Figure 5: Three Key Functions of Human Government).

518) Some churches possess the capacity to build schools, colleges, and universities. Others may focus on more charitable endeavors; but overall, the church does not possess the capital adequacy of government and corporations.

519) The church does not have the capacity to create employment empowerment zones in order to provide opportunities for employment and balanced economic growth within communities.

520) The most critical role the church should play is that of striving with all its might to mobilize the spiritual visionaries having God's armor and weapons of warfare.

521) The laws of nature to which *all* humanity are subject, place limits on what we can achieve in the physical world. Spiritual laws that the majority of the six billion world population subscribe to also set boundaries for us.

522) Human beings are endowed with an intelligent mind, and creative capacity, sufficient to change our circumstances and environment, and shape our destiny in the university.

523) My richest lessons come from the poorest people. They deepen my understanding of what really matters in life. I listen to their stories and they compel me to speak out—for their sake and ours. **-Mark Lutz** —Mark is Senior Vice President of Global Philanthropy at Opportunity International, a non-profit microfinance organization.

524) The recurring state of hopelessness around the world makes obvious the need for government intervention, not just as political, social, and economic imperatives, but also as a spiritual imperative, as well.

525) Society needs its rich; some would not eat had it not been for the rich. Jesus knew that many might lack the divine insight, as temporary custodians, to manage personal wealth, and national wealth; hence the reason for His admonition to the rich.

526) God in His wisdom, from the creation of the earth, took away the moral defense of rich individuals, societies, and nations.

527) God invalidates our moral arguments. God wants us to understand that many of the world's hopeless individuals and nations have neither boots nor straps.

528) The poor rely upon the generosity of wealthy individuals, corporations and nations. They also depend upon the administration of government social programs and upon the contributions of religious organizations, NGOs, family, friends, and strangers to meet basic needs of food, clothing, and shelter.

529) Hope through personal responsibility begins with a hopeful attitude. When we do, even the hopeless may envision rays of hope that shine through otherwise darkened clouds of life.

530) We must engage in the global struggle to create a better world. This struggle requires a new blueprint of hope for our survival.

531) The scientist, the doctor, the lawyer, the engineer, the professor, the politician, and the philosopher, and the ordinary person, feel a sense of hopelessness.

532) When we assume personal responsibility for God's creation, we begin the process of bringing hope to the world, not only for our race, culture, class, caste, nationality, or religion, but for others as well.

533) We must rise above the selfish motivations which guide our actions. We must consciously and consistently seek to purify ourselves of the tendencies to act on selfish impulses.

534) We must guard against inaction that can amount to shirking responsibility when we do nothing to bring hope to the lives of others.

535) Hopelessness is a well-defined condition in society with causes and effects that are both quantifiable and measurable.

536) We are responsible for our family dysfunction, delinquent children, abused children, abused husbands and wives and marriage breakdown.

537) We are responsible for the brutalities in the world by the way we live with our neighbor, because some of us are overly nationalistic, racist, or prejudiced.

538) We belong to this religion, or that religion, causing conflict with each other in defense of our gods.

539) The juncture at which eighty percent of the world's population finds itself is that we are powerless.

540) Regardless of the sophistication of Western and other developed nations, no nation (independently) can hope to protect itself from such threats, because they have far-reaching consequences for the entire global village.

541) Who is willing to say, unequivocally, that it is God's will that human living should be a hopeless journey from one unmanaged crisis to another?

542) God admonishes us to humble ourselves, and pray and seek His, and turn from their wicked ways, then He will hear from heaven, and will forgive our sins and heal our land (2 Chronicles 7:14) (Reference: *Five Foundations of Human Development* (FFHD) —Figure 15: God's Threefold Promise to Humanity).

543) When we obey God's Word, we release the trinity of God's spiritual purpose for our lives and our Earth, resulting in a corresponding open heaven and promises from God.

544) Despite God's manifold promises, whether religious or not, six thousand years of human history has shown that we continue to stumble in the darkness.

545) Nations' citizens must become acutely aware of the conditions under which other human beings live, and avoid justifications for inaction, or a moral defense to justify the social and economic state of our neighbors.

546) No one is immune to the devastating mental effects of hopelessness. Neither money nor material possessions, nor position, nor power, nor prestige in society can give us hope.

547) Throughout history, many rich and powerful individuals have ended their lives, crippled by fear and depression and overwhelmed by loneliness, yet there is a better hope in fervent prayer without ceasing.

548) Many challenges to individuals and nations over the ages have been caused by the unhealthy exercise of free will.

549) We have allowed race, culture, class, nationality, and religion, which should unite us, to be the catalysts that precipitate divisions among neighbors.

550) What if we stepped away from our religious dogmas and customs for a moment and focused on God, not the differences in our God or god(s), but on the universality of God?

551) What if adherents to religions decided not to wait on others to ascend to the hill where God's light from above could shine through us to light a path to Him?

552) Imagine if we prayed for our enemies, our leaders, our fallen brother or sister, or our weaker neighbor.

553) We have built civilized societies out of the ashes of the Dark Ages. The unquenchable light of idealism lives within and underpins our

hope for survival in the twenty–first century and in the new millennium.

554) Hope in God is one of the cornerstones of the Christian faith and of other religions. The world, with its riches and its wants, does not free us from suffering.

555) We have developed vast storehouses of human knowledge, and we declare our material achievements as progress, and high civilization, but are we capable of manufacturing hope?

556) Prayer is essential for the world and for the church, because it is the only way of making God and His redeeming love present in the world.

557) God entrusts us with the intellectual capacity to seek our own salvation. He has entrusted us with the church, His most precious possession, and we are its members (visible and invisible).

558) The physical and material needs and wants of our modern age lead some to pray for miracle healing, jobs, cars, homes, and even husbands and wives.

559) One cannot deny that physical and material needs are essential to our survival, but often we miss an important aspect of prayer.

560) Prayer connects us to God through the Holy Spirit. Essentially, God's righteousness is the bridge between us, and the things we need.

561) Matthew teaches that more important than our *wants* are our *needs*, but our wants often outstrip our needs. The questions facing us are how and for what should we pray?

562) Is it reasonable to demand of God the rewards of prayer when prayer is self–centered and self–concerned? Observing the dramatic rise in the "Gospel of Prosperity," God has become to us our personal provider of material things.

563) The underpinnings of our prayers are what we want God to do for us, or to provide for us, as opposed to daily worship, thankfulness for grace and mercy, and glorification of God. The Psalmist exalts: "Be exalted, O God, above the heavens; *Let* Your glory be above all the earth" (Psalm 57:11 NKJV).

"Let us not become weary in doing good, for at the proper time we will reap a harvest if we do not give up. Therefore, as we have opportunity, let us do good to all people, especially to those who belong to the family of believers" Galatians 6:9–10 (NIV). Jesus Christ cared for the poor: "All they ask was that we should continue to remember the poor, the very thing I was eager to do."

Galatians 2:10 (NIV)

564) **What is charity?** Charity is a spiritual command from God. In order to qualify giving as a charitable deed, it must originate both from love and from a sense of spiritual duty and responsibility.

565) This basic truth of our existence denies us any opportunity to free ourselves from our responsibility to the poor in society, regardless of their color, race, culture, language, nationality, or their religion.

566) This scripture suggests that alleviation of the suffering of the poor among us is an indispensable component and compelling evidence of spiritual disciplines.

567) When we make reference to the poor, our focus is on those who are impoverished due to circumstances beyond their control.

568) There is an inherent danger when we try to intellectualize poverty and suffering of fellow human beings. It renders us insensitive to the needs of those who suffer unjustly.

569) God of the universe understood before the foundation of the world that the poor and disenfranchised would face great poverty in the midst of great individual, national, and international wealth.

570) God has made the treatment of the impoverished of this world a basis upon which He judges the world and the basis on which one can enter into His kingdom (Matthew 25:31–40).

571) Western nations engage their religious, social, political, and legal resources to help uproot the remnants of social and economic injustice from their landscapes.

572) In the book of Deuteronomy God gives this directive: If there is among you a poor man of your brethren, you shall not harden your heart nor shut your hands from your poor brother" (Deuteronomy 15:7).

573) God, the Author of creation, understands how the poor in society arrived at their state of impoverishment. He understands the inequities of each generation and the human and natural conditions that lead to poverty.

574) God knew that human inclinations would perpetuate poverty in the world, therefore He commanded us to open our hands wide to our brother and to the needy in our land.

575) Tens of thousands of foreign aid workers make self–sacrificing contributions to feed the impoverished in under–developed nations, whose plight has endured for generations.

576) Unfortunately, the effects of the great kindnesses of individuals and organizations are temporary, overwhelmed by the next cycle of human tragedy.

577) Despite the aggregate of trillions of dollars in foreign aid and the continuing nature of poverty, such continued generosity is essential to alleviate hunger and starvation, temporarily.

578) Despite our great storehouse of human knowledge, our advancements in science and technology, and our great intellectual progress, we continue to feed the symptoms of poverty. There is a need for a deeper intellectual understanding of the causes of poverty and its endemic nature.

579) God has given us a conscience as our moral guide. His word further enlightens us rather than leaves us to determine our own actions based upon intellectual considerations.

580) The roots and trajectory of poverty seem to parallel the roots and trajectory of wealth creation, since poverty is an implicit side effect of our system of wealth creation.

581) From a historic perspective, some structured poverty has its roots in slavery. This has been the case in North America, the Caribbean, South America, Europe, and parts of Africa. These economic inequities of slavery and post–slavery extend into the eighteenth and nineteenth centuries of the industrial era.

582) Intentionally or unintentionally, political, social, economic, and educational exclusion helped to sustain poverty on a steady

trajectory, with its aftershocks resonating in the twentieth and twenty-first centuries.

583) Poverty is not a natural phenomenon in our world. Undeniably, some poverty has its origins in tribalism entering the world stage ill equipped. Racial prejudice, overt racism, and other forms of social and economic injustices underpinned "systems of exclusion."

584) Indigenous peoples throughout the world have fallen victim to some form of oppression by the stronger and more powerful of the earth. From a Western world perspective, these historic disadvantages began in the sixteen hundreds and extended into the mid-nineteen hundreds.

585) Our poor world nations are staggering under the burden of inefficient economies in the twenty-first century. Our poor nations are indebted to the powerful, developed nations in an unbalanced global economy.

586) Can our poor nations survive the compounding effects of man-made, complex, and natural catastrophes, while at the same time, confront new and emerging challenges?

587) Developed nations have the capacity to engineer their recovery from natural and manmade disasters, but underdeveloped and developing nations may never recover.

588) Many global conflicts have their origins in ancestral, territorial, racial, cultural, national, and religious differences.

589) Although some hope exists for rebuilding the physical infrastructure after a disaster, the greater challenge to humanity is to find ways to rebuild in the human realm.

590) The world has recorded examples of many conflicts that can span years and generations. Developed nations should use their genius to help poor nations find ways to resolve their internal and external conflicts.

591) Western nations strive to provide better neighborhoods for children to have opportunities for personal growth and religious freedom. Underdeveloped and developing nations refer to the exodus from the home land as a "brain drain."

592) Developed Western nations are not responsible for the drain of intellectual capital from underdeveloped and developing nations *to* developed nations.

593) The present social and economic crisis in underdeveloped and developing nations is indicative of the need for some form of rebalancing of the world's intellectual and resource capital.

594) When nations achieve some parity in development, and intellectual, economic, and material well–being, peace and harmony will be within global reach.

595) The rise of economic dislocation and the new war and environmental refugees have had a destabilizing effect on all nations.

596) The frequency and magnitude of catastrophes in our modern era, presents a great burden to already weak political and economic systems with vulnerable leadership and infrastructures.

597) There is an urgent need for a moral appeal to world leaders to seek peaceful means to avert the man–made disasters and to mitigate the uncontrollable ones.

598) The Church and other religious organizations must speak from a common moral platform, and seek ways to better understand the trajectory of poverty and its historic and present underpinnings.

599) A brief study of the history of slavery reveals that the reason for slavery was economics in the first instance. Undeniably, economic disadvantages have permeated structural poverty with structural advantages and disadvantages (Reference: **Eric Williams (1911-1981)**, *Capitalism and Slavery* (London: Andre Deutsch Limited © 1944 by Eric Williams)).

600) The church historians of the day made justifications and apologies for the church, likewise, the church dutifully supported acts that were contrary to God's spiritual purpose for our existence.

601) Western governments, unobstructed by the Western church, gained a financial foundation fostered by Black African slavery through free labor and the Triangular Trade.

602) Black African slavery through free labor provided the appropriate economic platform for Western power elites to support a major economic transformation from manual agricultural production to mechanization.

603) Western nations' economies have grown significantly through the genius of the Industrial Revolution (1800s – 1900s), capitalism, and modern education.

604) Despite the historic fact of the church's involvement in the slave trade, one must balance one's view regarding the abolitionists of 1783 and later, the English Evangelicals who were opposed to the slave trade.

605) The signing of The Emancipation Proclamation on January 1, 1863, signaled the beginning of the end to slavery in the United States of America, and eventually throughout the world.

606) The emancipation of Black African slavery throughout the colonies ushered in new challenges for survival for which post–slave populations were unprepared.

607) Western nations missed an opportunity, in the early eighteenth and nineteenth centuries, to equip and empower post–slavery populations for their survival in the new world as an extension of the moral triumph over slavery.

608) The survival of post–slavery peoples throughout the colonies hinged upon the call of God in their lives, as churches mushroomed across the landscape of post–slavery nations as a symbol of God's preserving power.

609) Mercifully, God made all human beings in His image with equal standing before Him (Genesis 1:26). It is upon this basis of God's universal spiritual equality that the indomitable spirit of human beings triumphs.

610) The Spirit of God's love is still plowing and reseeding our hearts with love, which is the only true way to roll back the dark shadow cast upon the world for centuries.

611) Despite the fact that we live in the twenty–first century, the widespread social, economic, and educational gaps foster division in the way in which various individuals and nations view human existence.

612) The prism from which individuals and nations tend to view human life throughout the world reveals social, political and religious values which are often at variance.

613) There are some market conditions in the world that perpetuate wealth for some as they unavoidably create poverty for others.

614) Capitalism and material progress bolstered the prosperity of the Industrial Revolution (1800s – 1900s), which ushered in a new era of wealth creation.

615) Western capitalism has demonstrated the capacity for great material progress on one hand, and great economic disparity on the other.

616) Capitalism created greater rewards of production into the hands of a few, but also at the same time, capitalism empowered a viable middle class.

617) Mass industrialization of the nineteenth, twentieth, and the early twenty–first centuries ushered in even greater changes in production through automation.

618) With great wealth for the industrialist and a new era of profligacy, capitalism became a word with negative undertones as the middle class began falling behind economically while wealth increased in the upper tier of society.

619) One can argue that two major economic systems are on the opposing ends of the modern economic spectrum: capitalism and socialism.

620) Interestingly, political systems of Western nations are rooted in these two opposing dynamics, as they engage in a recurring cycle between the models of leadership.

621) Those who promote socialism view capitalism as the cause of the economic ills in modern society and the diminishing value of the workers contribution to profitability.

622) Those who promote capitalism seek greater corporate profits and returns on shareholder investments with limits to regulations.

623) The tenuous balance among production, marketing, consumption, and profits can realize great benefits, when shareholder and stakeholder values are taken into consideration, as well.

624) Capitalism began to emerge in a new form in the twentieth century with corporations taking on transnational dimensions as they explore international markets for cheaper sources of labor to reduce the cost of production, and increase profitability.

625) Capitalism, has become a double–edged sword, first as the engine that facilitates material growth and prosperity, and second, as the mechanism which creates great disparity between rich and poor.

626) There is a need to develop new global economic models which encourage less superfluous wealth and more equitable distribution of the wealth created by production.

627) This new economy should promote linear growth to allow for meaningful implementation, adaptation, and assessment of fundamental human needs.

628) Linear pattern of growth might seem counter to human progress or even appear to go against the principles of capitalism, but the inherent benefits lie in more stable nations, sustained growth, and stable world economies.

629) The more serious concerns with capitalism lie in the gravitation of wealth to the wealthy and to the creation of a social and economic world imbalance which destabilizes nations and jeopardizes the international peace that we crave.

630) There was a time in history when we battled with other races, cultures, religions, and nations to gain territory, power and economic advantage. Today we are fighting against ourselves.

631) Peoples and nations are inextricably linked by virtue of human needs for material resources, trade and commerce, and environmental protection in the global village.

632) Western nations with a Christian heritage know that our wars are futile, and they only create human suffering, poverty, and a waste of material, human, and financial resources.

633) Growing poverty, hunger, and disenfranchisement around the world increase the need for charity. Hoarding of strategic, tactical, and operational resources perpetuates and precipitates the urgent need for charity.

634) We can delineate this world crisis as due to growth in population, knowledge gap, imbalance in trade, changing climatic conditions, natural disasters, and wars, from tribal and militia wars to our modern sophisticated wars with the most expensive and sophisticated modern technologies.

635) Many underdeveloped and developing nations have vast reserves of natural resources. What, then, is the reason for the disenfranchised and impoverished state of these nations?

636) We often fail to heed the lessons of history, of nations that concentrated wealth and power in the hands of a few and brought about the demise of their civilizations.

637) The modern world follows the same course of the great empires, which suffocated egalitarian growth of the masses and brought about their eventual collapse.

638) The current overwhelming need for charity is a symptom of something that has gone monumentally wrong with leadership in the world. Nations can seek every opportunity to promote fair trade with national and trans–national neighbors.

639) Debtor nations can use their financial resources to develop the human capital through the education of their populations, and change the trajectory of poverty, through creativity, innovation and political inclusion.

640) Creativity and innovation strengthen the output of manufacturing, which is the basic building block of modern economies, and this is true for all nations.

641) Many of the problems, which afflict nations, demand great moral, political, social, intellectual, technical, and materially based solutions.

642) Nations will benefit when the world's natural resources and global assets imbalance becomes a moral imperative, as opposed to a purely economic imperative.

643) Every economic upheaval that takes place in developed nations is a threat to the economic survival of underdeveloped and developing nations.

644) World energy prices have the most dramatic impact on the economic survival of underdeveloped and developing nations.

645) The church and other religious organizations can let their voices resonate around the world in a moral appeal to leaders of underdeveloped and developing nations to renounce autocratic and military style governments.

646) Developing and underdeveloped nations should follow the lead of Brazil and of the United States' 22nd Amendment, and enact term limits in their constitutions to two four–year terms in office.

647) The noble goals of charity are only a stopgap measure for these underdeveloped and developing nations, because observation shows that trillions of dollars in charity are not eliminating human suffering.

648) Charity is important and necessary, but it should not be a substitute for needed permanent solutions to national and international imbalances in knowledge and wealth.

649) Every citizen of every nation should pray that his or her nation would strive to avoid, to the greatest extent possible, humanly caused *or* humanly inspired calamities (Reference: *Five Foundations of Human Development* (FFHD) —Figure 4: Hierarchy of World Disasters).

650) *Reparation* is a word that we react negatively to, because it means accepting blame, but it is a word which has power to redeem and heal individuals and nations. *Love* is the only other word in the English vocabulary that has healing powers comparable to reparation.

651) When reparation becomes a legal obligation, as opposed to flowing spiritual and moral imperatives, it loses its capacity to heal wounds, and it causes division among peoples and nations.

652) Reparation can permanently restore most of the broken relationships in the world between nations.

653) When nations adopt a spiritual responsibility to all of humanity and in particular, to those nations that have suffered social and economic injustices, the need for charity should diminish.

654) Western churches and all religions should encourage all to atone for past atrocities against humanity and to voluntarily come to the table of reconciliation with our brothers in accordance with the Word of God.

655) The opportunity exists for Western nations to do good to those who are of the household of faith (family of believers) as God has instructed us in Galatians 6:10.

656) This spiritual perspective for reparation is unquestionably beneficial to national and international world stability and permanent healing.

657) Nations throughout the world should examine reparation as a spiritual imperative, as opposed to a legal obligation.

658) One could argue that, to a great extent, Western nations do compensate nations and have for decades, through opening their borders; through giving foreign aid; through allowing access to their great universities; and through many charitable and humanitarian responses to disasters.

659) The church and other world religious organizations should also recognize that poverty goes far beyond money. Spiritual, social, and

intellectual poverty have at least as devastating an impact on world communities as economic poverty.

660) Charity has its place, but there is an important distinction and advantage to reparation over charity. Charity in the broadest sense has the foundation of a response to humanitarian need detached from any underlying responsibility on the part of the giver.

661) Reparation, on the other hand, speaks to a different set of spiritual imperatives and moral connections between the donor and the recipient, thereby linking them spiritually.

662) Reparation among peoples and among nations can take the form of a structure of remedies that addresses specific areas of historical disadvantages with measurable goals and outcomes.

663) Money cannot buy sustained inner peace, happiness, or contentment, but on the other hand, lack of money relegates the poor and disadvantaged to a life of less than optimum nutrition, health, housing, transportation, education, and employment.

664) The phenomenal growth of national and international charitable organizations is a double-edged sword. On the one hand, it is testimony to the human spirit of compassion and on the other hand, it is, in part, due to our failed leadership in the world.

665) To a great extent, charity organizations are symbolic of our failed approaches to solving the phenomenal rise in world hunger, world suffering, world homelessness, and world-wide manmade, natural, and medical calamities.

666) Our vast storehouse of human knowledge calls into question our capacity to manage the challenges of our modern era, as we enter the global village with one unmanaged crisis after another.

667) With every passing decade, some of the same regions of the world face recurring disasters in never-ending cycles of natural and man-made calamities, while the generosity of the human spirit continues.

668) Arguably, there is a critical need for money and for temporary relief, but money alone cannot stem the root causes of humanitarian disaster, though it is an essential temporary solution.

669) It is worth mentioning that some of those who laborer in God's vineyard face great personal risk in parts of the world that have become a minefield of wars, disease, and other forms of seemingly, unsolvable human suffering.

670) New regions add to the collective need for intervention as new challenges confront emerging nations, individuals, families, groups, humanitarian organizations, governments, and non–governmental organizations.

671) Ancient man, perhaps the Akkadian (or Accadian) ancient Mesopotamia (now Iraq) from about 3000 B.C. until the time of Jesus; when struck by a disaster would have in all probability pointed to the heavens for an answer.

672) We build our cities on waterfronts; the poor and improvised build their vulnerable habitats along underdeveloped costal waterways, because they rely on fishing and other minor commerce as well.

673) The wealthy build their homes on beach fronts, along mountainsides and densely forested areas away from the crowded inner urban centers.

674) Catastrophic disasters can strike any nation with or without warning. The recent January 2010, Haitian disaster, a 7.0 magnitude earthquake, was indicative of how natural disasters can take on greater proportions due to lack of mitigation strategies.

675) Hurricane Katrina, which was perhaps one of the deadliest hurricanes in the United States, struck New Orleans on August 23, 2005 with damage estimated in billions of dollars.

676) No amount of money that we have to spend after–the–fact can parallel God's admonishment in Second Chronicles, chapter seven, verse fourteen, as our guiding principle for the preservation of humanity and the environment.

FOUNDATION 1
SPIRITUAL FOUNDATION
—1.5. PEACE (HARMONY)

"Peace I leave with you; my peace I give to you. I do not give to you as the world gives. Do not let your hearts be troubled and do not be afraid" John 14:27 (NIV). "Make every effort to keep the unity of the Spirit through the bond of peace. There is one body and one Spirit–just as you were called to one hope when you were called."

Ephesians 4:3–4 (NIV)

677) **What is peace?** The answer is as fundamental as the question. Peace is a facet of God, rather than of human beings.

678) God's Word enlightens: Peacemakers who sow in peace raise a harvest of righteousness (James 3:18).

679) When we comprehend and accept this most important fact, human civilization will have taken the first step toward peace.

680) Peace is not merely the absence of human conflict, but the imposition of the reign of love among human beings, which can only come from the heart of God.

681) Shalom refers to a state of family unity, peace with one's neighbors, and freedom from fear and anxiety. Shalom is contentment within our souls and with God (Numbers 6:26; Romans 5:1).

682) When we think of peace, visions of peaceful coexistence among nations come to mind, yet this peace eludes humanity, because only the joy of the Lord transcends peace.

683) From a biblical perspective, the peace that the authors refer to is the peace of God manifested through the Holy Spirit.

684) The prophet Isaiah wrote, approximately twenty–five hundred years ago: "The way of peace they have not known, And *there is* no justice in their way; They have made themselves crooked paths; Whoever takes that way shall not know peace" (Isaiah 59:8 NKJV) (circa 712 BCE).

685) Which nations can we say are responsible for the ravages of wars? Can we blame a nation's ideology, its politics, its religion, its race, its culture, its economics, its nationalism, or its pride?

686) We are nationalistic (even so, nationalism can be both positive and negative). We are African, American, Australian, British, Canadian, Chinese, French, German, Indian, Jamaican, and Russian – just to name a few nationalities.

687) We are White, Black, and Brown. We are adherents of Christianity, Hinduism, Jainism, Sikhism, Buddhism, Judaism, and Islam, just to name a few religions (Reference: *Five Foundations of Human Development* (FFHD) —Table 1: Major Religions of the World).

688) We are religious, but do our religions matter if our religions divide us, and set us apart, because of our superficial differences? Can our religions lead the way to peaceful coexistence and unite us as a human family?

689) We often forget that we are, first, members of the human family, with a common heritage. We often forget that we are the world composite of all of our needs, thoughts, feelings, hopes, and aspirations, and of our violent nature as well.

690) How can the international community of nations find peace? Is peace a military imperative as opposed to a spiritual imperative? Peace begins with God who is the source of peace (John 14:27).

691) If we miss this most important distinction, our desire for peace becomes a vain pursuit, marked by futility and frustration.

692) Jesus Christ came into the world to redeem man from sin, but we often forget that He also introduced the perfect way to peace as an example to humanity. What is this perfect way?

693) *Suffering for righteousness sake* (Matthew 5:10); this is the path of perfection of the saints, but human nature is incompatible with suffering for righteousness.

694) It may seem counterintuitive that when others have done us wrong, our response should be forgiveness and mercy.

695) One problem of our modern era is that we often permit temporary suffering to inspire anger in us, rather than to draw us closer to God's grace and mercy. Our perfect example, Jesus Christ, demonstrated a spirit of peace as an example to humanity.

696) Jesus Christ, in the New Testament (NT), offers humanity a new way to bring peace to a world that seems to be in perpetual conflict.

697) This new way calls for a new paradigm of religious teaching that focuses on the central authority of God and on the teachings and message of Jesus Christ to all of His followers.

698) The message of Jesus Christ and the Apostles points us to the reasons for the absence of peace, after six thousand years of human conflict.

699) Their message should provide a compelling reason to trust in God, but we must first win the "war of denial" of the authority of Jesus Christ and follow His path of forgiveness and mercy.

700) The church must, of necessity, strive in its actions to demonstrate Christ-like behavior to the world. War and retaliation by any nation first violates the dictates of our values, then disregards the authority of Jesus Christ.

701) "Blessed *are* the peacemakers, For they shall be called sons of God" (Matthew 5:9 NKJV). "But I say to you, Love your enemies, bless those who curse you, do good to those that hate you, and pray for those who spitefully use you and persecute you" (Matthew 5:44).

702) Many wonder why we should respond with love, forgiveness, and mercy when others offend us. Many might not be aware that God has accounted for every thought and every wrongdoing from the beginning of time.

703) The trust among nations has been broken repeatedly over past centuries. Genocide and great wars have shattered the hopes of humanity to live in peace and harmony.

704) We seem to place greater hope for peace in modern science and technology than we place in the important lessons of six thousand years of recorded human history.

705) Even for some adherents of Christianity, it seems extraordinarily difficult to practice the teachings of Jesus Christ, which state that peacemakers are called the Sons of God (Matthew 5:9).

706) Each one of us must act in the interest of the survival of humanity and write and speak to the issues that confront us in the twenty-first century.

707) The Holy Scriptures, ancient prophets and great philosophers of yesteryear have forewarned us of time of great tribulations and great

wars among nations. In acts of defiance we have purposely chosen paths that all but guarantee fulfillment of the prophetic writings.

708) We formulate justifications in order to maintain our hope for peace through advancements in science and technology, but these advancements bring great fear among peoples and nations, because of the destructive capacity of some technologies.

709) God knew that in the twenty-first century, fear would be one of the most dominant human preoccupations and that humanity would doom itself to warfare, trying with all of its gifts and advancements to eradicate fear through arsenals of modern weapons.

710) God knows His creation and in His infinite wisdom, He gave us a force more powerful than fear – *faith*. No other action equates the exercise of the power of faith in God.

711) Faith is more than an intellectual activity. Faith is an entity. Faith is a substance. Faith is an antidote to fear. Fear without faith incapacitates individuals and nations.

712) When nations equip themselves with God's Spirit of love, joy, peace, patience, kindness, goodness, faithfulness, gentleness, and self-control, they will be prepared for peace.

713) When nations equip themselves with weapons of mass destruction, they are preparing for war rather than peace. This preparedness brings fear of each other and takes us further away from the noble goals of peace that we strive for.

714) The great horrors of wars over past centuries have not inspired humanity to veer off the path of violence and to veer onto the path of non-violence.

715) Observing the conflict among nations over the past six thousand years provides us some evidence that world nations, reacting to fear of each other, bring us ever closer to the brink of catastrophe with the horrors of ever greater wars than those experienced in *World War I (1914–1918)* and *World War II (1939–1945)*.

716) Paradoxically, some who promote wars as the way to peace often use *World War I* and *World War II* to justify their arguments, but can we justify the repeat of such catastrophes in our modern era, in which we claim modern enlightenment?

717) Whether or not well founded, the world lives in hope that peace is within the reach of the next peace plan, peace mission, peace treaty, or peace pact. How confident ought we to be?

718) Over the past century, there have been numerous peace initiatives, peace marches, and the formation of organizations dedicated to peace, but our efforts have not ushered in a sustained period of lasting international peace and harmony.

719) Humanity can have freedom from fear, but it requires a right relationship with God, righteousness, the power of authenticity among leaders, and justice among human beings.

720) Imagine if we sincerely believed that life was always leading toward a higher good and that God was in control of human affairs.

721) We live in a world that seems to indicate that some level of armament is essential to act as a deterrent against some neighbor.

722) If we use violence as the means to achieve peace, would we not have to use violence as the means to maintain peace? More importantly, can nations truly achieve or sustain peace through violence?

723) No one would deny that this is a crossroads at which ancient civilizations have stood, and at which we stand in the modern age.

724) The international community of nations expends, in the aggregate, hundreds of billions of dollars in armaments per year in a quest to tilt, or maintain the military balance in order to bring peace to the world through deterrence.

725) Western Christian nations and other nations are familiar with the words of the Psalmist, who admonishes: "Unless the LORD builds the house, They labor in vain who build it; Unless the LORD guards the city, The watchman stays awake in vain" (Psalm 127:1 NKJV) (circa 975 BCE).

726) God clearly distinguished, for our edification, the Old Covenant and the New Covenant. He left no doubt regarding his admonishment, warning, and reward for obedience to His Word. Unfortunately, we have not fully comprehended or heeded God's advice and instructions. We have not adhered to the advice of our Creator — God.

727) We have (consciously or sub–consciously) accepted conflict as innate and unavoidable, as global villagers come into their own, each nation with its own political ideology.

728)   We have made civilization into a grand competitive arena in which the strong survive at the expense of the weak.

729)   After six thousand years, we have not learned to live in peace and harmony among nations. We did not, and do not, understand the benefits of fellowship with the human family.

730)   We think of ourselves more highly than we ought to. We have divided society by tribe, sect, caste, nationality, race, color, education, intellect, age, and by social and economic status.

731)   We have gone down the road of gross intolerance to each other as we wage war against each other in the name of material progress and peace.

732)   Material wealth and power over others have directed our paths. We have exploited other human beings, in particular, the innocent, the young, the elderly, the weak, the poor, the sick, and the disenfranchised, often for our own personal gain.

733)   Democracy promises to build a better world with peace, security, and justice for all, which are its noble goals. Democracy, has nearly accomplished these goals that are, indeed, reachable as we strive to elevate our democratic ideals.

734)   Is it possible to achieve the noble goals of our democratic ideals? Assuredly! But it is only possible when God's Theocracy underpins the ideals of our democracy.

735)   The compatibility of these two ideals holds the greatest promise for a better world with peace, security, and justice for all; these are the stated goals of democracy.

736)   In our quest for universal peace and harmony, world nations stockpile huge arsenals of weapons of mass destruction (to greater or lesser degrees) and, instead of peace, we have harvested wars for six thousand years past to the present.

737)   History shows that during the Middle Ages, a belief in God was strong and pervasive among Christians in Europe and among Muslims in the Middle East and North Africa.

738)   Historical records show that followers of Christianity and Islam killed each other in their military campaigns for approximately 200 years and well into the fifteenth century.

739) Religion has played a significant role in attempting to bring about peace. Pure religion is still our only hope, and God's wisdom is the only attribute that will effectively guide our pursuit for peace.

740) Advances in science and technology have increased our reliance upon earthly wisdom in our twenty–first century. Science will not save us. There is a need to understand the dramatic changes that are taking place throughout the world.

741) There is an enormous discontent among peoples and nations that is expressing itself in different ways. A great spiritual hunger is developing in various parts of our world. Present political, social, and religious conflicts, wars, and rumors of wars and the accumulation of armaments are symptomatic of this hunger.

742) Who or what is responsible for the chaos in the world? Can we, by reliance only on our own wisdom, avoid the descent into another global war – *World War III?*

743) Man will bring civilization to the brink of annihilation, but can science bring us back from the brink? Assuredly not! God will have to intervene and take control of His creation. Is *World War III* inevitable? Can we afford the outcomes of yet another great war?

744) The way to peace is framed in explicit Biblical guidelines: "Blessed *are* the Peacemakers, for they will be called the sons of God" (Matthew 5:9 NKJV).

745) "When a man's ways pleases the LORD, He makes even his enemies to be at peace with him" (Proverbs 16:7 NKJV). According to God's Holy Word, it is possible to have lasting peace, and it is certain that lasting peace will come.

746) Observing various civilizations and religious, one cannot doubt that humanity has earnestly tried to achieve peaceful coexistence among nations, and that we continue to strive despite our failures.

747) Regardless of our great passion for peace; to a great extent we have failed. Our forefathers have not left us a legacy of peace, and *our* legacy will be as theirs.

748) The reason for human conflicts and wars are far more deep–rooted that the political, racial, cultural, economic, territorial, material or social struggles we observe in daily life.

749) History has shown that humanity has not consistently applied God's universal love and justice to pursue the way of peace.

750) Despite the boons of science and technology, better education of the masses, access to religious knowledge, and the proliferation of peace organizations, we have failed to engender peaceful co-existence.

751) We have placed our reliance in government, yet, we must all pursue peace. It is not simply a responsibility of governments and statesmen.

752) Our modern civilization is coming into alignment with the description of the prophetic scriptures (Hosea 4:6–7 NKJV).

753) Undoubtedly, we need to re–examine the Holy Scriptures and find God's direction and the spiritual purpose of our existence. Christ enabled the reconciliation between God and human beings that results in perfect peace.

754) God inspired the Apostle Paul to look into the future from two thousand years ago. Paul describes the last days as perilous times, times of crass materialism, moral decadence, idolatry, and a false spirituality that denies the true power of God (2 Timothy 3:1–5).

FOUNDATION 1
SPIRITUAL FOUNDATION
—1.6. HUMILITY (MEEKNESS)

"Rich and poor have this in common: The Lord is the Maker of them all" Proverbs 22:2 (NIV). "Humility and the fear of the Lord bring wealth and honor and life" Proverbs 22:4 (NIV). ". . . God opposes the proud but shows favor to the humble. Humble yourselves, therefore, under God's mighty hand, that he may lift you up in due time. Cast all your anxiety on him because he cares for you. Be self–controlled and alert. . . ."

1 Peter 5:5–8 (NIV)

755) **What is humility?** Humility means *meekness* and is the most significant aspect of the original and only true relationship between human beings and God.

756) Humility does not demand that we humiliate ourselves or eliminate character or personal integrity, but rather that we give preference and honor to others.

757) The humble individual puts aside personal ambition and adopts a disposition of humility and honor to God.

758) The Apostle Peter, writing to believers struggling in the midst of persecution, encouraged them to conduct themselves courageously for the person and the program of Christ.

759) Peter turned his attention to the younger people saying: "Likewise you younger people, submit yourselves to *your* elders. Yes, all of *you* be submissive to one another, and be clothed with humility, for *'God resists the proud, But gives grace to the humble'* " (1 Peter 5:5 NKJV).

760) Our submission to God and to each other allows us to grow in spiritual maturity, but pride often impedes our spiritual growth.

761) When we respect people for who they are at their current station in life, we can build more effective relationships based upon mutual trust and respect.

762) The universality of humanity will come from different colors, races, cultures, nations, and continents, and God will be the final judge.

They will come from different periods in history, and from different denominations.

763) The scripture reveals: "(Now the man Moses was very humble, more than all men who were on the face of the earth)" (Numbers 12:3 NKJV).

764) Insightful observation leads us to understand that lack of humility in relation to each other is typical of the human condition, such as our social and economic class status, race, and culture.

765) Lack of humility can cause us to view others who are not as prominent as us as undeserving of our respect and attention. These attitudes give rise to pride, which suffocates our humility.

766) Pride erodes our humility and misguide us causing us to regard humility as weakness and as an undesirable quality.

767) Do not set your mind on high things, but associate with the humble. Do not be wise in your own opinion" (Romans 12:16 NKJV) (circa CE 57–58).

768) Whose guidance should the world follow? God points us to the greatest act of humility through the suffering and death of His son Jesus Christ.

769) True humility comes when, in the light of God, we walk in humility, thinking of ourselves as nothing. It is denying ourselves of the world's self–promotion and allowing God alone to elevate us.

770) To lose oneself in God is the ultimate act of humility. Only then will we no longer compare ourselves with others and be able to meet other individuals as one who is nothing, seeking and claiming no personal status.

771) The challenge of humility *or* servant–hood begins with recognition that all human beings are equal in God's sight, with equal opportunity for redemption and for living a life of fulfillment through a relationship with Him.

772) Our family, social class and creed have no influence on our standing before God.

773) History teaches that there is a compulsion to exhibit pride in our relationships with our neighbor.

774) We sub–consciously, sometimes even consciously, set up barriers to human relationships, nurturing negative patterns of behavior against others.

775) Many individuals and nations never partake of the great benefits that humility brings to the table of civilization. The great lessons of humility are forgiveness, mercy, patience, compassion, humility, and servant–hood.

776) Our lack of humility toward others whom we might deem inferior, causes us to deny them love, compassion, justice, service, opportunities for employment, and fair compensation.

777) Rather than the relentless pursuit of service to other human beings, the pursuit of self–elevation leads us on a path of inhumanity and lack of humility.

778) There is no greater, more dangerous human condition that we should avoid than the spirit of pride.

779) The wise king Solomon, of Proverbs, equates pride with evil. Solomon reveals: "The fear of the Lord is to hate evil; Pride and arrogance and the evil way, And the perverse mouth I hate" (Proverbs 8:13 NKJV) (circa 961 BCE).

780) Human pride influences the decisions that are made daily. Pride undergirds all selfishness, all human suffering, all jealous behavior among families and friends, and all broken marriages.

781) Pride is the root of too much of the violence that occurs in the institutions of the streets.

782) Pride can also be the catalyst for national and international conflicts. Pride is a spirit that we can only conquer in the spiritual realm.

783) When we conquer pride we unlock the power of humility, which promotes peace and harmony in our lives, families, communities, nations, and the world.

784) Pride has its roots in our weak human nature. When we give in to the mastering nature of pride, it leads down the path of hopeless struggle that eventually overtakes and overwhelms us.

785) We can find deliverance from pride and be saved from its destructive force, which often overwhelms us, societies, and nations.

786) Solomon, the supreme of Israel's wise men, admonishes: "Pride goes before destruction, And a haughty spirit before a fall. Better to be a humble spirit with the lowly, Than to divide the spoil with the proud" (Proverbs 16:18–19 NKJV) (circa 961 BCE).

787) God, in his infinite wisdom, did not leave us without examples of humility and servant–hood.

788) Jesus Christ in His human state demonstrated the ultimate act of humility prior to his departure from earth.

789) Christ summons His followers to servant–hood, even as we expose ourselves to those things of this world that nurture our pride, such as our grand homes, our executive careers, and our expensive automobiles.

790) Jesus is telling us that we need to serve each other and persuade our pride to take flight.

791) He has given us a new model of leadership where the leader serves those whom he or she leads (family, corporation, or nation) and adopts a new understanding of humility in relationships.

792) Humility (meekness) in daily life begins when we truly see how God is all and when we make ourselves available for God to be all in our lives.

793) It is only by the relentless exercise of humility in daily life that human beings begin to achieve true nobility.

794) In the presence of God we demonstrate submissiveness of heart and an attitude that we assume pleases God, but God is calling us to a different posture in our horizontal relationships with others.

795) What a fascinating thought, that the only measure of our love for God is our everyday fellowship with other human beings, regardless of color, race, culture, nationality, or social and economic class.

796) The true test of our humility is an empirical measure of the treatment we give to those whom we might regard as lower in standing than us – religiously, politically, socially, financially, physically, or intellectually.

797) Our love for God is but a delusion, unless it can measure up to the test of daily life with all of humanity.

798) Our humility before God has no empirical measure or value, except that it prepares us to reveal the humility of Jesus Christ to others.

799) Genuine humility is that which we demonstrate in our daily conduct, as opposed to our posture before our God or god(s), in prayer and veneration.

800) It is only in our unobserved moments that we demonstrate who we are and that others can see what we believe. The minutiae of daily life are the tests of eternity, because they prove what spirit possesses us.

801) The daily test of our humility is how, when tested, we humble ourselves in the presence of others. It is the mark of the humble individual.

802) Nations of the world are meeting at the crossroads of the civilization that has become a global village. Circumstances beyond any nation's control have shuttled us into the global village relatively unprepared.

803) Nations are unprepared to address the issues that confront them, such as religion, culture, race, social and economic class differences, and political worldviews.

804) No one denies that some nations have great scientific and technological capacity, but being prepared for the challenges ahead requires other non-technical attributes, as well.

805) Can the church respond to the new secular and religious challenges that confront it?

806) Western civilization finds itself at a juncture of incompatible directions, from religious, racial, social, cultural, educational, political, technological, and economical perspectives.

807) Who, or which nation has the capacity and capability to guide us through the uncharted territories ahead (Reference: *Five Foundations of Human Development* (FFHD) —Table 8: Example of Capable Guides and Outcomes from their Guidance).

808) The true development of nations reflects the humility of Jesus Christ to promote peace and harmony among nations.

809) God is challenging Christians, who blissfully profess to give themselves for Christ, yet sometimes find it difficult to give up self-seeking and self-interest to seek the good of others as first imperatives of our existence.

810) The challenge of the modern Christian church is to demonstrate the virtue of the humility of Christ, the most prominent among the virtues, the graces, and powers through the Spirit.

811) We must look on our neighbor in every state of affairs as God's instrument for our sanctification as never before.

812) We must exercise the humility that Jesus displayed as He confronted those who would persecute Him. We must have such faith in God that nothing of self inhibits our dedication to service to our neighbor.

813) God wants us to count ourselves least while we seek to be like Jesus Christ, who counted Himself a Servant, Helper, and Comforter, to others, even to the lowliest and most unworthy that He encountered while on earth.

814) We allow the symptoms of problems, such as violence, terrorism, poverty, hopelessness, or juvenile delinquency to challenge us while we miss the deeper, underlying flaw in the human spirit.

815) The great fallen empires are evidence of this. We now face the "final option" in the twenty-first century.

816) God knew that humanity would be at this impasse, and He therefore instructed Matthew to provide us with the "final option," after we had realized the futility of mere mortal solutions. "But seek first the kingdom of God and His righteousness, and all of these things shall be added to you" (Matthew 6:33 NKJV).

817) Our progress in the physical mastery of our world yields great comforts, great advances, and great benefits, although the real solution to our many challenges lies elsewhere.

818) God's Word teaches that He is able to do exceedingly, abundantly above all that we ask or imagine, (including everything above), according to the power that works in us (Ephesians 3:20) (John 14:12–13).

819) Ancient King Solomon, of Israel, sought wisdom from God, and God granted him immeasurably more than he had asked or imagined. What does the world seek from God?

820) What do you and I seek from God? Unlike our asking a favor of someone, a servant attempting to appease a master, an employee asking for a pay raise, or a young soldier nervously standing a breath away from a Major General, God's Word teaches us thus: "Let us therefore come boldly to the throne of grace, that we may obtain mercy and find grace to help in time of need (Hebrews 5:16 NKJV).

FOUNDATION 1
SPIRITUAL FOUNDATION
—1.7. PATIENCE (LONGSUFFERING)

"Consider it pure joy, my brothers, whenever you face trials of many kinds, because you know that the testing of your faith develops perseverance. Perseverance must finish its work so that you may be mature and complete, not lacking anything" James 1:2–4 (NIV). Be patient, then, brothers, until the Lord's coming. See how the farmer waits for the land to yield its valuable crop and how patient he is for the autumn and spring rains."

James 5:7–8 (NIV)

821) **What is patience?** Why is it necessary to be patient (longsuffering)? What is this state of being that is vital to better relationships among individuals, families, friends, societies, and nations?

822) What are the characteristics of a patient person? The answers can be found in the greatest testimony to patience, the Gospel of Matthew. The Sermon on the Mount is perhaps the most complete commentary for humanity covering every aspect of Christian living (Matthew 5:1–12).

823) "Blessed are you when they revile and persecute you, and say all kinds of evil against you falsely for My sake. Rejoice and be exceedingly glad, for great *is* your reward in heaven, for so they persecuted the prophets who were before you" (Matthew 5:11–12 NKJV).

824) The Sermon on the Mount is probably the scripture closest to the heart of adherents of Christianity. It puts in perspective the entire mission of Jesus Christ and provides perfect direction for patience in the twenty–first century.

825) Though many rehearse the Beatitudes and write and preach the insightfulness of their message, the Beatitudes are more than words; they are the spiritual keys to daily practice of the teachings of Jesus Christ.

826) Collectively, the Beatitudes constitute the sum total of the teachings of Jesus Christ and the fulfillment of His message to His followers, and they can be viewed as the Decalogue of the New Testament (NT).

827) The most important teachings of the Beatitudes call our attention to the need for patience (longsuffering).

828) Patience is probably the most lacking of all of the human virtues in our challenging and fast–paced lifestyle.

829) Somewhat perversely, those most closely related to us present the greatest test of our patience yet are the ones with whom we exercise the least amount of patience. They are our children, our husbands, our wives, our parents, our grandparents, and our friends.

830) Most of us, if not all of us, have displayed impatience, and some of us still struggle with impatience.

831) Jesus Christ presented himself as the perfect example of patience and self–control to those who would follow Him. In the face of great provocation, rather than retaliate with anger and impatience, He exercised forgiveness and mercy.

832) Unlike human beings, Jesus did not yield to the circumstances of persecution and trials. His message and His conduct together were the revelation of the will of God to the world.

833) When others offend us, our natural inclination is to react with impatience and anger. We are still unaware that there is a conflict within us between the spirit and the flesh.

834) Patience is one of the most indispensable requirements of peace and stability in our emerging global village.

835) Without the exercise of patience, the racial, cultural, religious, social, and economic crossroads of our current civilization will lead to future genocide and wars among nations.

836) Perceptive observation and the clear records of six thousand years of history should make us acutely aware that patience, kindness, goodness, faithfulness, gentleness, and self–control are necessary for meeting such challenges in the future.

837) Our vision of a global village could become another fleeting illusion in our eternal quest to govern ourselves and find hope for humanity.

838) Is it possible for nations to co-exist in peace and harmony? Certainly! Imagine just for a moment leaders and citizens alike coming to the realization that human intellect alone cannot nurture the virtues that are essential for our survival.

839) The casual observer can comprehend that the challenges of our modern era can lead to impatience.

840) Impatience and lack of self-control can potentially lead to familial, societal, national, and international conflict.

841) When we open the windows to the panorama of human history, what do we see? When we understand the causes of the events chronicled, what do we learn?

842) Scholars in our twenty-first century will describe the human legacy as a *graveyard of indifference* toward our neighbors, exacerbated by impatience and intolerance.

843) Impatience can result in genocide within nations and between nations, and can be consummated by nations. Can world nations afford the present and future cost of indifference to each other?

844) Examine the records of history, as you ponder the following questions: Why do we think that somehow our failed approaches in the past to governing God's creation will work in the future?

845) Why do we work under such difficult circumstances to perfect what six thousand years of history teaches us will inevitably fail?

846) The failings of the past are not a result of some quality of leadership, lacking back then, but that has now been developed.

847) The failings of the past are also not due to ignorance about the physical world or about sociology or economics, now understood better in the twenty-first century.

848) Rather, they are due to the failure to guide ourselves and our societies in accordance with Christ's teachings and the teachings of the great prophets.

849) History provides us with insight into past civilizations, how they lived and, more importantly, how their leaders and their empires came to an abrupt and violent end.

850) Some of these leaders denied God, and the existence of God. They overstepped the natural limits of their leadership and authority.

851) Some leaders overworked the masses. They depleted their farmland. They destroyed their ecosystems, and they assumed dictatorial power. Most critically though, they lacked the fruit of the Spirit of God, against such there is no law (Galatians 5:22–23).

852) Many of the great empires and their leadership have left behind unflattering lessons of history.

853) When we think of these historic empires and their leadership, we can only imagine the awesome power they once wielded.

854) Why did these great empires collapse? Could it be the result of an unexplained phenomenon? Can we learn from the past when we misinterpret human weakness as greatness?

855) Nations have rejected God's knowledge. They have failed repeatedly to comprehend God's role in their worlds, preferring their earthly power.

856) There were perhaps five reasons for the collapse of every empire in history. *(1)* Empires rejected God's knowledge; *(2)* empires failed to comprehend God's principles for His governing authorities; *(3)* empires failed to incorporate God's purpose for those they governed; *(4)* empires failed to recognize the dominion of nations and; *(5)* empires failed to elevate the masses to some meaningful level of social, economic, and political participation in the affairs of the nation.

857) Ancient leaders failed to recognize that their repeated abuses were incongruous with God's law, which governs human behavior and the survival of mankind.

858) History will label us the impatient generation. Our busy lifestyles have caused some of us to grow impatient, lacking in tolerance and self–control.

859) Common, everyday activities have become a stressful experience as we hurry to and from work on busy, overcrowded highways to pick up our children from school or from babysitters and then to hurry back home to prepare supper.

860) We demand instant relief from illnesses; cosmetic surgery to obtain instant youthful looks; drugs to enhance athletic abilities; quick diets to lose pounds, and national lotteries to obtain instant wealth.

861) We expect instant responses to our needs and wants. Our wants reflect our impatience, and our desire to alleviate our own suffering causes us to seek instant healing and miracles for our ailments.

862) Christians may view suffering as God's response to our operating outside of His will for our lives, but most understand that one can be in the perfect will of God yet, like Job, find that suffering comes upon us suddenly.

863) Rarely do we consider that some suffering may bring us closer to the perfect will of God.

864) Indeed, suffering may perfect us. To the contrary, many call upon God to alleviate their suffering, according to their timing, rather than according to God's.

865) Suffering should foster an attitude of patience. The Holy Bible assures us that God does not cause the suffering that occurs throughout the world.

866) God does not bring trials upon human beings to make us suffer for wrongdoings, but our seeds of wrongdoing may result in the harvest of the fruits of suffering.

867) We must exercise patience in tribulation to achieve victory over spiritual depression and gloom (Matthew 5:11–12). Patience allows us to maintain faith in God regardless of our circumstances.

868) Patience is not static. Patience requires endurance. We may exhibit patience for a time and then our patience wanes.

869) Jesus Christ came to the world not to elevate Himself in the eyes of His disciples or the world, but to take upon Himself the burdens of our transgressions and to manifest the ultimate act of patience in suffering.

870) The world stands in awe at God's grace, mercy, and patience for humanity. The patience of God provides opportunities for human beings to assess their spiritual standing with Him as they repent of wrongdoings and conform to His purpose for their lives (2 Peter 3:8–9).

871) God created us with a free will and with freedom to choose, including freedom to accept or reject His grace and mercies.

872) Many throughout the world reject the message of Jesus Christ, but despite the rejection of His message, God continues to extend His

grace, mercy, and patience with open arms, as He awaits our decision.

873)   In our mortal weakness, we need God's constant assurance to help us to maintain patience and endurance.

874)   Without such spiritual and mental help, we lose our capacity for patience and endurance. We face a complex world of undulating states of acceptance and rejection; caring and uncaring; hope and hopelessness; fortune and misfortune; and faith and fear.

875)   These challenges to our patience occur within our workplaces, among peer groups, and within marriages and family relationships.

876)   Ironically, it is within these environments that we seek acceptance and solace, and the patience of others.

877)   We live in an age in which culture teaches that the great virtues are self–awareness, self–esteem, and self–actualization.

878)   In the pursuit of our self–rewarding behavior, we diminish the value of selflessness and the virtues of patience, self–control, and endurance.

879)   We must recognize that each one of us is responsible for the suffering of others, for the genocide, the wars, the hunger, and the brutality in the world.

880)   With God's enabling power, we have the potential to create a better world with peace and happiness, not just for ourselves, but also for our neighbors.

881)   Each one of us is both individual and society. It is not by exclusion of others, but by including more of others, that we broaden the narrow sphere of self and set out on the path of understanding the need for patience.

882)   This new paradigm helps to engender better relationships between individuals and nations.

883)   We need God's enabling power, because we are rational, yet irrational, we are happy, yet unhappy, we are peaceful, yet violent, we are calm, yet erupt like volcanoes, sometimes with little provocation.

884)   Often uncontrollably, we are a strange mixture of pleasure, hate, fear, aggression and domination.

885) With God's enabling power, we are also capable of exhibiting the fruit of His Spirit – love, joy, peace, longsuffering (patience), kindness, goodness, faithfulness, gentleness, and self–control (Galatians 5:22–23).

886) "May the God who gives endurance and encouragement give you a spirit of unity among yourselves as you follow Christ Jesus, so that with one heart and mouth you may glorify the God and Father of our Lord Jesus Christ" (Romans 15:5–6).

THOUGHTS TO ENLIGHTEN AND EMPOWER THE MIND

2001 QUESTIONS AND PHILOSOPHICAL THOUGHTS TO INSPIRE, ENLIGHTEN, AND EMPOWER OUR WORLD TO LIMITLESS HEIGHTS

SF

—FOUNDATION 2 MORAL FOUNDATION

FOUNDATION 2
MORAL FOUNDATION
—2.1. LEADERSHIP (GUIDANCE)

"Let the peace of Christ rule in your hearts, since as members of one body you were called to peace. And be thankful. Let the word of Christ dwell in you richly as you teach and admonish one another with all wisdom, and as you sing psalms, hymns and spiritual songs with gratitude in your hearts to God. And whatever you do, whether in word or deed, do it all in the name of the Lord Jesus."

Colossians 3:15–17 (NIV)

887) **What is leadership?** What qualities make a great leader? A leader is someone who knows that servant–hood and humility are the core strengths of leadership.

888) A servant leader knows that when he or she makes available equitable opportunities for growth, his or her followers benefit from enhanced mental and productive capacities.

889) There is a growing body of individuals in every walk of life expressing some level of discontent with leadership in our modern era. Many search for leadership worth following.

890) They search for a new leadership that is authentic, and can engender, sustain, and nurture societies and nations, but only he or she who serves is qualified to lead.

891) What are the moral considerations of a leader? A leader is acutely aware that fear cannot effectively stimulate cooperation, ambition, initiative, or creativity in others.

892) A leader recognizes that the existence and moral growth of individuals, societies, and nations depends upon the moral imperatives of leadership (Reference: *Five Foundations of Human Development* (FFHD) —Figure 18: Three Key Attributes of Human Leadership, —Figure 19: Three Key Attributes of Human Development, and —Figure 20: Three Key Recognized Human Limitations).

893) When the exercise of leadership conforms to God's plan for humanity, He enables both the leader and the nation.

894) In a general sense, one can view leadership from two distinct perspectives: *(1)* leadership which derives its authority from human beings; and *(2)* leadership which derives its authority from God.

895) Regardless of the origin of leadership and its inherent authority, leadership should never be the imposition of one's will upon others.

896) God, who is the supreme authority for humanity, does not impose His will on humanity.

897) Western nations have built their political structures upon the principles of New Testament (NT) Christian thought. Nevertheless, Western nations have, within their history, particular tendencies to oppose the will of God.

898) Writers of the great constitutions and national anthems of Western democratic nations must have known, either by spiritual discernment, intuition, or by intellectual insights that a nation's guidance by a superior authority is crucial to leadership and the nation's survival.

899) There is a natural tendency for us to assume that what qualifies the individual as a leader is his or her position of power, election to an office, or personal attributes – erudition, charisma, or courage.

900) One naturally assumes that being the head of an organization or institution equates to leadership.

901) Is leadership inherent in positions of authority? Not necessarily. Leadership begins with spiritual discernment, spiritual development, and the recognition of human limitations.

902) The Apostle Paul teaches us that God's guidance ought to be at the heart and center of leadership, but this does not occur naturally. Leaders must seek God's guidance in order to effectively manage His creation.

903) The evidence of this need underpins Western nations' constitutions, and national anthems, which recognize freedom, justice, and preservation and protection as the inalienable rights of every human being.

904) True leadership, is the exercise of moral duty without regard to color, race, culture, language, religion, nationality, or social or economic class. This leadership perspective can only come from a heart informed by God.

905) **Henry Grady Weaver (1889–1949)**: "The Romans were never able to solve the problem of true constitutional government. But their partial recognition of human rights under law brought the problem into the open and was not without value in leading to its solution some 1,400 years later."

906) **Henry Grady Weaver (1889–1949)**: "Try to rewrite the Declaration of Independence without reference to the Christ axioms. You'll find it can't be done."

907) Despite the noble goals of world nations, the reality of human leadership often falls short of our intentions.

908) Leadership may bear conscious or subconscious prejudice against others with whom we have no common bond or heritage, and this has been an integral part of our recorded history for six thousand years.

909) Leadership is a way of life, which brings increasing opportunities to transform ourselves as we give unwavering service to those whom we lead.

910) Positions of authority do play a part in leadership, but only from the point of view of appointment, because the essentials of leadership are its functions.

911) A peculiar observation, among autocratic leaders, is the succession of power from father to son. One might be inclined to conclude that their symbiotic relationship is a function of deoxyribonucleic acid (DNA).

912) The essential prerequisite of leadership, is to motivate others from the inside. This type of leader creates opportunities for others to be part of the intellectual pool, to participate in the process, and to share in the rewards of production.

913) Over the past several decades, Western nations have made great efforts to ensure that leadership and authority are unbiased and transparent, particularly in the public services and in public corporations.

914) Western nations have, over the centuries, written and amended constitutions and Charters of Rights and Freedoms, enacted civil rights laws and crafted employment equity laws for the protection of citizens.

915) Nations in the international community, recognizing the need for a world body to promote world peace and harmony and cooperation

among nations, created the League of Nations after *World War I* in 1919.

916) The League of Nations was then replaced by the United Nations (UN) after *World War II* in 1945. This international global organization is essential for the advancement of world peace and harmony among sovereign nations.

917) In 1946, the ©UN created The United Nations Educational, Scientific and Cultural Organization (UNESCO) branch, which is located in Paris, France. This important world organization provides hope to the world in areas such as culture, education, science, and communications.

918) In spite of such world bodies, we still struggle with unsolved problems from past centuries, as we face new and emerging problems of a future for which we are manifestly unprepared.

919) Modern civilizations are at the same major crossroads of culture and religion that have challenged leadership in the past.

920) This is our defining moment of the twenty-first century. The new dynamics of the modern world demand new ways of looking at civilization, not just through economic prisms, but through religious, moral, social, and cultural prisms of the twenty-first century.

921) Leadership styles of the past do not hold out hope for our survival in this new period of world history. We are making new history, ushering in new and emerging challenges to leadership.

922) Religious leaders speak of a universal God and of the unity of the human family. These religious principles are fundamental to universal leadership. Is God universal to religions?

923) Evidence of divisions among religion and among religious denominations demonstrates that world religions do not share the same concept of God, or religious tenets, which is a challenge to religious leadership in the world.

924) It is only when we grasp a common concept of God as God of the universe that leaders of nations will inadvertently grasp the concept of the oneness of humanity, which alone can unite us.

925) Despite our modern era of leadership councils, and leadership training and development, a great leadership deficiency seems to exist in every sphere of human endeavor.

926) One would naturally assume that our universal God would have a universal influence on all of humanity, and would be present in all of our institutions, but the paradox of religion is its history of exclusivity.

927) It seems as though the universality of our God, or god(s), and our all–encompassing love for humanity, diminish within the most important of our national and international institutions.

928) If we do not practice, daily and consistently, the core principles of our religions, in every institution and organization, can our religions have any meaningful effect?

929) There is a need to shift to a new standard of leadership that incorporates our religious virtues in all facets of human endeavor, in *all* of its universality.

930) Our leaders in the modern age must have the capacity to help us emphasize our religious belief by practice; our faith by works; our happiness by joy; our tolerance by love, *and* our need for revenge by the need for justice and mercy.

931) Many world leaders demonstrate great moral capacity in response to natural catastrophes, such as storms, floods, earthquakes, or famine, but at the same time, world nations seem to be incapable of avoiding human catastrophes such as genocide, wars, and other man–made disasters.

932) Our religious leadership must go beyond our churches, chapels, cathedrals, monasteries, synagogues, temples and mosques and enter the gates of our great institutions where we can practice and measure the values to which we subscribe through our religions.

933) The perspective of leadership as servant–hood is a paradox for some leaders in our modern era, because the world does not view leaders as servants.

934) Servants are considered lowly and submissive and such a posture is expected, even demanded, from them. Those who employ servants rarely allow their servants to make decisions regarding their workload and routine.

935) Imagine for a moment the Chief Executive Officer (CEO) of one of our mega–corporations being regarded as a servant to his or her follows.

936) The history books are a testament to leaders whose empires collapsed as their leadership came to a brutal end. These bloody

leadership transitions often paralleled the way in which leaders rose to power.

937) In ancient times, conquest was the rule rather than the exception, and wars raged across the feudal countryside throughout the Middle Ages when leadership and authority were absolute.

938) Leaders of Western democratic nations and other nations of the world do recognize the superiority of God and afford their citizens freedom to worship their God or god(s).

939) The efficiencies of modern democracies do translate into some level of self–governance by their citizens. Democratically elected leaders possess a range of the requisite leadership qualities.

940) Leadership behavior conveys the impression that leaders are unaware that their governments are temporary. God permits them for a time.

941) All authority over creation begins with God, for He is the supreme authority. Most of humanity subscribes to a belief in the spiritual existence of God, gods, or a divine being, because we did not create ourselves and neither can we account for our existence as a natural phenomenon.

942) The keys to successful leadership begin with servant–hood and humility; yet, we often seek qualities and attributes such as education, intelligence, charisma, or loyalty as the mark of great leadership.

943) Leadership by ideology, as opposed to leadership by council, can have dire consequences. Leaders like Napoleon (1769-1821); Hitler (1889-1945); Mussolini (1883-1945); and Stalin (1878-1953) occupied positions of great power.

944) Alexander the Great (circa 356–323 BCE) was a remarkable leader and general, but only because God used him to fulfill certain aspects of His purpose in the world. History also teaches that his life came to an unfortunate early end at the young age of thirty–three.

945) Irrespective of leadership styles or systems of human government, in a general sense, leaders are convinced that they are doing the right thing and the best for the nations they govern.

946) Presidents and prime ministers lead our democratic systems of government in the West. Western democracies have elevated Western civilization to relative heights of religious, social, educational, and economic enlightenment.

947) Democracy has also elevated Western nations to a new age of freedom with liberty and justice for all. Freedom and liberty include limits for the greater good of all, and justice strives to extend to its full universal dimensions.

948) Some leaders view democracy as a system that naturally offers equal opportunities to all, despite evidence of inequality and inherent advantages and disadvantages in society.

949) Visionary leaders recognize that all members of society do not possess equal capabilities or opportunities for achievement.

950) Visionary leaders recognize the inherent limiting, self-limiting, and socially limiting circumstances that impact the lives of many individuals.

951) When leaders adopt an autocratic leadership style, which disregards the important lessons of history, as seen in some developing and underdeveloped nations, they unwittingly suffocate the growth of their nations.

952) Democracy was also birthed in violent revolutions, as it swept through Latin America and Africa over the past centuries. The dawn of the twenty-first century has ushered in another series of violent democratic revolutions in North Africa and in the Middle East.

953) Unless a leader understands God's divine spiritual purpose for human existence, which informs moral leadership over the nation, human leadership becomes futile. This type of ineffective leadership has been the hallmark of many nations over the centuries, recorded in the archives of human history and the human psyche.

954) When we examine the "flight recorder" from the wreckage of human history, the most important piece of evidence is a male dominated leadership.

955) Where are our nurturing and caring "mothers of civilization?" Where are our "keepers of compassion?" "Where are our prayer worriers?" Has our male leadership relegated (theoretically) *fifty percent* of the world's population to silence? (Reference: *Five Foundations of Human Development* (FFHD) —Foundation 2: Moral Foundation–Leadership Lessons in History).

956) How do we know that the great compassion of our "mothers of civilization" does not hold the key to human survival? One can argue that men occupy greater than eighty percent of all of the positions of high leadership and authority in the world.

957) Throughout history, women have faced many challenges, from labor and social exclusion, gender and sexual exploitation to political and corporate exclusion.

958) Women have agitated for change in various movements, including (but not limited to) feminism, the Women's Rights Movement, feminist rebellion, social feminism, and gender equality legislation.

959) Over one hundred years ago, in 1909, began the recognition of women's place in society through the National Women's Day. March 08, marked another historic day for women, International Women's Day (first celebrated in 1911).

960) The current state of our world demands that we begin to make new history that includes women to a much greater extent than we have experienced in the past.

961) There is no doubt that the courage of many great men have brought us out of the Dark Ages and into the Industrial Era (1800s–1900s).

962) Men have used their genius to engineer better living through artificial intelligence, from the micro–wave oven to jet engines. Men have given to humanity great institutions of learning, great governmental institutions and great peace organizations.

963) Many great men have labored to find cures for human illnesses. Pharmacologically, modern medicines have all but eradicated and brought under control such diseases as smallpox, the bubonic plague, yellow fever, and even polio (poliomyelitis).

964) Despite these achievements, in terms of a fruitful life for all, the scales are imbalanced against women and children whose voices have the least impact on the direction of nations.

965) Caring mothers, fathers, and children must not simply stand by and watch the wreckage of God's creation continue unabated with repeated patterns of failed male–inspired leadership.

966) Repeated patterns of failed leadership have had less to do with academic achievement, charisma, and nationalism and more to do with our failures to unquestioningly acknowledge and accept God's spiritual guidance.

967) The world has now passed through the aftermath of these two great wars: *World War I (1914–1918)* and *World War II (1939–1945)*, as well as through acts of genocide, slavery, colonialism, apartheid, and

countless other conflicts over the decades and into our twenty-first century.

968)   We are careful to avoid meaningful dialogue on the advent of the next great *World War III*, because we know intuitively, and by academic and empirical observation, that the possibility is real and frightening.

969)   Leaders of nations throughout the world should be on guard against the allure of nationalism and self-interest, which can lead down paths of leadership indifference.

970)   The great wars in ancient and modern history have revealed the weakness in human nature and have shaken the bedrock of confidence in the capacity of human beings to provide moral leadership in the world.

971)   When we veer from the path of love, compassion, patience, mercy, and forgiveness for others, not only do *we* suffer, but also our grandparents, our parents, our wives, our children, our grandchildren, our great grandchildren and great, great grandchildren suffer as well.

972)   When things go wrong in a nation, the citizens look toward their government for assurance of leadership, but where can governments look for leadership? Where can leaders find trustworthy guidance? (Reference: *Five Foundations of Human Development* (FFHD) — Figure 9: God's Hierarchical Model of Authorities for Humanity).

973)   To conclude that nations are self-governing contradicts the fact that most of the world's population subscribes to a superior authority, and Western nations acknowledge God's guidance as the cornerstone of their constitutions.

974)   National anthems throughout the West recognize God's supremacy. Prayers at official government proceedings recognize God's sovereignty. State funerals reflect God's presence in our mortal and immortal lives.

975)   The visible presence of churches, chapels, cathedrals, monasteries, synagogues, temples, and mosques in our nations is a testimony to our belief in a superior authority.

976)   Despite these demonstrations of faith, beliefs, and practice, past centuries have been rife with revolutions, uprisings, acts of genocide, and wars. The present is rife with civil disobedience, modern warfare, militia wars, and terrorism.

977) Enlightened leaders follow God's guidance for their leadership; it results in their increased capacity to stimulate national growth and national peace and harmony.

978) The divine inspiration of Paul's writing provides sufficient evidence that without God's guidance and direction human beings cannot direct their own lives. Furthermore, the prophet Jeremiah affirms: "O LORD, I know the way of man *is* not in himself; *It is* not in man who walks to direct his own steps" (Jeremiah 10:23 NKJV) (circa 622 BCE).

979) We have tried philosophy, religion, mysticism, cultism, humanism, spiritualism, and political systems, but have we found the answer? After thousands of years of applying human leadership alone, Jeremiah's statements are still meaningful and relevant, and provide us with reasons to examine our human failings.

980) Jesus knew that it takes great moral courage to lead in this world; therefore He reminds us of the trials that believers will face (Matthew 5:11–12 NKJV).

981) There is no doubt that leadership in the twenty–first century demands great exercise of the fruit of the Spirit. Leaders understand that they are leading for the next generations.

982) History teaches us what we were like in the past, and could be in the future. If our world leaders, and visionaries, predispose the next generation to violence as a solution to human problems, history will not be kind to us.

983) History will present greater lessons of human suffering than we experienced in the past, because world nations have a much greater capacity for global warfare than in the past, aided by weapons of mass destruction.

984) We possess great hidden spiritual, moral, social, intellectual, and physical capacities. Likewise, our great secular and religious universities and seminaries of higher learning can aid us on the intellectual front through the power of dialogue.

985) We have access to God's capable guidance through His Holy Spirit; through Jesus Christ; and through His hierarchical authoritative structure for humanity (Reference: *Five Foundations of Human Development* (FFHD) —Figure 1: The Triune God (Godhead).

FOUNDATION 2
MORAL FOUNDATION
—2.2. AUTHORITY (POWER)

"Everyone must submit himself to the governing authorities, for there is no authority except that which God has established. The authorities that exist have been established by God. Consequently, he who rebels against the authority is rebelling against what God has instituted, and those who do so will bring judgment upon themselves."

Romans 13:1–2 (NIV)

986) **What is authority?** Human authority is an unmerited gift from God. How should one exercise human authority? Are there limits to human authority? Is there an ultimate authority?

987) There are two fundamental perspectives for viewing authority: *(1)* SPIRITUAL AUTHORITY is inherent in Jesus Christ our Lord and Savior; His authority comes from God the Father (Matthew 28:18). *(2)* SECULAR AUTHORITY is inherent in human beings and enabled by tens of thousands of human laws.

988) The greatest gift from God to human beings for the formulation of just nations *is* human authority, enabled by the authority inherent in Jesus Christ.

989) God in His infinite wisdom has prearranged a hierarchy of authority to provide us with structured relationships with our earthly authorities, earthly institutions, and Him.

990) God has set the limits of human authority. God in His infinite wisdom did not give human beings dominion over each other (Genesis 1:26).

991) Despite God's admonishment, nations have dominated other nations, and human beings have dominated other human beings to the injury of God's creation.

992) The autocratic leaders of the ancient world held absolute power and authority over their kingdoms.

993) The governments of modern Western nations have decentralized power and authority; this demonstrates that progressive governments recognize the need for various levels and limits to human authority.

994) God foreknew that ultimate human authority would pose an inherent danger to authority, itself and to those who are subject to authority.

995) The essential exercise of authority begins with righteousness, and righteousness comes from God, through right relationship with Him and obedience to His Word.

996) The book of Romans, chapter thirteen, verse one, points us to God's Theocracy, in which He leads through authorities; He appoints human authorities under His guidance.

997) The word *theocracy* originates from the Greek word "theokratia." The root words of *theocracy* are *Theos* (God) and *kratein* (to rule). Combined, they mean "rule by the deity."

998) The leader appoints a cabinet to serve the people, and human authority can thus effectively operate under divine appointment by God, subject to His will.

999) Estranged from the will of God, the authority of His appointed agents will fall short of the ideal aim of service to humanity.

1000) The church is God's agent with the moral authority to speak on behalf of its founder Jesus Christ. The Holy Bible provides explicit written instructions for our edification, and more significantly, for our survival.

1001) When we face personal, family, and national crises, we often acknowledge God's existence, but we neglect to avail ourselves to His guidance when everything seems to be going well for our nation and for ourselves.

1002) We often deny God an invitation as a key subject matter expert (SME) in our decision-making. His seat is *vacant* at the family table, corporate boardrooms, and at major national and international forums, when things are going well.

1003) Figuratively speaking, God's does not deny us His presence, but His plans are generally at variance with ours.

1004)   Ironically, when something goes wrong with our plans, we immediately call upon our God or god(s) to be our moral guide for the moment.

1005)   God extends His grace and mercy to us always, despite our neglect. He offers us an unfettered opportunity to come to Him in times of personal, national, and international crises.

1006)   Without God's intervention in all of our plans, there is no guarantee of peace, safety, or security of nations. With such clear scriptural admonishment, why would we not seek His trustworthy guidance in every human endeavor as a proactive strategy?

1007)   God has given us unfettered access to His infinite knowledge, wisdom, and understanding through His Word and through the teachings of His Son Jesus Christ.

1008)   God's authority was not sufficiently applied, as various forms of authorities ruled autocratically over their subjects.

1009)   Autocratic leaders purported to be godlike in authority, and often they would require that all of their subjects worship them or their gods.

1010)   Autocratic leaders failed to recognize the insufficiency of human authority; now they and their gods lie as silent witnesses, as part of the wreckage of human history, and as monuments to their folly.

1011)   Those who opposed the authority of the ancient world met with punishment, exile, imprisonment, or death. Fear, mistrust, anarchy, and rebellion resulted in bloodshed.

1012)   The blood of Christian martyrs stains the pages of religious history. The passage through the Middle Ages to our twenty–first century is littered with kingdoms that were governed by the weakest of God's creation.

1013)   In contrast, in Western democratic nations and other emerging democracies, the citizens elect their leaders who hold office as presidents and prime ministers.

1014)   These constitutional democracies follow the laws of the land to guide the democratic process, which gives protection to citizens, from each other and from their own governments.

1015)   A belief in God as the supreme authority for Western nations has a stabilizing effect upon Western nations and upon nations in other parts of the world.

1016) Despite our belief in God, oftentimes, some of us, and some leaders, veer from the path of forgiveness, humility, and mercy (Luke 24:13–35).

1017) Notwithstanding six thousand years of recorded history, with examples of nations' rise and fall over the centuries, many nations, including Western nations, still demonstrate their reluctance to trust in God's leading, judgment, guidance, and authority.

1018) Our legacy of religious, racial, and cultural divisions and wars contradict our belief in a sovereign God whom we claim undergirds our great Western constitutions and Western democracies.

1019) The empirical evidence demonstrates that many nations, including Western nations are at a critical crossroads of retaliation and religion.

1020) We are often tempted to choose retaliation, rather than trust in God. This retaliation is a road strewn with delusions that many ancient civilizations have traveled with no return.

1021) The great monuments of destruction and our archives testify to this fact. Our twenty–first century is merely a continuation of our journey throughout God's creation.

1022) It is the year twenty eleven, of the Christian Era. We have taken the path of retaliation and have arrived at the modern world. We are confronted with challenges within families, within institutions, within neighborhoods, within corporations, within religious organizations, and within and among nations.

1023) The failure of some human authority over the centuries reflects a growing disenchantment with human leadership and reflects the great intellectual starvation that is occurring throughout the world.

1024) Unlike human authority that operates on principles of suppression, either by intellectual resolve or unintentionally, the result is the same – a repeat of history.

1025) God's authority incorporates love, kindness, humility, sharing, caring, compassion, and meekness, and appeals to higher moral imperatives.

1026) Rather than a world that is gaining confidence in human authority, the world is questioning the human capacity to rule itself. The failure of human authority is a paradox.

1027)   Why have we not been able to effectively satisfy fundamental human needs beyond material needs, despite the available educational, intellectual, financial, technological, and scientific resources?

1028)   Nations that recognize the supreme authority of God, and adhere to His principles, are better able to understand, manage, and solve fundamental human problems.

1029)   Human authority and its rebellion against God have only brought misery, insufficiency, suffering, starvation, and death. On the other hand, His authority, fortified by His immutable law, the Ten Commandments, and other related biblical and religious principles, will bring abundance, peace, material, and spiritual prosperity.

1030)   One who seeks knowledge of God's supreme authority might enquire how we can know His will for our peoples and nations. We can know God's will for our lives when His love motivates us to obey His commandments and to do according to His will.

1031)   Can human authority be effective outside of God's authority? It is essential to answer this question as the world moves closer to a global village with mass migration of peoples, as well as to the movement of information, jobs, technology, and money across and between continents.

1032)   Can hundreds of thousands of human laws be as effective as God's immutable law for governance in the global village?

1033)   Human beings have over the centuries demonstrated the spiritual, moral, social, and intellectual capacity to rise from the Dark Ages into the enlightened era of the twenty-first century, relatively speaking.

1034)   Human progress has elevated civilization to new heights, and the limits of progress are still not in sight. It highlights an ideology of authority which we have taken for granted as the ultimate solution to human problems.

1035)   Whenever something goes wrong with society, there is a call for more human authority.

1036)   Have we found peace and security in human authority or in more authority? Have we found it in the authority of the modern church, in world religions, or in our gods? Have we found it through modern education or political authority?

1037) Have we found peace and security in our great religious and secular universities and world institutions? Have we found it by incarcerating millions of individuals worldwide? Have we found it in peace pacts, peace treaties, peace marches, and civil rebellion?

1038) What is the basis of authority upon which all of human civilization must rely? The basis of authority lies within the Word of God. When we adopt this basic premise, only then will a new world of reforms spring forth and lead to the creation of national and international peace and harmony and the lives of fulfillment that we crave.

1039) Global leadership and authority in the twenty-first century must go far beyond human authority and allow the attributes of the Spirit of God to infuse human authority.

1040) The Spirit of God infuses love, joy, peace, patience, kindness, goodness, faithfulness, gentleness, and self-control. This infusion transcends unbiased judgment and an ideology that promotes the survival of all of humanity.

1041) A global village cannot be viable in an atmosphere of self-interest. In order to function effectively as a global village, developed nations must adopt principles of universality such as equitably sharing in the fruits of creation.

1042) We must be mindful that we are merely temporary custodians of God's great wealth. Likewise, history teaches that human genius alone did not derive the great wealth of some developed nations.

1043) The exploitation of human beings and natural resources and the imbalance of power played important parts in wealth accumulation, as chronicled in Eric Williams' *Capitalism and Slavery* (Williams 1944).

1044) God has granted Western nations and various other nations the privilege of being the "provisional custodians" of a small portion of His earthly wealth.

1045) God has also opened a small window to His spiritual intelligence to enable us to manage and to care for His creation.

1046) God has provided us with all of the guidance necessary to promote and maintain unity among neighbors. Evidently we have not closely examined His plan for a global village, because our version differs, both in theory and in practical application, from His (Ephesians 4:4–6).

1047) The global village of the twenty-first century demands authority that recognizes the need to balance national self-interest and national selflessness, as mass immigration presents new challenges to nations.

1048) The consequences of the flow of intellectual capital from developing and underdeveloped nations are rarely considered. Developing and underdeveloped nations struggle to rebuild from the deficiencies that this flow creates as capital financing poses a problem to them.

1049) Developed nations can help developing and underdeveloped nations to cope with the collateral effects of their diminished capacities.

1050) The greatest hope for world stability is to first build capacity for social and economic stability and peace from within nations.

1051) Great leadership is three dimensional; it demands a critical balance among *(1) education, (2) intelligence,* and *(3) experience,* sustained by such moral imperatives as honesty, integrity, fair dealing, empowerment of subordinates, and the sharing of the fruits of success.

1052) The values of human intelligence and experience are evidently not explored to the same extent as education in managing corporations. This is evident when we examine the downfall of otherwise viable corporations, even mega-corporations.

1053) Lack of education was not attributed to the collapse of the world economy at the beginning of the twenty-first century. We must examine the deeper reasons, lest we repeat history.

FOUNDATION 2
MORAL FOUNDATION
—2.3. ENLIGHTENMENT
(REVELATION)

"This is the message we have heard from him and declare to you: God is light; in him there is no darkness at all. If we claim to have fellowship with him yet walk in darkness, we lie and do not live by the truth. But if we walk in the light as He is in the light, we have fellowship with one another, and the blood of Jesus, his Son, purifies us from all sin."

1 John 1:5–7 (NIV)

1054) **What is enlightenment?** How does one achieve enlightenment? In the context of the moral foundation, enlightenment is a moral imperative for human development.

1055) In this discourse, enlightenment does not refer to the *Age of Enlightenment* described by post–medieval times. It refers to the enlightenment that comes from the light of God.

1056) The operative word concept is "light; to shed light, to enlighten." God alone can enlighten us, because He is a God of light.

1057) The **Age of Enlightenment**, or the Enlightenment, was an era that began in the eighteenth century and lasted about a century and a half. It began at the close of the Thirty Years' War (1648) and ended with the French Revolution (1789).

1058) One can consider the word *enlightenment* to have an absolute meaning. This means that one is enlightened or one is not.

1059) God's enlightenment changes us, and the benefits of His enlightenment lead us to walk in new directions. Our mannerisms, speech, habits, and general behavior take on new meaning.

1060) God created human beings with the intellectual capacity to be enlightened, because we are His highest creation.

1061) God gave us the power to reason, the power of imagination, the power to be creative, and the power to use past experiences to guide us to paths of enlightenment (revelation), peace, and harmony.

1062) Revelation is the disclosure or unveiling of something hidden. Without His revelation, He appears to be hidden or non–existent.

1063) When God shines His light on us, and we are receptive to its influence, it automatically elevates us to a new realization of His spiritual purpose for our existence.

1064) Our goal, therefore, is to allow God to permanently transform us by the light of His love and redemption. This transformation gives us the moral strength to live every day, from the moment of revelation, on, in newness of life.

1065) Enlightenment provides access to His divine knowledge, wisdom, and understanding as we adopt new behaviors toward our neighbors (horizontal relationship) and toward our daily communion with Him (vertical relationship).

1066) God's transformation of our lives enables us to strive daily to remain in the light of new knowledge and to resist all earthly temptations.

1067) Enlightenment (revelation), therefore, signifies that one has access to God's divine knowledge, wisdom, and understanding which help us to grow in stature and in progress, both in the physical and in the spiritual realms of our lives (2 Timothy 3:16–17).

1068) Our greatest revelation is the understanding that we are first and foremost spiritual beings, living temporarily in our physical bodies.

1069) The roots of a tree are connected to the earth and draw nutrients from the earth to sustain the life of the tree. Likewise, the roots of our spiritual being are connected to God who sustains human life.

1070) A tree will die when its roots are taken out of the earth. Similarly, when we separate ourselves from God we affect our capacity for fulfilled living and we die spiritually.

1071) There is a spiritual hunger in us that only God can satisfy. We are made alive first as spirit before we become alive in our mortal bodies (Jeremiah 1:5).

1072) The first imperative of human development ought to be our spiritual enlightenment. This is the highest form of enlightenment and it transcends other forms of enlightenment such as moral, social, intellectual, or physical.

1073) God knew that human beings would honestly seek to be enlightened, however He also knew that we would interpret our material, scientific, and philosophical advancements as enlightenment. Hence, Jesus spoke these words: "I am the light of the world" (John 8:12 NKJV).

1074) Scientific intelligence has largely replaced the search for God's enlightenment, and it has taken us along dual paths in our search for enlightenment.

1075) God knew that our scientific achievements, material wealth, and intellectual achievements would distract us and cause us to move farther away from His marvelous light.

1076) God knew that some would misconstrue the quantum leaps from the Middle Ages to the ages of philosophy, reason, intellectualism, and information as enlightenment.

1077) We must therefore differentiate between our spiritual enlightenment, which comes from God, and our social, political, intellectual, and scientific enlightenment, which comes from the human intellect.

1078) To be enlightened means to walk daily in the light of God. When we walk with Him, we are not afraid of the darkness of the world. Our light shines so that others see a path that leads to Him.

1079) Jesus Christ instructs: "Let your light so shine before men, that they may see your good works and glorify your Father in heaven" (Matthew 5:16 NKJV) (circa CE 27). The Apostle Paul counsels: "For you were once darkness, but now *you are* light in the Lord. Walk as children of light" (Ephesians 5:8 NKJV) (circa CE 63).

1080) We know that we are on the enlightened path to God when His righteousness permeates us, and a compulsion within us causes us to seek our higher good and we begin to live a moral life.

1081) Morality today, in our laws and in our media, has become associated with standards of sexual behavior. The word *morality* brings to mind the liberation of the modern age, but there are other broad facets of the word *morality* which we ought to consider as well.

1082) We often forget or even sub–consciously downplay behavior that is unfair, unethical, unjust, dishonest, or uncharitable as conduct which falls outside of God's moral framework for humanity.

1083) Moral enlightenment is critical to moral behavior, moral authority, and moral leadership in the world.

1084) Moral leadership and authority have the capacity to determine the nature of human survival; but what are the principles of moral enlightenment which can set us on the right path of moral relationships with our neighbors?

1085) It is not sufficient to consider just being a good person by extending goodness to friends, family members, and individuals of whom we have a high opinion.

1086) The true measure of goodness comes from our relationships with those with whom we are unfamiliar, and with those of a different race, color, religion, culture, language, and socio–economic background.

1087) Enlightened human relationships must come from a heart informed by God, as opposed to the head informed by human intelligence. From the heart, human goodness derives its intuitive nature, though God nurtures it by His goodness toward us.

1088) Jesus Christ knew that the absence of a relationship with God would cause hardship and suffering in the world and result in the breakdown of our relationships with our neighbors. He prepared His disciples by establishing a simple code of love for God and for neighbor as the first imperative of human goodness (Matthew 22:37–39).

1089) Righteousness does not come naturally; it is a result of moral enlightenment, which requires diligent and daily practice. Hence, to walk in the moral light of God, human beings must practice human goodness.

1090) Imagine a world blind to color, race, culture, nationality, religion, and social and economic class. This is what human goodness demands.

1091) Imagine the billions of dollars that nations spend correcting problems due to relationships which have gone monumentally wrong – resulting in genocide, war, hunger, dislocation, medical costs, and rebuilding of infrastructures.

1092) Imagine the redirection for the advancement of humanity as a whole, of the billions of dollars saved through the avoidance of such human calamities by enlightened individuals and nations, and through our daily practice of good works.

1093) Our obedience to God's principles allows us to reap the benefits of His promises (peace, joy, provision, protection, and enlightenment) and divine insight.

1094) Human governments and citizens operating under the light of God can accomplish what tens of thousands of human laws, and billions of dollars, can only partially realize.

1095) Human laws are necessary, but they do not cultivate overall goodness in human beings. Obedience to human laws largely cultivates compliance, based on fear of censure or punishment by other human beings, rather than fear of God as a first imperative for human behavior (Psalm 111:10).

1096) God knew that some human beings would obey the law because of conscience, others would obey because of fear, some through knowledge of His Word, and that still others would not obey at all.

1097) God's enlightened government, complemented by an enlightened people, is a prerequisite for nations to flourish. Systems of government can only grow and flourish by the voluntary involvement of their citizens.

1098) God's righteousness empowers us in every human endeavor. The spirit of cooperation results in a decrease in conflict between parents, families, neighbors, societies, and nations.

1099) Nations place their trust in human laws as the primary mechanism of ensuring civil societies (as they should), but human laws cannot supplant God's law.

1100) We know from religious teachings that leaders of ancient nations that called their nations to prayer and fasting have benefited from God's intervention (Jonah 3:5–10).

1101) God has promised to listen to our prayers and to relent. He promises to forgive the sins of individuals and nations and to bring about their rebirth. "If we confess our sins, He is faithful and just to forgive us our sins and to cleanse us from all unrighteousness" (1 John 1:9 NKJV).

1102) God's revelation through King Solomon for His people applies to our nations today; God gives His assurance: "if My people who are called by My name will humble themselves, and pray and seek My face, and turn from their wicked ways, then I will hear from heaven, and will forgive their sin and heal their land" (2 Chronicles 7:14 NKJV).

1103) God is telling us through His Word that He *will* relent when we are in obedience to His will and when our prayers reach up to heaven.

1104) God wants us to experience lives of fulfillment but where does such a life begin? The answer lies in acquiring knowledge, wisdom, and understanding of His purpose for our existence, which opens the doors to His enlightenment.

1105) The mechanism by which human beings acquire knowledge is through education; however, for education to be enlightening (revealing), it must of necessity encompass religious, moral, and social elements, as well as traditional academics.

1106) Education ought to be thought of as enlightenment, as a first imperative of learning. This new approach to education as enlightenment can have a significant impact on the academic structure of our educational institutions.

1107) Nations of the world that are lagging technically could bring themselves within the family of progressive nations if wholesome education were made generally available to all of their citizens.

1108) All nations can advance socially, intellectually, and economically with some level of parity when nations deploy education equitably; when it is wholesome; and when it is made generally available to all segments of populations.

1109) Educational enlightenment helps individuals, societies, and nations to see beyond the narrow sphere of self and to widen their vision beyond individual, family, color, race, culture, religion, and national boundaries.

1110) The important national value of academic success is the great opportunity it provides to translate our successes into the lives of others less fortunate than ourselves.

1111) Success and successful living have been mentioned numerous times in this book, but never in the context of personal material worth or the material worth of others.

1112) What is success? Success is God's love enabling us to live in the temporary while producing the eternal in others.

1113) Success is Doctors Without Borders (Médecins Sans Frontières), an international, independent, medical, humanitarian organization that delivers emergency aid to people affected by armed conflict, epidemics, natural and man–made disasters, and exclusion from health care.

1114) Throughout his epistle to Jewish believers, James integrated true faith and everyday practical experience by stressing that true faith must manifest itself in works of faith.

1115) God's Word reverberates in our world of superfluous wealth and power as it did in ancient times.

1116) Perhaps God is using the emerging global village to enlighten humanity to its, and to His, universality. We are bringing nations together digitally, while God is bringing us closer into one universal whole.

1117) God's enlightenment is a necessary ingredient for better families, societies, and nations. It is the only hope for individuals and nations as we seek answers to challenges in the natural world where His marvelous light awaits us at the end of the corridor.

1118) God wants us to look beyond the surface of our natural world and see the good in human beings that is not visible, except through spiritual eyes.

1119) God extends His uncompromising love to us; His unquestioning forgiveness awaits us every morning we rise; His inexhaustible grace and mercy are always available to us.

1120) All God asks is that we seek forgiveness daily for wrongdoing, step into the light of His Word, and allow Him to guide our path to His spiritual purpose of our existence and His enlightenment.

FOUNDATION 2
MORAL FOUNDATION
—2.4. RESPONSIBILITY (DUTY)

"So then, each of us will give an account of himself to God" Romans 14:12 (NIV). "We who are strong ought to bear with the failings of the weak and not to please ourselves. Each of us should please his neighbor for his good, to build him up. For even Christ did not please himself" Romans 15:1–3 (NIV). "Do not conform any longer to the pattern of this world, but be transformed by the renewing of your mind."

Romans 12:2 (NIV)

1121) **What is responsibility?** How do individuals in the modern world relate to their responsibilities? Are human beings altogether responsible for their behavior?

1122) We ought to examine our responsibilities to children, family, society, neighbor, government, nation, and most importantly, to God. Responsibility is real and is toward the Word of God as opposed to merely being an academic discourse.

1123) When we think of responsibility, we rarely give thought to our higher order of accountability, and so we often misunderstand the two different concepts.

1124) The first premise, with regard to our responsibility and accountability, is that we are first and foremost accountable to God. Second, we are accountable to our neighbor. Third, we are accountable to the integrity of the environment (the land) that sustains life.

1125) The interchangeability of *accountability* and *responsibility* often blurs the distinct differences between the two concepts. Distinction between these words is vital to the understanding of how we communicate with each other and impute culpability.

1126) ACCOUNTABILITY: The individual who is ultimately answerable for the outcome of an activity or situation, even though he or she may delegate the activity to another. One who is accountable can also be responsible for the outcome.

1127) RESPONSIBILITY: The individual who is charged with the primary role in the performance of a specific duty or the execution of a certain task. It can also have a more narrow, cause–and–effect meaning. The responsible person may not necessarily be accountable or liable for the outcome.

1128) The root of all forms of accountability and responsibility begins with parents' accountability and responsibility for their children's upbringing. This is certainly the most common example in society in which individuals have both roles.

1129) Parents are accountable to God for the upbringing of their children. Likewise, they are responsible for training their children and responsible for the outcomes of their children's behavior until the children reach adulthood. It is a *twofold* function, which involves the nurturing of children.

1130) Often intuitively, from the moment the newborn child arrives in the home, parents begin to prepare him or her to leave the home to form a separate family relationship and relationships with the outside world.

1131) Parents' exemplary guidance is the most important part of the child's preparation process. Parents institute by their actions the whole idea of guidance.

1132) The demarcation line between accountability and responsibility for child and youth behavior is often a complex matter for the judiciary in the modern age.

1133) In many jurisdictions, parents are held accountable for the behavior of children until they reach the age of sixteen years old. Parents also assume other forms of accountability until children reach the age of eighteen years and yet other accountabilities, until young adults reach twenty–four to twenty–six years of age.

1134) Parents have perhaps eighteen years in which to instill knowledge, wisdom, and understanding to enable the child to live a fulfilling life that honors God and gives service to humanity.

1135) It is implicit in raising children that there are levels of accountability and responsibility which parents and children should be acutely aware of.

1136) More important, it is God's command that children honor their parents. The Old and New Testaments state that children have paramount responsibilities to parents. Twice in the scripture God has intervened to make explicit His command to children.

1137)   Approximately four thousand years ago God gave a revelation to Moses and Israel in which He commanded children: "Honor your father and your mother, that your days may be long upon the land which the LORD your God is giving you" (Exodus 20:12 NKJV) (circa 1426 BCE).

1138)   Approximate two thousand years ago God gave a revelation to Paul for the church. God also promised two significant benefits that children would inherit for their obedience to parents: children would have long and happy lives (Ephesians 6:1–3).

1139)   Obedience is the most important word for children to understand, and it equates to children's responsibility. It is the beginning of the journey from responsibility to accountability.

1140)   Children are the seeds of society. In fact, the nurturing of these seeds is critical in the early stages of child development.

1141)   The child who has not learned to obey his or her parents is like a seed that does not develop well or produce wholesome fruit (Reference: *Five Foundations of Human Development* (FFHD) —Figure 23: Eight Environmental Influences on Children and Youths).

1142)   If the child does not obey his or her parents, who are God's representatives for the family, he or she will not learn to obey societal authority and certainly will not learn to obey God, who cannot be seen.

1143)   God in His infinite wisdom knew that the instruction of children would be the ultimate determinant of the religious, social, and economic stability of families and nations.

1144)   Some youths find themselves answerable to the judicial system at an early stage of their development. Parents, churches, the education system, the judicial system, and society seek to understand who is accountable for children's behavior.

1145)   Children and youths live in a society that makes the rules for them with little participation or input from them. From the media, to politics, to education, to religion, to healthcare, to the management of corporations, adults dictate most, if not every aspect, of the lives of children and youth.

1146)   Children often witness a willingness by modern society to accept less than high integrity as a natural product of modern bureaucracies and the modern way of doing business in politics and in corporate affairs.

1147) Impressionable children accept less than high–integrity behavior as the norm, and this expectation consciously and sub–consciously forms part of the child's psyche and intellectual makeup.

1148) The news media reports that there are many problems facing the nation's youth. They tell us of smoking and drinking at an early age and that young people are forming their relationships with the law at an early age.

1149) Parents tell us that youths are unprepared for the critical responsibility of early romantic relationships, marriage, and the raising of children.

1150) Some members of society point to child rearing in a single–parent environment as being a major contributor to these problems. Some point to weaknesses in their religious and social upbringing.

1151) Children and youths attempt to mirror our materially driven lifestyles; and our acquisition of wealth and power as the overriding imperatives of adult behavior.

1152) The struggles among youth reflect the struggles of adults. These struggles are not unique to single parent homes. Regardless of family composition, *all* experience some level of influence from the modern world.

1153) Educational institutions once had a responsibility far beyond academic information literacy. They had a responsibility to shape and develop moral character in the lives of their students.

1154) The shift to a new model of materially based education fostered new, scientific approaches to teaching and learning. This new model spawned a new era of technological advancement and material progress as the first obligations of progressive nations.

1155) Western Christian nations have abandoned their long heritage of religious instruction in their public schools, and this decision has been upheld by Western constitutions, which are the hallmark of their democracies.

1156) God knew that human beings would have great challenges in maintaining religious traditions in the modern era.

1157) God did not create human beings and then leave us to figure out our accountabilities and responsibilities within His creation.

1158)   There is a need to shift to a new benchmark of religious principles and values regarding our accountabilities and responsibilities toward each other.

1159)   The institutions of human beings (marriage, family, government, politics, education, religion, and business) have intrinsic links to all human endeavors.

1160)   A new world order of principles, values, and responsibilities must recognize a broader perspective of the human family and incorporate the spirit of co-operation, both by head and by heart.

1161)   How can we rest comfortably in the presence of God, whom we claim to love and worship, when the vast majority of the world's population lacks basic medicines, food, clothes and shelter?

1162)   God's counsel to the strong that we bear the infirmities of the weak is not simply a social or intellectual exercise. This responsibility is basically spiritual, and it flows from the heart. It transcends all visible differences in color, race, and culture.

1163)   The church has two distinct functions to fulfill; the first is to prepare the lives of its members for their eternal destiny (1 Thessalonians 5:23; 2 Thessalonians 2:1-3), and the second, to work in pursuit of favorable human relationships in all regions of the earth using all available religious, moral, social, intellectual, and economic means.

1164)   Our responsibility to God, family, neighbor, society, government, and the environment then becomes the first obligation of human existence.

1165)   We must preoccupy ourselves and imbue our minds with the pursuit of our responsibilities and accountabilities to God, to authority, to family, to nation, to neighbor, to authority, and to the environment; otherwise, modern civilization will collapse in the dust like past civilizations.

1166)   We must grow beyond divisions between parent and child, husband and wife, and among family members, friends, neighbors, societies, nations, and most importantly, the division between God and us.

THOUGHTS TO ENLIGHTEN AND EMPOWER THE MIND

2001 QUESTIONS AND PHILOSOPHICAL THOUGHTS TO INSPIRE, ENLIGHTEN, AND EMPOWER OUR WORLD TO LIMITLESS HEIGHTS

—FOUNDATION 3
SOCIAL FOUNDATION

3.1. RELATIONSHIP (RELATIONS)
3.2. RACE AND RACIAL PERSPECTIVES (ONENESS)
3.3. BEHAVIOR (CONDUCT)
3.4. SELF—ESTEEM (SELF—CONFIDENCE)

FOUNDATION 3
SOCIAL FOUNDATION
—3.1. RELATIONSHIP
(RELATIONS)

"Be devoted to one another in brotherly love.
Honor one another above yourselves. Never be
lacking in zeal, but keep your spiritual fervor,
serving the Lord" Romans 12:10–11 (NIV). "Rejoice
with those who rejoice; mourn with those who
mourn. Live in harmony with one another. Do not
be proud, but be willing to associate with people
of low position. Do not be conceited."

Romans 12:15–16 (NIV)

1167) **What is relationship?** Do human relationships play a critical role
in the nature of our survival?

1168) Relationship with God is our highest form of relationship, and it is
a spiritual relationship. Our relationship with God our Creator is
the model for all other relationships.

1169) God has defined our relationship with Him in His Word, therefore
there is no ambiguity regarding how we should communicate with
Him and cultivate human relationships (Matthew 22:37–39).

1170) There is a tendency to view relationships from a generic
perspective, but we understand spiritually, morally, socially,
intellectually, and intuitively that there are many distinct types of
relationships.

1171) Each relationship requires a distinct set of conditions to be
wholesome and fruitful. Nevertheless, there are behaviors that we
exhibit that impair our relationships, either intentionally or unintentionally or by our actions or inactions.

1172) Most, if not all, relationships break down because we fail to
establish agreements on expectations and because of the unrealized
expectation of either one or both of the parties.

1173) We engage in relationships in our personal, public, private, and
professional lives, but we often neglect to establish and agree on the
expectations we have of the relationship.

1174) We suffer daily from the negative effects of our relationships with others in such circumstances as these: separation and marriage breakdown, family disagreements, sibling rivalry, contract violation, and business failure.

FOUR FOUNDATION PRINCIPLES TO ENABLE HUMAN RELATIONSHIPS

1175) **Principle 1**: Diligently learn about the individual, people, or nation with whom we desire to build a long–term relationship.

1176) **Principle 2**: Acquire as much experiential knowledge as is necessary to gain a thorough understanding of the individual, people, and nation with whom we desire to build a long–term relationship.

1177) **Principle 3**: Apply the knowledge of the individual, people, and nation with whom we desire to build a long–term relationship, with trust, respect, prudence, and honest communication.

1178) **Principle 4**: Practice patience, understanding, forgiveness, compassion, and reasoned judgment when things do not go our way with whom we desire to build a long–term relationship.

1179) When we neglect any one of these four principles, it can lead to relationship breakdown, separation, jealousy, prejudice, intolerance, and violence.

1180) From an international perspective, the breakdown of relationships between peoples and nations leads to the severing of international relationships as well.

1181) Unfortunately, it only requires one of the two parties in the relationship to violate the principles of that relationship to result in relational breakdown.

1182) We can only benefit from the fruits of effective relationships when we fully embrace and practice the four principles of relationships.

1183) Our earthly relationships can become tenuous with time and circumstances. Relationships can change from one day to the next and can lead to breakdown of communication between siblings, parents and children, husbands and wives, employees and employers, and even more problematic relationships between nations.

1184) If we are unable to establish and maintain a relationship with God, who loves us unconditionally, it is inconceivable that we can establish and maintain wholesome relationships with others whose love for us (and ours for them) is unavoidably conditional.

1185) Social intelligence enables human social relationships; spiritual intelligence enables our spiritual relationship with God the Father and His Son Jesus Christ.

1186) This relationship with God is critical, and it establishes the basis for the nature, purpose, and endurance of all other human relationships.

1187) Lasting mortal relationships pose a great challenge to individuals and nations, regardless of their level of sophistication, social and economic status, or system of government.

1188) Despite the noble goals of international peace organizations and peace agreements between and among nations, the global community struggles to avoid the breakdown of relationships.

1189) Breakdown of international relationships have been the catalyst for the genocide, war, terrorism, and territorial and religious conflicts that the world has experienced over past centuries.

1190) When civil societies break down, the costs to national and international economies are monumental.

1191) Why are our relationships fragile and threatened when we arrive at positions of disagreement? Our reliance on the human intellect alone is the primary cause of our tenuous human relationships.

1192) Modern educational enlightenment and the growth in world religions have not been sufficient to mitigate international conflict, and engender an "Age of Peace."

1193) We have chosen the same path for centuries and have only managed to elevate the military option as our path to peace with devastating results. The evidence that God's spiritual nature is no longer working within us is then reflected in our outward violent reactions to other individuals and nations.

1194) With much ease we adopt an unforgiving attitude, an uncaring, unloving, and even prejudiced nature.

1195) The danger we face when we relinquish our relationship with God is that we are no longer constrained by His will for our lives and by the Holy Spirit who guides us.

1196) Unintentionally, perhaps intentionally, we allow the demands of our materially driven lives to draw our attention away from God and His nurturing relationship.

1197) When we neglect to give honor to God, all other relationships are weakened; we fail to honor and obey our parents; we fail to serve others; we fail to obey authority; we fail to manage God's creation.

1198) The integrity of broken bonds of relationships lead to feelings of betrayal, yet our human nature compels us to break the bonds of our relationships, even when the relationship is with the highest – God.

1199) How do we begin to understand why we behave the way we do, knowing the negative consequences? The psychologist and the sociologist may have scientific answers, but there are non–scientific (spiritual) answers as well.

1200) Our broken relationships arise from some of the more negative characteristics of our nature, such as disobedience, pride, greed, obduracy, and impatience.

1201) These negative attributes of our nature, rather than produce the fruits of God's love and enhance our relationships, are factors that contribute to broken relationships with parents, husbands, wives, family, friends, neighbors, employers, society, and nation.

1202) The peace of God within brings us to a higher understanding of our relationship with Him and with our neighbor.

1203) This understanding is essential to harmonious relationships and cooperation, beginning within the family. For this reason God has special admonishments for the family (husbands, wives, and children).

1204) The nucleus of the family is the marriage of husband and wife within it, which is ordained by God. He has established the family for His purpose; hence, He provides the basis upon which to build important human relationships. God admonishes the family, beginning with the husband and wife.

1205) Marriage is the primary foundation of all human relationships. Is it not profound that the Holy Bible focuses on the relationship among husbands, wives, and children?

1206) Marriage is the only human relationship that God instituted and which must be solemnized before witnesses.

1207)   Marriage is the nucleus of the human family, society, and nation. Therefore the bond of marriage demands special attention to lessen the potential for breakdown of the marriage relationship and the potential negative and lasting impact on children.

1208)   Marriage breakdown impacts the stability of families, societies, and nations, and its effects spill over into the international community.

1209)   Some young adults engage in early marriage relationships and live–in arrangements to fulfill the need for companionship and for their economic survival. For some youths, these relationships occur before they establish their careers or are intellectually, emotionally, socially, or financially mature.

1210)   For better or for worse, many of us do get married, and based on copious statistical data, the trends seem to indicate that many marriages fail to deliver the wholesomeness intended.

1211)   Marriages greatly increase their probability of success when couples adhere to God's five foundations of marriage and when they subscribe to principles of marriage relationships.

1212)   Separation and divorce trends will continue in light of the ever–increasing stresses of daily living and of earlier romantic relationships.

1213)   Romantic marriages and wedding planning are important aspects of the marriage, but the first canon of marriage is the spiritual bond.

1214)   God ordained marriage and He established five foundations to stabilize marriage relationships such as: *(1) companionship; (2) completeness; (3)enjoyment; (4)procreation;* and *(5)protection.*

1215)   These above five foundations are intrinsic to the reality of the bonds of marriage. Our constant awareness of and response to these foundations strengthens the bond of marriage.

1216)   These five foundations are not formulated for our own expectations in marriage, but for our mutual expectations.

1217)   These five foundations help us to build bonds of friendship based upon our mutual need for companionship, completeness, enjoyment, procreation and protection. In addition, married couples desire a union which will sustain love and romance, security, long–term compatibility, and shared responsibility for raising children.

1218)   Although married couples seek the best of social relations, often they do not take the time necessary to evaluate their relationships in terms of longevity or of changing demands. For instance, mothers (wives) still bear the heavier burden of responsibility for raising children, caring for their welfare, and maintaining an overall stable household.

1219)   These responsibilities and accountabilities in marriage are part of the total commitment that the couple must contemplate in order to ensure a successful marriage.

1220)   Unlike past generations, couples today have access to a battery of marriage counselors, youth counselors, and religious counselors. The probability of a successful marriage increases when the couple seeks professional marriage counseling prior to the marriage.

1221)   The biblical view of marriage affirms the presence of a divine element in marriages. Marriage must not be confused with a wedding ceremony, which only solemnizes and symbolizes a couple's commitment.

1222)   Marriage represents a unity of mind, soul and body; it likewise involves an understanding of God's purpose for spousal union. Husbands and wives are no longer two, but one flesh (Matthew 19:5).

1223)   Marriage is the only human relationship ordained by God; hence, it is the most important relationship outside of our relationship with our Creator, God. A stable international community is rooted in stable nations. Stable nations are rooted in stable families; as well, stable families are rooted in stable marriages.

1224)   When the couple maintains constant awareness of the five foundations of marriage, and when they engage in consistent daily practice of the principles of marriage, it helps to create stability within the marriage.

1225)   When we neglect to define responsibilities and accountabilities within marriages, it strains the relationship and can result in domestic disharmony.

1226)   In marriage, as in all relationships, the power of dialogue creates opportunities for building mutual trust and friendships, which provide a good starting point for couples contemplating marriage.

1227)   Marriage stability is a central building block of stable families and stable nations. Western governments place a great emphasis on the welfare of children.

1228) Enlightened leaders know that the social and economic stability of their nations is a function of the nurture, care, and opportunities that society, beginning within the family, extends to children.

1229) The family was once a safe haven from the fears and inadequacies of its members. Today the shrunken family unit appears to be too small and fragile to accommodate the concerns of its members.

1230) The new form and structure of families challenge its ability to manage the social, housing, and economic concerns of its members.

1231) The demands for greater amounts of freedom and independence, rather than interdependence among its members, pull the modern family apart. Why has the family changed in size and viability?

1232) Families of generations past offered their members a more centralized unit, often with several generations living in the same household.

1233) Families of generations past, operated within a framework of high moral and religious values and subscribed to personal discipline, interdependence, and respect for each other.

1234) Today, in our affluent middle class or lower income families, some members are in need of an escape from family violence, abuse, loneliness, impoverishment, over–crowding, or despair.

1235) Depression in children and adults is indicative of internal and external stressors on the family.

1236) The modern family seems to be in a state of major adjustment, which may have begun during the Industrial Revolution (1800s–1900s).

1237) The Industrial Revolution ushered in new ways of life and financial and material prosperity for the masses. It also ushered in the commuter age and great mobility of individuals, which resulted in separation of parents from children for long periods of time.

1238) The financial fortunes gained from the new era afforded a range of options for family members seeking to move out of crowded, centralized homes to establish their independence.

1239) Family members in the modern era appear to view themselves much less as part of a central unit than did previous generations. Many are engaged in a struggle for self–fulfillment and independence rather than for interdependence.

1240) A new individualism is invading the family unit. Parents' pre-occupation with work and careers create opportunities for children and young adults to gain early independence, long before children and young adults are equipped to make independent judgments on important social issues.

1241) There is a relaxing of discipline by modern parents, due to more progressive approaches to caring for children. Some might postulate that the relaxing of standards in the discipline of children has contributed to the various current patterns of youth delinquency.

1242) Compassion for children lives within all of us. Many divorced couples re-marry into families with children, and they often provide them with the love and care that all children deserve.

1243) Regardless of the forms of family that emerge in the future, the family will survive. The natural desire for human companionship will prevail in spite of family violence and broken marriages.

1244) Needless to say, for better or for worse, many of us do get married; hence, the critical need to strengthen the institution.

FOUNDATION 3
SOCIAL FOUNDATION
—3.2. RACE AND RACIAL PERSPECTIVES (ONENESS)

"From one man he made every nation of men, that they should inhabit the whole earth: and he determined the times set for them and the exact places where they should live. God did this so that men would seek him and perhaps reach out for him and find him, though he is not far from each one of us. 'For in him we live and move and have our being.'"

Acts 17:26–28 (NIV)

1245) **What is racism?** Where did this social phenomenon that is so hard to define come from?

1246) Why has racism been such a constant crisis in multi–racial societies when our religious philosophies teach that all human beings are born equal?

1247) Is racism a pre–existing condition at birth, as opposed to being a derived social condition? Is there a cure for racism?

1248) Why are we characterized by race, as opposed to being characterized by the fact that we are all human beings, created by God, and are all members of the human family? Are there any positive benefits of racism?

1249) The Bible educates us that we are one blood: "And He has made from one blood every nation of men to dwell on all the face of the earth, and has determined their preappointed times and the boundaries of their dwellings" (Acts 17:26 NKJV).

1250) Racism is a spiritual, moral, and social condition with no redeeming value. It is an aberration of the human spiritual nature; it is not a natural condition of our existence.

1251) God's enlightenment is the only permanent cure for racism, and it is available to anyone with the desire to obtain it.

1252) Looking through the windows of history, one cannot help but wonder why superior education, intelligence and character do not transcend such a human aberration.

1253) Why did all humanity not benefit from a superior guidance and steer itself toward the fruits of God's love?

1254) Unless God directs our lives, we are powerless against the pervasive nature of racism and of other human ills that we must be on constant guard against (Galatians 3:23–29).

1255) Scientific investigations teach: "All human beings belong to a single species and are descended from a common stock. Copyright © UNESCO 1979, (United Nations Education, Scientific and Cultural Organization). Declaration on Race and Racial Prejudice (Adopted by the General Conference of UNESCO at its twentieth session Paris, November 1978), Article 1, p. 11.

1256) Three perspectives provide a broader approach to the understanding of race (Reference: *Five Foundations of Human Development* (FFHD) —Figure 21: Three Hierarchical Perspectives on Race). The three perspectives on race are: *(1) Religious; (2) Scientific and (3) Observable* – seem to confirm intrinsic linkages among all humanity.

1257) Accusations of prejudice, discrimination, and intolerance may occur within a racial grouping, but these occurrences may not have a racial component. However, when these same acts occur among different races, society views them as acts of racial prejudice, racial discrimination, or racial intolerance.

1258) No one race perpetrates these hard–to–define acts. All races display similar tendencies. This has been the challenge, and continues to be a challenge for any nation of different racial groupings.

1259) The act of racism causes mental and/or physical suffering to the victim. It is a most destructive and disreputable condition of any nation.

1260) There is no known natural cure or antidote to racism, including human law. Human law can only temporarily constrain the practice of racism, because the strength of laws is in legal capacity rather than in moral capacity.

1261) What exactly is the root cause of racism, and what are the belief systems that perpetuate it? Racism has its roots firmly planted in the belief that some races are superior to others in *natural intelligence* and *character.*

1262) Racism is primarily a product of the assumption of racial and cultural superiority.

1263) Religious, intellectual, empirical, and scientific observation cannot demonstrate that any race has superior value or superior patterns of behavior (such as, love, patience, kindness) over another.

1264) Every race falls short of these superior qualities (the fruit of the Spirit) that God looks for in them.

1265) Intellectual and empirical observations, augmented by historical records, lead to the conclusion that all races demonstrate similar positive and negative behavioral characteristics and potential for human failure and greatness.

1266) Let us engage ourselves intellectually in this most important discourse on race. Observably, all human species are born either "equal," "unequal," "equally unequal," "unequally equal," or "unequally unequal."

1267) In every continent, every country, every city, every village, and every indigenous area and in every history book, observable evidence of a common human heritage exists.

1268) Combined world travel, experiential knowledge, and intellectual and empirical observation teach us that there are more similarities in human beings and their behavior than there are differences.

1269) Biblical, scientific, and observable evidence point to the same origin and destination. The wise King Solomon informs: "Then the dust will return to the earth as it was, And the spirit will return to God who gave it" (Ecclesiastes 12:7 NKJV).

1270) We are basically spiritual beings trying to master human experiences. Out of the spiritual comes love and fruitfulness.

1271) Every race and every culture reflects its fears, tears, suffering, joys, hopes and aspirations. These common reflections have led to the conclusion that all races possess equal capabilities for great good and great evil.

1272) Some races and cultures may exhibit behaviors that are different from others, and some of those behaviors may even be contradictory.

1273) One might hypothesize (through observation) that variances in human behaviors could be attributable to the conditions under which a person was born, where he or she lived, and to what degree he or she received either positive or negative nurturing.

1274) One can further hypothesize that the main difference between any two human beings is in their response to wants, needs, or nurturing, or in their reactions to fear or emergencies.

1275) Children are born into the world without an intellectual understanding of race, color, culture, religion or nationality. Family differences such as poverty, culture, dress, and language have little impact on young minds.

1276) Visible differences are first recognized from a point of view of childish curiosity, but first lessons in intellectual understanding of race would most likely come from the parents.

1277) Racism is the way we discriminate between others of a different race or culture and then translate our attitudes of those others into the minds of young children.

1278) Positive behaviors can result from a positive posture. Likewise, a negative posture might bring children into conflict with other races and cultures.

1279) Our racially insensitive behaviors may begin in our homes, our neighborhoods, the primary school classrooms, the schoolyards, or in competition on the playing fields.

1280) Western nations, along with their Christian heritage, have also had a history of racist practices as demonstrated during the post Black African slavery of the sixteenth to nineteenth centuries in the colonies, in Africa, in the Caribbean, and in the United States of America.

1281) Western governments, private organizations, individuals, and the church have all labored to eliminate racism in society. The signing of The Emancipation Proclamation on January 1, 1863, signaled the beginning of the end to slavery in the United States of America, and eventually throughout the world.

1282) Abolition of slavery introduced new forms of racism, which translated into a new order of discrimination and inequality which then engendered racial conflict.

1283) The struggle for racial equality became an international symbol of the struggle for respect and dignity for all human life, and it continued through the mid 1900s.

1284) In 1948 a Universal Declaration of Human Rights declared the rights and dignity of all human beings. This was followed by ©UNESCO statements and declarations in 1950, 1951, 1964, 1967, and 1978.

1285) Paradoxically, governmental institutions had to enact into law, alienable rights that all human beings were born with.

1286) Approximately one hundred years after the signing of the Emancipation Proclamation, a Historic US Civil Rights Acts was signed in 1964, by then US President Lyndon B. Johnson (1908 – 1973), who served as the thirty–sixth President of the United States from 1963 to 1969.

1287) The past half–century has marshaled in a new portrayal of racial harmony in the Western world, but this new era did not come about exclusively from the goodness of the human heart; rather, hearts and minds prevailed.

1288) How would we know when we had achieved racial equality? We would know when the imposition of the heart had triumphed over the imposition of the law.

1289) The twenty–first century depicted a major turning point in the history of the United States of America. In November of 2008, Barack Hussein Obama (born August 4, 1961) was elected the forty–fourth and current President of the United States of America.

1290) Black Africans, American Blacks and Whites, and peoples around the world view a Black American presidency as a racial triumph rather than as a social, moral, or intellectual triumph.

1291) **Edward Gibbon Wakefield (1796–1862):** "The reasons for slavery wrote Gibbon Wakefield, are not moral, but economical circumstances; they relate not to vice and virtue, but to production."

1292) Despite our predisposition to emphasize race, intellectual observation teaches that human beings are not born with inherent prejudices and racial intolerance.

1293) We learn, nurture, and perpetrate such behaviors, often temporarily constrained by human laws. It is only by the grace of God, and His enlightenment that His light transforms us and we experience a new personality of love for humanity.

1294) Discrimination can also take the form of denial of opportunity on the basis of age, gender, access to housing, or employment practices. These acts may or may not have a racial component.

1295) Discrimination can be subtle, or it can be highly visible as in an all Black or all White fraternity where, even if one gains membership, feelings of discomfort may accompany one's presence, rather than feelings of accommodation.

1296) Are we really different, and does being different physically, constitute a catalyst for conflict? In the quest for knowledge and understanding of who we are as a human species and where we have come from, many scientific disciplines have examined this question.

1297) Archeologists travel around the globe, painstakingly unearthing secrets of past civilizations. They dig down through the depths of ancient ruins and burial sites to unearth tools of trade, weapons of warfare, and pottery for storage, cooking, and eating.

1298) Archeologists also attempt to reconstruct history through patterns of birth, life, death, and burial. They search through archives of ancient writings that can provide clues to the evolution of civilizations, arts, cultures, customs, and religious practices.

1299) The study of sociology and psychology blend scientific and humanistic approaches. Sociologists study systems made up of relations among people, such as families, formal organizations, ethnic groups, or countries and their politics.

1300) These studies are an attempt to understand human relationships and the mechanisms that create, perpetuate, and maintain the social balance that maintains civilization.

1301) Social movements, legal and economic systems, institutions, organizations, and cultural forms are also the subjects of study in sociology. Have the goals of sociology helped us to unravel the mysteries of race and racism?

1302) Sociology, psychology, and other studies in human behavior, whether scientific or observational, teach that the human species is a paradox. It is not that we are inherently good or evil, but that we are socially and ethically the most adaptable of all living organisms.

1303) An understanding of the spiritual purpose for our existence provides us with a starting point for understanding the human species.

1304) A child that grows up Christian, Jewish, Muslim, Hindu or Buddhist will display behaviors and customs that are characteristic of the family culture and religious heritage.

1305) A child that grows up in an Indian, Chinese, African, American, Israeli, or Italian home will display behaviors consistent with the home culture and customs.

1306) During our formative childhood years, we rarely recognized, understood, or preoccupied ourselves with color, race, culture, or physical differences.

1307) Racial prejudice has afflicted individuals and nations, and still frustrates the international community despite great efforts to contain its devastating effects on human survival.

1308) Throughout history, people of different racial groupings have had great difficulties accepting each other as equals.

1309) Paradoxically, inequality and lack of empathy exists within common racial groupings on the basis of class or color stratification.

1310) This phenomenon leads to the conclusion that color differences pervade human relations to such an extent that any study regarding race and racism must necessarily examine the impact of color as a prime factor.

1311) Are we different and does being different physically, constitute a catalyst for conflict?

1312) Our experiences as human beings shape us. Within the limitations of our genetic makeup and natural propensities, all human beings are the product of religious, moral, social, racial, cultural, and physical conditioning and environment.

1313) The real human dilemma then involves a conflict of differences. Wherever there are differences, there is a potential for conflict, whether the differences be inherent, such as race or color, or whether they be cultural or economic, such as social and material standing.

1314) Negative images and opinions of others often place children and adults in poor relationships that nurture anger and hatred, and frequently lead to outright religious, cultural, and racial conflicts.

1315) For six thousand years, accentuated by religious and cultural differences, our world has been a virtual battleground for genocides, racial wars, political wars, class wars, and even territorial wars involving the same race and color.

1316) Our preoccupation with our visible, physical differences seems to define and characterize our existence. Many immigrants identify themselves first, by their country of origin, and second, by their adopted country.

1317) Minority cultures, must express their desire to understand, embrace, and integrate themselves into the majority culture, which means moving outside of their cultural comfort zones, and earnestly accepting the host culture.

1318) Minority cultures must be mindful of the great generosity of developed nations that have embraced all cultures over the centuries.

1319) Parents must help their children to gain a better understanding of the blessing of God that permeates all nations that formulate laws to protect the rights of the individual and of the collective rights of all citizens as well.

1320) The Holy Bible counsels: "For you, brethren, have been called to liberty; only do not *use* liberty as an opportunity for the flesh, but through love serve one another" (Galatians 5:13 NKJV). "Let each of you look out not only for his own interests, but also for the interests of others" (Philippians 2:4 NKJV).

1321) Who we are begins in the spiritual (Ecclesiastes 12:7). Human hands have not formed us; neither can human genius explain scientifically how human life came into being.

1322) The Holy Bible teaches that all human beings were made from one blood; every nation of men to dwell on all the face of the earth (Acts 17:26–29). What a powerful and moving testimony to the origin of the human species! As well, it is an admonishment toward humility.

1323) Imagine just for a moment; a world in which God did not make us one blood, and set a pre–appointed time for us to die or limit our boundaries and habitation on earth (Acts 17:26 NKJV).

1324) This is the starting point for the modern scientific search for understanding of our spiritual existence. The Holy Bible presents *immutable truths* regarding the origin, purpose, and limitations of human existence.

1325)   Despite scientific discoveries of the vast and incomprehensible universe over past centuries, human knowledge is infinitesimal and limited to the material realm.

1326)   The scientists must also join the search from non–scientific perspectives as well, knowing that we are on a journey about which no scientific enquiry can inform humanity of the beginning or the end with absolute certainty.

1327)   Scientific research, of necessity, must help humanity to better comprehend its commonalities, while taking the main focus off the conflicts that underpin our differences, in hope of generating a better understanding of our unique place in the universe.

1328)   In researching the subject of Race, Racism and Racial Harmony, the most valuable scientific tool is a booklet entitled: "Declaration on Race and Racial Prejudice," adopted by the General Conference of UNESCO at its twentieth session in Paris, 27 November 1978.

1329)   Science presents multiple perspectives regarding the origin of the human species, and how we relate to each other socially, unconstrained by external factors such as color, race, culture, and nationality.

1330)   The desire for race and harmony is the focus of numerous other disciplines such as anthropology, sociology, and psychology that attempt to help human beings to better understand, cope with, and build better communications with each other and with nations.

1331)   We are really not different from each other when we observe human behavior from religious and scientific perspectives and from intellectual observation.

1332)   The desire for racial harmony is a definite preoccupation of human beings. We must continue our great moral efforts through humanitarian struggles to attain a higher understanding of the collective needs of humanity.

1333)   We have an opportunity to create "new history" as we push the envelope on our educational, intellectual, and scientific capabilities; rather than to repeat the history of past civilizations.

1334)   The mass media of our modern age can be the greatest agent for the eradication of all forms of racial stereotypes. The proliferation of radio, television, and internet media communications can help elevate understanding of the interconnectivity of the global village.

1335) The mass media can be the greatest force for good, when attention to the greater public good is a first imperative.

1336) The mass media can foster the cultural, religious, and racial harmony we desire and seek. More importantly, the mass media alone, facilitated by modern digital electronics, has the capacity to disseminate global communications instantaneously to combat all forms of misinformation that might be contrary to the public good.

FOUNDATION 3
SOCIAL FOUNDATION
—3.3. BEHAVIOR (CONDUCT)

"Therefore, prepare your minds for action; be self–controlled; set your hope fully on the grace to be given you when Jesus Christ is revealed. As obedient children, do not conform to the evil desires you had when you lived in ignorance. But just as he who called you is holy, so be holy in all you do; for it is written: 'Be holy, because I am holy.' "

1 Peter 1:13–16 (NIV)

1337) **What is behavior?** Behavior is the way in which we conduct ourselves both in private and in public.

1338) Our behavior reflects our composite self. It is outward action that suggests who we are internally. It speaks of our nurturing, our values, our beliefs, our tolerances and intolerances, and of our empathies.

1339) God of the Bible provides His creation with the explicit instructions and guidance necessary to promote life–saving behaviors, which ensure peace, harmony, and cooperation among individuals and nations.

1340) Observably, human behavior is rather complex to discern. It is only God's Holy Word that can predict with certainty the outcomes of human behavior based on the violation of His directives.

1341) We have in some measure accepted human behavior as rational and controlled but at times, random and often uncontrolled.

1342) We seem to take for granted, and to justify to some degree, hate, envy, jealousy, bigotry, racism, prejudice, greed, aggression, competition, and violence as acceptable in some circumstances.

1343) The natural response to these human behaviors is the demand for more human authority, but human authority has not managed to control the more base nature in us.

1344) Observing human behavior, one can surmise that despite our nurturing, there is a tendency to respond with some level of aggression when someone does wrong to us.

1345)   When something goes wrong within our society, we look to our governments for answers, because governments have the macro–administrative mechanisms to address problems of society.

1346)   What is the impetus behind human behavior, good or bad? The family is the tree from which all members of society have sprung. The communist, the socialist, the dictator, the conservative, the liberal, the democrat, and the republican came from within families.

1347)   The judge, the lawyer, the policeman, the delinquent, and the offender all are the products of families. The scientist, the engineer, the doctor, the nurse, the principal, the teacher, and the student all have their roots within the family.

1348)   The murderer and the victim also have roots within the family foundation. The family then becomes the first place to look when something goes wrong in society, but not the only place to look.

1349)   From the moment a child is born, he or she begins to experience the effects of his or her first social environment – the home.

1350)   The traditional and cardinal rules for raising children once were a display of good manners, personal discipline, responsibility, respect, and cooperation with one or both parents, family members, and/or others.

1351)   Family love and care for each other were once the hallmark of family relations, particularly in caring for infants and elder family members.

1352)   Respect for family elders and law and order were, at one time, customary within families. In other words, social behavior was once, and is now, paramount to the stability of the family and to society.

1353)   In generations past, the family offered its members a more crowded centralized unit which operated within a framework of moral and social principles and values.

1354)   Peer pressure was less significant. The influence of schoolmates was generally positive. In our modern era, youth are susceptible to, and often engage in, social behaviors which society labels as delinquent.

1355)   The growing child's many hours in school allowed for teachers to be significant influences on his or her behavior.

1356) The decline in youth behaviors may have links to a need to escape from family violence, abuse, loneliness, despair, depression, and/or boredom.

1357) The family unit ought to provide the most stable and nurturing environment within which to grow. This stability within the family is important, because it translates to stability in society as well.

1358) Families in our highly mobile era may not view themselves as integral building blocks of societies, but they are the building blocks of society, with children at the nucleus.

1359) The intrinsic link between family and society is evident when the breakdown in the family and consequential breakdown in society is observed.

1360) Modern enlightenment seems to take us further apart from our responsibility toward each other, as our first and foremost "spiritual duty."

1361) The view of the family is more or less in the context of a unique social entity. Families tend to identify themselves in the context of race, culture, religion, nationality, and social and economic class.

1362) The independence of members, rather than their inter-dependence, leads to family fragmentation, as each member strives to cope with the stresses of his or her daily life.

1363) Some family members seek solace outside of the family, as opposed to within the family, which further weakens family cohesion and likewise, the cohesion of society.

1364) The Holy Scriptures, in the book of Proverbs, provides specific instructions to humanity and particularly to youth regarding their behavior.

1365) The book of Proverbs is a comprehensive guide to human behavior. It provides simple instructions and explanations in clear and understandable language. It also defines principles of godly behavior and delineates rewards and consequences for human behaviors that violate the law of God (Leviticus 26:1–46).

1366) God recognizes that we do not have a natural inclination to pursue His wisdom. Furthermore, when we pursue wisdom, it generally occurs in the latter years of life.

1367) Despite our access to God's divine knowledge, His wisdom and His understanding, our society has arrived at its present state of affairs with overwhelming religious, social, and economic problems, despite growth in human knowledge, growth in Christianity, and growth in world religions over the past century (Reference: *Five Foundations of Human Development* (FFHD) —Table 1: Major Religions of the World).

1368) The proliferation of tens of thousands of human laws penned by nations to maintain a tenuous social balance among individuals, societies, and nations provides sufficient evidence of the weaknesses of human laws unaided by God's law.

1369) God has made His laws available to us through His Holy Word, written by the prophets and Apostles, and taught in the Christian church. What's more, in light of our access to God's knowledge, wisdom, and understanding, why haven't nations throughout the world risen to the apex of moral and social behavior?

1370) Do our faith, our belief, and our practice accentuate the practice of Western Christianity and the behavior it displays?

1371) Observe the day, Sunday, when millions of Westerners go to church to worship the universal God. Although the Christian church has significantly improved its image over the centuries, empirical observation suggests that it is still the most segregated day with regard to church attendance.

1372) Sunday is not only a day on which we racially segregate, but a day of intellectual and doctrinal differences as well. The image of the Christian church and its adherents is critical to the image we project to society.

1373) Our religion should have the capacity to present a perspective on human behavior that transcends color, race, culture, and nationality. Yet the various groupings reflect color, race, cultural, and intellectual stratification, as well as social class differences contrary to the aims of a unified body.

1374) Walking with God and entertaining strangers places us in a different realm mentally and physically. It can make us both uncomfortable and fearful, because it tests our assertions regarding our spiritual standing, as people of God.

1375) Christ in us produces faith, self–discipline, and visible love seen in good works. Why would Jesus Christ place challenges before us knowing our human weaknesses? Why would God admonish us to associate with those whom we view as different from us, or threatening to us?

1376) God foreknew that as human knowledge and material wealth increased, human behavior would change. Knowledge and wealth can cause great social, economic, and religious divisions, hence His counsel against our reliance upon human wisdom.

1377) Our behavior and our daily lives become a witness to the fruits of His love, as we include others more into our lives. This behavior demonstrates to the world that God's love is in us, as we display love outwardly.

1378) Spiritual disciplines (such as, fasting and prayer) do not take the place of social responsibilities toward the weak of our societies.

1379) True religion does not allow us the liberty of developing moral defenses to free ourselves from guilt regarding the poor in society regardless of whether they are of another color, race, culture, nationality, or social and economic class.

1380) The Holy Scripture intrinsically links the existence of human civilization to the concerns of the needy.

1381) God has seen the affliction of the poor from the beginning of time. In His infinite wisdom, He has chosen to defend the poor, because He has seen the exploitation of human beings that has taken place throughout human history.

1382) God listens to our broken promises to eradicate poverty, hunger, and human suffering, repeated every decade. He has seen our great moral efforts, and our great injustices throughout the centuries to the present. His omnipresence and His omniscience should act as a moderating force on human behavior.

1383) God knows our compulsions, our sincerities, and our insincerities. He knows that our responses to human suffering might be social and economic, as opposed to our response to His spiritual command.

1384) God's Word ensures us that by giving and sharing with those less fortunate; we reap the rewards of His love, peace, protection, healing, light, and the joy which is our salvation (Habakkuk 3:18).

1385) Perceptive observation points us to a new reality that seems to be emerging with the incidence of youth poverty on the Western horizon as well as with the incidence of destitute children in other parts of the world.

1386) In generations past, the poor and afflicted were the aged and forgotten of the human species. Our twenty-first century has ushered in a new segment – a young, impoverished class alongside a young, affluent class in society.

1387)   Many impoverished teenagers voluntarily or involuntarily are living on the streets away from the protection of the home environment. Others are living in public shelters and elsewhere in conditions that might not be altogether wholesome.

1388)   Some youth are the working poor, some with young children to care for, at a stage when they themselves could benefit from parental nurturing.

1389)   Many attribute the new segment of impoverished youth to the behavior of some youth who do not respect the authority and guidance of their parents.

1390)   Knowingly or unknowingly, our youth are listening, and modeling adult behavior. Youth behavior, similar to adult behavior, is constrained either by human law, by human goodness, or by obedience to God's law; the latter comes from the transformation of the human heart.

1391)   Human laws and human goodness are but temporary constraints against wrong behavior. This critical knowledge should be the starting point of any attempt by societies and nations to affect youth behavior.

1392)   We must be mindful that the offences that are alarming to parents and society and which youths commit, mirror offenses that adults commit as well (Reference: *Five Foundations of Human Development* (FFHD) —Figure 24: Three Key Categories for Dialogue with Youth and Figure 25: Four Key Empowerment Categories for dialogue with Youth).

1393)   On the surface, material demands appear to have the dominant influence on youth behavior, however, there is also a great spiritual hunger going on among our youth; they are not intellectually aware of their inner longing nor of the emptiness that can only be satisfied when they realize their spiritual purpose in life.

1394)   God's admonishment to youth is profound. His instruction to youth is to get wisdom. It is the preeminent foundation upon which life–respecting and life–saving behaviors stand.

1395)   **The Book of Proverbs** is designed both to prevent and to remedy ungodly lifestyles. The Proverbs are the product of the wisdom given to Israel through Solomon, of Proverbs literature (931 BCE).

1396) **Survey of Proverbs:** "Proverbs is the most intensely practical book in the Old Testament (OT), because it teaches skillful living in multiple aspects of everyday life.

1397) Our earnest prayer, supplication, and open-mindedness informs of His divine wisdom. Seeking knowledge, wisdom, and understanding without open-mindedness demonstrates the lack of a diligent search.

1398) To the natural intellect it may sound naive to think that somehow the pursuit of God's wisdom is the path to permanently correct human behavior.

1399) The Holy Scripture informs that there are consequences to transgressing God's law. Is it possible for individuals and nations to base their survival on God's law? The Holy Spirit can empower human beings to live the true meaning of the commandments.

1400) Can we live without hate, envy, jealousy, bigotry, racism and prejudice? Can we live without greed, aggression, competition and violence as the natural way of human existence? Assuredly we can!

1401) We must believe that despite the challenges of past civilizations and despite our current challenges, the indomitable spirit that lives within human beings has enabled modern civilization to rise up out of a dark past to overcome human suffering, such as the misery that resulted from slavery, apartheid, genocide, wars, and colonization.

1402) The past must be our greatest teacher to ensure the survival of future civilizations.

1403) Fundamental principles of morality found in religions of the world help us to survive from crisis to crisis.

1404) The ethical and spiritual springs of human life can prevent the world from entering into another moral crisis, on the scale of *World War I (1914–1918)*, and *World War II (1939–1945)*.

1405) Our denial of our capacity to overcome human crises, and rise above our differences in ideology, politics, culture, nationality, and religion often impedes our spiritual moral, social, and intellectual growth.

1406) We may place our confidence in science and technology, in our material wealth, and in our gated communities. We place our confidence in various forms of authority and human laws. Yet we know intuitively, and within our spirit being that only God's laws enable human behavior.

1407) The all-knowing God has made provision for replacing human government from the beginning of time because of human weakness and refusal to submit to His will.

1408) God used the synoptic gospel writer, Luke, to inform us that Jesus Christ, whom heaven has received, will return to restore all things, according to His Holy prophets (Acts 3:18–21).

1409) God also used the prophet Isaiah to advise us that He will be the architect of the future government, and Jesus Christ will be His authority over all the earth.

1410) Human governments have an express and limited purpose on earth and likewise a limited capacity within themselves to affect human behavior or to manage God's creation without His enabling guidance.

1411) Without God's theocratic model upon which to frame our democratic models and other systems and structures, the world cannot experience true liberation or live peaceful and fulfilling lives, which are gifts from God.

1412) The world cannot through human intellect achieve such a liberated state of being, because liberation begins with a change of the human spirit being (Ezekiel 36:27), which alone can permanently transform human behavior and bring about a new era of secular and spiritual authority.

FOUNDATION 3
SOCIAL FOUNDATION
—3.4. SELF–ESTEEM (SELF–CONFIDENCE)

"For you created my inmost being; you knit me together in my mother's womb. I praise you because I am fearfully and wonderfully made; your works are wonderful, I know that full well. My frame was not hidden from you when I was made in the secret place. When I was woven together in the depths of the earth, your eyes saw my unformed body. All the days ordained for me."

Psalm 139:13–16 (NIV)

1413)   **What is self–esteem?** Self–esteem is one of the most important attributes of human existence.

1414)   Self–esteem is an internal concept by which one identifies oneself and is underscored by feelings of superiority or inferiority; a general result of comparison with others transcends high or low self–esteem.

1415)   What are the effects of low self–esteem on individuals? Why do some children and adults suffer from low self–image, self–worth, and self–esteem?

1416)   Is positive self–esteem something that human beings can develop without the help of other individuals and society at large?

1417)   Some individuals consider *self–image, self–worth,* and *self–esteem* to be synonymous, but self–image and self–worth are predecessors of self–esteem.

1418)   We tend to associate self–image, self–worth, and self–esteem with our material well–being and with the physical image we project to society.

1419)   An individual who displays high self–esteem is outgoing, highly socialized, and self–confident in dealing with others.

1420)   Individuals with high self–image project themselves in a manner in which they desire their friends, peers, and associates to perceive them.

1421) Regardless of how we esteem ourselves (high or low), the act of comparing ourselves with others is a common denominator. The way others look, how they dress, what they possess, and whom they associate with, in some way speak to our self–esteem.

1422) The image of ourselves that we see in the mirror is often in contrast to the magazines and television images of movie stars and models.

1423) The phenomenon of looking at one's self through the images of the media serves to perpetuate two different responses. **First,** individuals with high self–esteem use the images to boost their self–esteem. **Second,** individuals with low self–esteem are further challenged by the comparison to their own image, and this comparison then acts as a negative rather than a positive impulse.

1424) Self–esteem begins within the family. Children are generally born into homes with happy and loving parents regardless of parents' circumstances or of environment of birth.

1425) We have no say as to the family we are born into, and the environment in which we grow can have positive or negative impact on our overall development in terms of *self–image, self–worth* and *self–esteem.*

1426) Children may not be aware of these mitigating situations, or of how their parents' circumstances may be shaping their lives and images of themselves.

1427) In generations past, children and adults identified themselves simply as persons. There was little pretence about who we were on the outside.

1428) Unlike adults, children have little control over their nurturing. Yet their formative nurturing has a direct influence on their self–image, self–worth, and self–esteem.

1429) Parents who have a high regard for the success of their children inspire and motivate them. Conversely, parents who have low expectations of their children may not express the same level of enthusiasm for success for their children.

1430) In our modern era, there are an inordinate number of audio, visual, and physical images that may impact the way children and adults view themselves, physically.

1431) The ideal images compel them to compare and evaluate themselves with others, in terms of color, looks, height, hair, weight, size, clothes, and even education and intelligence.

1432) The material demands and social pressures of our modern era often shake the confidence and self–esteem in children and adults.

1433) The rapid changes taking place in society have an impact on the intellectual and emotional growth of children. The transition from youth to adulthood seems to occur at a pace that is incompatible with youth development and understanding of real world phenomena.

1434) Essentially, the growth of children and search for self–esteem in all of its dimensions is actually a search for fulfillment in God.

1435) Self–esteem from God's perspective is different from our perspective. There is a definite gap between secular and religious perspectives on the teachings and understanding of self–esteem.

1436) We were created in God's image with inherent abilities and intellectual capacities that only human beings have. God, having created us in His image, enables us to rise above physical differences. We therefore ought to exhibit the same self–worth.

1437) The self–esteem gap that we refer to occurs as a result of conscious or subconscious choices to appropriate measures that contradict our greater significance as creations of the living God.

1438) High self–esteem comes from our vertical relationship with God. A weak vertical relationship with God negatively impacts our horizontal relationships with our neighbors.

1439) When we reflect on our own lives, each of us can remember a period in our childhood and youth when we felt somewhat withdrawn and lacking in vitality, self–image, self–worth, and self–esteem.

1440) There is nothing wrong with self–enhancement, but the problem arises when we begin to worship the *creation* more than the *Creator.*

1441) The demands and influences of modern societies can become an obsession, and some youths may succumb to wrongful behavior in a quest to satisfy their material wants.

1442) The intuitive nature of parents often helps them to detect signs of low self–esteem in children. Family members and others such as teachers, ministers, and the family physician, might also observe and respond to changes in children's behavior.

1443) Generally, parents and family members view changes in youth behavior as inevitable phases in their social development, but they often miss important signals of low self-esteem in their children.

1444) A materially driven society reinforces this perspective of attempting to elevate self-esteem in children and adults, rather than establishing an internal measure of our worth in the image of God (Genesis 1:26).

1445) Color, race, and culture may not appear to be obvious factors affecting self-esteem, yet these human characteristics, including language and nationality can add force to low self-esteem in children and in adults.

1446) One can surmise that at every level of society, all human beings have, at some time, exhibited feelings of low self-image, low self-worth, and low self-esteem, simply because we are social beings.

1447) From the poor, dispossessed, and disenfranchised to the wealthiest of individuals, even brief periods of low self-esteem can cause individuals to lose self-control and to adopt self-destructive behaviors.

1448) Low self-image, low self-worth, and low self-esteem afflict us and can take us to the edge of human powerlessness and hopelessness.

1449) **Gary R. Collins (2007):** Members of minority groups often are made to feel inferior due to racism that degrades people because of their skin color or ethnicity and systematically denies access or privilege to one racial group while perpetrating access or privilege to members of another racial group. Gary R. Collins PhD., *Christian Counseling–A Comprehensive Guide*, Third Edition (Nashville, TN: Thomas Nelson, 2007), p. 429.

1450) Consciously or sub–consciously, an individual may be comparing his or her state to that which is perceived to be better. We compare our way of life to others as we search for fulfillment. This search is generally in the material and physical realms, as opposed to the spiritual realm, because this is where our natural compulsions lie.

1451) We admire, and in some cases we idolize, some individuals for their looks, their shape, or their athletic prowess, as we diminish our godly image.

1452) Why are we always comparing ourselves to others? Do we not risk becoming someone with an identity crisis, rather than someone who seeks to enhance his or her image in the light of God's image? Is comparison not the primary cause of the internal conflict that leads to low self-esteem?

1453) The undeniable fact is that we are who we are on the inside. When we compare ourselves to others, are we not forgetting that fact? Is it not a waste of our energy, which should be directed toward our development as human beings made in God's image?

1454) The term *role model* is often misinterpreted to mean anyone who presents a positive image in society and whom we esteem as a good example for our children, our youth, and ourselves to follow.

1455) Role modeling requires a deep understanding of the role model's beliefs, methods, styles, and thinking. Hence, parents and older siblings ought to be the definitive role models, because of the intimate relationships we have with them.

1456) Role models appear to be gender specific. Males and females project different images and values and provide nurturing which is reflective of their gender.

1457) Where are the male role models in single parent families, headed mostly by women? Where is the traditional home with the two-parent family?

1458) The two-parent family is alive, and is still the majority stakeholder in raising children, notwithstanding the family has taken on new compositions in our modern era.

1459) In our highly mobile generation, men have greater opportunities to start new lives, thus limiting women's chances for reconciling failed marriages.

1460) In most nations, there is recognition and a national awareness of vanishing male role models in homes and in schools. This awareness calls for collaboration between family and society to address solutions to this dilemma.

1461) Some divorced and single mothers express loneliness and feelings of being betrayed by their husbands or partners. These feelings lead to apprehension, and their children's behavior may reflect the mother's feelings.

1462) Some single or divorced mothers develop great resolve to perform dual roles of mother and father in the absence of the male parent role model.

1463) Empirical observation shows that girls have a higher exposure to the "perfect" images in magazines, on television, and in music videos than do boys. These images are apt to influence girls' self–esteem and behavior, which may manifest in lifestyle illnesses such as bulimia and anorexia.

1464) Boys tend to externalize their response in the form of simple, disruptive behaviors all the way to outright violent and self–destructive acts.

1465) Delinquent male youth behavior is a preoccupation of modern society. This primary focus on male youth delinquency and contact with the justice system leads society to place a greater focus on the problems of self–esteem in boys.

1466) Youth incarceration is a reflection of ineffective development of our youth. Effective development of our youth ought to encompass their spiritual, moral, social, intellectual, and physical development, as well.

1467) The types of education, nurturing, and goals and expectations we establish for our boys and girls are the foundations of the men and women they become.

1468) In the absence of scientific investigation, intellectual observation could point us to some traits that are inherited from parents and grandparents.

1469) **Mahatma K. Gandhi (1869–1948):** "Children inherit the qualities of the parents, no less than their features. Environment does play an important part, but the original capital on which a child starts in life is inherited from its ancestors." The Philosophy of Mahatma Gandhi, Copyright © 1953. The University of Wisconsin Press, Ltd. Chapter 1, *Background of Gandhi's Philosophy*, p. 3.

1470) Gandhi makes a very interesting observation that can aid us in nurturing our children. When we examine his statements, Gandhi seems to be telling us that children inherit their parents' genes, traits, financial and business acumen, material worth, and even vulnerability to some illnesses.

1471) The original capital that children inherit from their parents is transferred through wealth, political affiliation, family cohesion, cultural synthesis and religious heritage.

1472) Gandhi's message helps us in the twenty–first century to understand the reasons for many of our racial, cultural, religious, and class prejudices, which have caused untold human suffering throughout his and our lifetime.

1473) It is important to underscore that the majority of children are well–nurtured, and are productive members of society who make great contributions in every field of human endeavor, but we also need to examine other forms of nurturing.

1474) World nations send their boys to engage in wars of aggression and to curtail aggressors, and children lose their fathers. Our daughters and mothers lose a great many fathers, partners, brothers, sons, and husbands, who often were the finest and brightest of their generation.

1475) For some youths, street values may be acceptable as a substitute for the values of home and other institutions.

1476) Have we ever stopped to think that the roots of the challenges our boys face may be attributable to their *self–worth*, *self–image*, and *self–esteem*?

1477) The challenges that our boys face did not occur overnight; therefore, they require multiple and long–term solutions, the scope of which are very significant.

1478) The collaboration between parents, religious institutions, learning institutions, business and industries, and all levels of government is needed to arrive at solutions (Reference: *Five Foundations of Human Development* (FFHD) —Figure 26: The Hierarchical Self–esteem (Universal) Pyramid).

1479) It is only when *all* of our institutions work together that society can begin the process of reversing the conditions which precipitate and sustain low self–esteem in our children.

1480) One might postulate that self–esteem is not a condition that only affects children or youth. Self–esteem can move along a trajectory and affect the feelings we have about ourselves at any stage of our lives and at all levels of the self–esteem pyramid.

1481) The individual must be constantly conscious of his or her environment, and how he or she is being positively or negatively motivated. Similarly, those who have control over the environment must be constantly aware of and responsive to the effects of the environment on others.

1482) Positive self–esteem begins with inner joy and outer happiness. The individual must begin with the assurance deep within his or her heart that God has ordained his or her steps (Proverbs 16:9) and that personal happiness should never be dictated by external influences.

1483) Building self–esteem and seeking happiness in oneself also means bringing happiness to others. It means self–improvement (spiritual, mental, and physical) as one helps to improve others.

1484) Positive self-esteem self–improvement in all aspects of our lives. Our mannerisms, our character, our personality, our moods of discouragement must all be conquered by the consciousness of our divine image of God.

1485) The responsibility for childhood behavior begins at home. The home is the first institution of accountability. Parents are responsible for the behavior of children, and it is a spiritual responsibility, not one that simply relates to parenting.

1486) Religious institutions may seem like unlikely places to promote self–esteem in children and adults, but they are probably the most important institutions for the promotion of self–esteem.

1487) Paralleled only by the home and the school, religious institutions provide hope, the basis for hope, and the faith that changes mental attitude and promotes hopefulness.

1488) The modern church to a great extent is a multi–cultural environment. This environment presents unique opportunities for cross–cultural discussions in self–esteem from religious perspectives.

1489) Positive self-esteem could contribute to positive rewards for business and industry in terms of human interaction, participation, creativity, and productivity.

1490) Positive self-esteem in individuals creates potential benefits for their corporations and themselves when they display confidence and self–assurance in business matters.

1491) Education is a key factor in combating low self–esteem, both from an academic and from a godly perspective. Religious education focuses on spiritual values, which neither material needs nor material wants circumvents or frustrates.

1492) The school curriculum is an essential medium through which to incorporate lessons in self–esteem. When children are knowledgeable about their culture, their history, and their family heritage, their positive self–esteem is enabled.

1493) Governments provide assistance in the form of financial incentives to businesses and industries that have a youth focus. Governments, like other national institutions, have a particular interest in the stability of youth.

1494) Government is the only institution with the apparatus to address challenges for our youth on a grand scale, and it's the only institution that can realize the greatest benefits outside of the family.

1495) It will take nothing less than a national and international state of emergency to rebuild some of the important structures for the benefit of future generations.

1496) Nations can engage in collaborative national strategies with other sectors of society with the focus on elevating the self-esteem of children.

1497) Positive self-esteem can lead to successful living. It can enable us to cope with and manage the many challenges in our lives, such as personal health, marriage, work-life, career, and family.

1498) We should strive to make these principles a part of our daily consciousness and an integral part of the national as well as the individual psyche.

1499) When these principles of success become our conscious and sub-conscious guides, the image, worth, and esteem of individuals and nations should rise to great heights, and lives of fulfillment could become the natural way of living.

THOUGHTS
TO ENLIGHTEN
AND EMPOWER
THE MIND

*2001 QUESTIONS AND PHILOSOPHICAL THOUGHTS
TO INSPIRE, ENLIGHTEN, AND EMPOWER OUR WORLD
TO LIMITLESS HEIGHTS*

—FOUNDATION 4
INTELLECTUAL FOUNDATION

4.1. INTELLIGENCE (INTELLECT)
4.2. EDUCATION (LEARNING)
4.3. KNOWLEDGE (UNDERSTANDING)
4.4. CAPABILITY (ABILITY)

FOUNDATION 4
INTELLECTUAL FOUNDATION
—4.1. INTELLIGENCE
(INTELLECT)

"For the message of the cross is foolishness to those who are perishing, but to us who are being saved it is the power of God. For it is written: 'I will destroy the wisdom of the wise; the intelligence of the intelligent I will frustrate.' Where is the wise man? Where is the scholar? Where is the philosopher of this age? Has not God made foolish the wisdom of the world?"

1 Corinthians 1:18–20 (NIV)

1500) **What is intelligence?** Is intelligence the same as education, knowledge, wisdom, or understanding? Is human intelligence the same as spiritual intelligence?

1501) Where does intelligence come from, and why is it essential for us to have intelligence to live successful lives?

1502) Can we be trusted to take care of our own destiny and survival without intelligence? (Reference: *Five Foundations of Human Development* (FFHD) —Figure 28: God's Hierarchical Intelligent Structure for Humanity).

1503) Human intelligence is a life–saving gift from God. Unlike animals that are limited to instinctive behavior, intelligent human beings have the capacity to promote good or evil in the world.

1504) Human intelligence guides our decision–making with regard to the nature and purpose of every human action and endeavor. Our connection to God's source of spiritual intelligence is through the Holy Spirit, which is the mind of God.

1505) Unfortunately, our knowledge of science and technology, derived from modern education and human intelligence, seems to place a barrier between spiritual intelligence and human intelligence.

1506) During our daily conversations, we might use the words intelligence and education synonymously. Generally, it is assumed that an individual who possesses a high degree of education naturally possesses a high degree of intelligence.

1507)   Education and intelligence originate from two distinctly different sources. The first source, **education,** is the sole prerogative of human beings. The second source, **intelligence**, begins with God. God has granted us, the highest of His creation, special blessings of intelligence.

1508)   The design and development of educational policies, standards, curricula, training methods, and outcomes are within the control of human beings.

1509)   We have unfettered opportunities to address national needs and priorities by the use of education, which is the mainstream of human development.

1510)   The endowment of modern education and human intelligence can lead to smugness, pride, vanity, aloofness, and feelings and displays of superiority.

1511)   The Bible educates us that there is a distinction between human intelligence and spiritual intelligence, but that we can achieve spiritual intelligence from God.

1512)   We must seek to comprehend the spiritual truths that come from above (heavenly wisdom) in order to aid us in our ability to manage His creation.

1513)   The highest form of intelligence is spiritual intelligence, which comes from God. Spiritual intelligence transcends and empowers all other forms of intelligence, such as moral, social, scientific, and leadership intelligence.

1514)   Spiritual intelligence gives us divine insight into God's divine knowledge, wisdom, and understanding, which are prerequisites to moral leadership and authority in the world.

1515)   Spiritual intelligence enables human beings to understand things that the natural mind cannot comprehend, because only the spiritual mind can discern those thing that are spiritual (1 Corinthians 2:10–14).

1516)   Human intelligence is limited to material knowledge; hence we have great capacity to create artificial intelligence in machines, but without spiritual intelligence, we can only see life in a haze; we cannot effectively manage God's creation.

1517)   Despite the awesome storehouse of human knowledge in the twenty–first century, why are we unable to create a world of peace and harmony? God has not constrained human intelligence. He endowed us with free will as free moral agents to seek His higher spiritual intelligence and purpose for our lives.

1518) God does not deny us the capacity for great intelligence or great minds. He did not constrain the great human mind of Amadeus Mozart (1756–1791); of Sigmund Freud (1856–1939); of Alexander Graham Bell (1847–1922); or of Albert Einstein (1879–1955).

1519) God did not constrain the minds of the modern age that gave us the telephone, produced the atomic bomb, and developed high-speed trains, electronic communications, the television picture tube, and the silicon chip.

1520) God provided us with every aid necessary to manage His creation and to live fulfilling lives. He has also opened to us His book of scientific insights (the Holy Bible) to provide us with the beginnings of our understanding of scientific matters.

1521) Scientific benefits to the modern world have been nothing short of phenomenal. Conversely, spiritual progress, the most important form of progress, seems to be in an embryonic stage when compared to scientific progress.

1522) How do human beings account for our deficiencies in spiritual progress (Galatians 5:22–23) in light of the growth in Christianity and other world religions over the centuries?

1523) Spiritual progress is not a measure of our educational, intellectual, or religious awareness or learning but of obedience to God's Word.

1524) If our search is for material knowledge, human intelligence, and scientific answers to our existence, then intellectual and scientific curiosity alone will direct our steps.

1525) If our search and desire is for the true knowledge of God, we then have to seek knowledge and insight from our greatest teacher, authority, and guide – Jesus Christ, who leads us to God through the Holy Spirit.

1526) Ironically, many of us rarely see the need for capable guidance; even young people fail to grasp the fact that God our Creator made us interdependent beings.

1527) Whether we are aware of it or not, we depend upon the lessons, nurturing, experiences, maturity, and the intellectual, social, moral, and spiritual guidance of others.

1528) Long before we are capable, we let go of the metaphorical hands of our parents, and as adults, we let go of the hands of our elders. Regrettably, we also let go of the hands of our Lord and Savior Jesus Christ, whom God has appointed as our capable guide.

1529) Current global trends should awaken us to the need for a new spiritual and intellectual revolution in the way we look at our lives.

1530) We can no longer view our lives through the prisms of yesteryear; rather, there is a need for a new revolutionary approach to manage the rapid changes that are taking place throughout the global village.

1531) We must attempt to view the twenty–first century through the inspired writings of the Holy Bible, which was written by the prophets over two thousand years ago.

1532) The past century gave us heroes, leaders, and revolutionaries who, through their vision of society or the world and with great personal conviction, made personal sacrifices to achieve their goals.

1533) Great heroes, leaders, and revolutionaries appear on the national and international landscape with new systems of belief, new ideologies, and new visions of hope for a better world, but the world often disappoints them.

1534) We immortalize our great heroes, leaders, and revolutionaries; we build monuments in their honor, and create national holidays in their names, but we need to be more attentive to their legacy in terms of the practical application of their values and principles.

1535) **Mother Teresa (1910-1997),** "We think sometimes that poverty is only being hungry, naked and homeless. The poverty of being unwanted, unloved and uncared for is the greatest poverty. We must start in our own homes to remedy this kind of poverty."

1536) How should we celebrate the great compassion displayed by the legendary Mother Teresa of Calcutta? Should we not try to keep in mind her legacy of compassion as we go about our daily lives?

1537) There is no doubt that our great heroes, leaders, and revolutionaries of the past century had great scientific, military, moral, religious, and social intelligence. Yet no one individual, race, culture, or nation can claim the sum total of intelligence; only God can, as revealed through His Word.

1538) There is a great compulsion in us to lean on our own understanding, based upon the natural intellect (Proverbs 3:5–6).

Hence, we struggle in the darkness of not knowing or not realizing that we are missing out on the great benefit of God's superior intelligence to guide our path.

1539) Have we ever considered the positive impact we could have on the world if we collaborated on platforms of intelligence of pure religion, athletics, journalism, arts, culture, music, and science and technology?

1540) All knowledge comes from God; therefore, He can bring us to the deeper things in life and elevate our understanding beyond the material realm of our existence.

1541) The natural mind can only discern natural things; hence, the quantum leaps in material education and science and technology have not been sufficient to release the super intelligent powers in us.

1542) We have the capacity to develop material intelligence, because we operate in the material realm, but where can we find superior intelligent guidance and direction in the twenty–first century?

1543) The Spirit of God, through Jesus Christ, is the key that unlocks our super intelligent nature. We are born with a certain materialistic intelligence, for which education is the key to open windows of creativity in us.

1544) Releasing God's spiritual intelligence enables our human intelligence and unlocks the doors to His knowledge, wisdom, and understanding for the advancement of our peaceful coexistence and fulfillment.

1545) Individuals in the twenty-first century cry out for a brave new frontier of intelligent leadership that recognizes the limitations of human intelligence.

1546) We need leadership that recognizes our *fallacy of adaptation*. God created the world with finite amounts of resources to sustain human life throughout the ages.

1547) Adaptation is a "double–edged sword." On the one hand, we increase food production, but on the other hand, we often diminish quality and raise food safety concerns regarding animals grown in factory farms.

1548) Nations seek adaptive solutions, which include the development of mega poultry, cattle, and pig factories, as opposed to conventional farms, where animals roam free, as they feed on God's natural food supply.

1549) We may applaud ourselves for the human genius that allows us to advance our science and technology in order to satisfy our needs and wants.

1550) Human societies have exhibited unrestrained consumption and unquenchable thirst for materialism, without complete regard for the impact on the world's eco-system.

1551) With projected growth in world population as well as in world consumption patterns, one could postulate that if eighty percent of the world's population were to consume resources at the same rate of consumption as the wealthy twenty percent of the population, some of the world's finite resources would be depleted (Reference: *Five Foundations of Human Development* (FFHD) —Figure 29: Decline in Finite World Resources versus Population Growth and Consumption).

1552) Arguably, Western nations consume 80% of the world's production of food, fuel, and material goods. Likewise, as other major nations come on board in the global village, their citizens will adopt patterns of consumption similar to those of the West.

1553) The exponential rise in global consumption and in human needs and wants will diminish our capacity to adapt at rates which will be compatible with the expansion in global population and in production cost.

1554) Some underdeveloped and developing nations have vast acres of underdeveloped lands, but they lack the critical science and technology needed to produce foods economically and on a national scale.

1555) Many underdeveloped and developing nations cannot compete in the transnational food marketplace.

1556) We refer to our species as the intelligent species, not recognizing the limitations of our intelligence. We have taken for granted human intelligence as our exclusive guide.

1557) We have, to a great extent, neglected the need for a superior intelligence to guide us. Six thousand years of recorded history has demonstrated our weaknesses through acts of genocide, slavery, wars, colonization, apartheid, and exploitation of our neighbors.

1558)   Our storehouse of human knowledge provides great benefits for humanity in most specialties of human endeavor. Modern education upholds human knowledge, but the knowledge of past generations may be of modest value to present generations.

1559)   Today's new knowledge surpasses yesterday's knowledge, which no longer has any practical value to our modern material world. In contrast, God's knowledge is for eternity.

1560)   Wisdom is having experience, knowledge, and understanding together with power to apply all three with prudence, practicality, discretion, and common sense.

1561)   Wisdom is the heart and center of moral and intellectual judgment; it is an attribute that God imparts to His people. Without God's wisdom, our guide becomes material education and knowledge.

1562)   Wisdom is critical to leadership and authority. It is also important to the individual in order to make wise choices in life. Often, human beings lament, "If only I had known," but knowing does not necessarily mean that wise actions will spring from human knowledge.

1563)   Wisdom is evidenced in the wise and prudent choices that are made, and these choices must be consistent with the commandments, statutes, rules, laws, and guidelines that govern human behavior.

1564)   Understanding is the quality of having insight and good judgment in general matters, such as an insightful power of abstract thought or the ability to logically follow through or project a line of logical thought and reasoning.

1565)   Understanding is not intuitive, but is a gift from God. "Trust in the LORD with all your heart, And lean not on your own understanding; In all your ways acknowledge Him, And He shall direct your paths (Proverbs 3:5–6 NKJV).

1566)   Understanding is a prerequisite to solving problems in the natural and spiritual realms of our lives.

1567)   Without understanding, life becomes an accumulation of unresolved human problems despite academic and scientific prowess and despite the growth of world religions.

1568) One must seek to understand and not assume that one does understand. For instance, we memorize scripture verses, but learning knowing by rote does not equate to understanding or knowledge.

1569) In order to gain knowledge and understanding, we must clear our minds of *all* unhealthy thoughts, *all* negativism, *all* pre–conceptions, *all* racism, *all* prejudice, *all* judgments, *all* unrighteousness, and *all* fears that set up barriers to listening, learning, and understanding.

1570) Nations cry out for new frontiers of leadership intelligence that can demonstrate both natural and spiritual intelligence.

1571) Individuals seek leadership that will incorporate God's knowledge, wisdom, and understanding. Individuals also seek leadership that will embrace good judgment, intellectual reasoning, and logical ways to analyze and solve problems that have had a stranglehold on nations for centuries.

1572) Human intelligence is inherent in the intellect; training can develop some of these characteristics, but the basic ingredients are God's knowledge, wisdom, and understanding that come from above.

1573) The book of Proverbs provides detailed instructions for us to deal successfully with the practical affairs of life. It gives wise maxims and divine perspectives essential to a successful life.

1574) Why do individuals and nations struggle to fulfill the purpose of a hierarchical world of social and economic class differentiation?

1575) An imbalance of wealth concentration, within and among nations in the world, manifests in poverty, and social and economic upheavals and global unrest (Reference: *Five Foundations of Human Development* (FFHD) —Figure 32: The Hierarchical Wealth and Population (Universal) Pyramids).

1576) Poverty leads to feelings of powerlessness. Powerlessness causes negative actions and reactions that resonate in civil unrest.

1577) Our wise benevolent God has provided for humanity everything that it needs and that in great abundance; this fact negates any need for us to struggle for mastery at all (Genesis 1:20–31).

1578) The price of our struggles will rise as the concentration of wealth increases in some sectors of the world and as the gap widens between the *haves* and *have–nots* among individuals and among nations.

1579) Why are these impermanent economic advantages necessary to human survival when the all-knowing God has provided us with such abundance?

1580) When we use our resources intelligently and preserve the environment, the abundance of air, fuel, food, land, and water will sustain the needs of all human beings and provide us with satisfying lives.

1581) God has made His wealth of knowledge, wisdom, and understanding available to human beings to enable them to solve problems and to live in harmony with each other and among nations.

1582) Leadership in scientific intelligence among the nations seems to be the greatest driving force today, even challenging religion for the most prominent position in the lives of human beings.

1583) Our hope for the twenty-first century seems to lie in another outburst of economic or scientific revolution.

1584) The rapid transition of scientific intelligence that fueled the Industrial Revolution (1800s-1900s) presents strong arguments in favor of new growth in science and technology.

1585) We live in a world of electronic marvels, but at the same time, we face a great and impending peril. As we make progress in the physical sciences and in the material realm, and as we create more luxuries for ourselves, we fall into the trap of self-reliance and we fall victim to the illusion of self-sufficiency.

1586) Rather than giving thanks to God for the advances made possible through the use of His gift of human intelligence, we turn a little more away from Him each time we unravel one of His mysteries.

1587) It seems that our faith and devotion to God ebb each time we solve a problem or make great advancements; why do we think that we no longer need God when there is no progress made *apart* from His gifts, His mercy, and His love? God alone enables our progress.

1588) Beneficial technology, such as Global Positioning Systems (GPS), can now relate the location of animals, people, places, and things. Medical scientific literature informs us that Magnetic Resonance Imaging (MRI) machines can detect diseases throughout the human body.

1589) We refer to modern wars as operations in theaters, as opposed to battlefields. The mention of ancient battlefields conjures pictures of the savagery of war, and the brute that is in us.

1590) Unintentional death of the innocent and unintended catastrophic destruction is referred to as *collateral damage*; this euphemism desensitizes us to the fury of wars.

1591) Despite the great benefits of artificially intelligent machines, unlike human beings, machines lack imagination, human creativity, and a mind for God to inspire with His superior intelligence.

1592) Can artificially intelligent machines ask questions, speculate, investigate, reason, or draw conclusions based on feelings and emotions?

1593) Can machines learn from experience and respond to new challenges beyond the purely statistical level, or can they demonstrate wisdom or understanding?

1594) Do machines have consciences that dictate their actions or that can arouse compassion and empathy for the suffering of human beings?

1595) Human beings alone are unique in the universe, and our unique position has led us to place ourselves at the center of all things. Our creations, rather than our Creator, are the focus of our existence.

1596) Our great scientific intelligence and creative genius have propelled human beings to godlike self–images, believing themselves capable of solving all human problems.

1597) Scientific intelligence has convinced some that solutions to all human problems are within the human brain and that science and technology will also find answers to the origin and formation of the universe.

1598) Today, scientific intelligence challenges spiritual intelligence, but many are not aware that God has only made available to humanity a finite amount of His knowledge. He alone is the Lord of all knowledge (1 Samuel 2:3).

1599) Our hope now rests in human education, human knowledge, and scientific intelligence. For instance, our hope for eliminating diseases now tends to rest in the human genius.

1600) God allows humanity to experiment with nature and human lives. The history of the world repeatedly teaches us that God is in control, but rather than working with God we tend to work apart from Him, thus limiting our opportunities for His strictures and for our safety and successful lives.

1601) Only faith in God guarantees us His beneficence (Matthew 9:29). "Trust in the LORD with all your heart, And lean not on your own understanding; In all your ways acknowledge Him, And He shall direct your paths" (Proverbs 3:5–6 NKJV) (circa 961 BCE).

FOUNDATION 4
INTELLECTUAL FOUNDATION
—4.2. EDUCATION (LEARNING)

"My son, do not forget my teachings, but keep my commands in your heart, for they will prolong your life many years and bring you prosperity. Let love and faithfulness never leave you; bind them around your neck, write them on the tablet of your heart. Then you will win favor and a good name in the sight of God and man."

Proverbs 3:1–4 (NIV)

1602) **What is education?** How do individuals and nations measure the benefits of investments in education?

1603) What are the goals of education? Does education end at graduation? Are great expenditures in modern education approaching the point of diminishing return?

1604) These questions may appear to demand academic answers, yet we can also find non–academic answers to the questions when we reach beyond the traditional boundaries established over many decades.

1605) The authors' perspective demands an openness of mind, as we engage in new thinking beyond the horizon of the twenty–first century.

1606) Education is a human construct. In a general sense, Boards of Education (BOE) decide for the masses. This is the cycle of education.

1607) As a human construct, education has been a powerful tool for the overall good of citizens and nations and, likewise, as a tool to exploit the masses.

1608) Any nation that denies its citizens the rights to education, denies itself and the world opportunities for intellectual growth and advancement.

1609) Education is responsible for the phenomenal growth in human knowledge. Nevertheless, the afore–mentioned, thought–provoking questions need answers to realize new returns for nations' great expenditures in education.

1610) Education is analogous to the horizon that appears to drift further away as we move toward it. Education is not a finite concept, nor is it an event to be achieved, nor does it end at graduation.

1611) Without education, our spiritual, moral, social, intellectual, and physical growth would be limited, as would also be our material wellbeing.

1612) Education is the base from which to build stable nations, but our view of education must take us beyond the natural inclination of thinking about education as, principally, a pursuit of academic information literacy (Reference: *Five Foundations of Human Development* (FFHD) —Figure 34: Non–integrated Religious Environment in Public Schools by Virtue of Non–integrated Religious Instruction) (—Figure 35: Integrated Religious Environment in Public Schools by Virtue of Integrated Religious Instruction).

1613) Education must have the inherent capacity to mitigate lifestyle challenges such as obesity, smoking, drug abuse, child and elder abuse, and reckless driving.

1614) Education must have the inherent capacity to correct social ills such as employment inequity, racial and religious intolerance, and social injustice.

1615) Education must have the inherent capacity to alleviate the conditions which inspire violence, genocide and wars; it must alleviate the fear that overwhelms individuals and nations; and it must alleviate anxiety for the future.

1616) Education must help mitigate the primary causes of divorce and its consequential impact upon the lives of children.

1617) Education must be all–encompassing. It must shield us from compulsions toward the fear, hate, jealousy, inadequacy, and greed that our material life fuels.

1618) Education must shield us from the dangers of discontentment with our looks, our bodies, our suffering, and our existence.

1619) Education must provide hope through a belief in human intelligence, enabled by God's spiritual intelligence and in human capabilities, enabled by His capable guidance.

1620) A new precedent in education must have the capacity to redirect nations from paths of intolerance to paths of tolerance, from mistrust to trust, from greed to moderation, from shareholder values to stakeholder values, and from violent wars and genocide to love and respect for sovereign neighbors.

1621)   Modern education has reached an apex in its capacity to provide for the material needs of humanity; it has recycled itself for decades, generally pursuing the same goals as student becomes teacher.

1622)   Modern education needs to be wholesome in order to achieve a passing grade. It has a failing grade in its capacity to liberate us religiously, morally, socially, and intellectually.

1623)   Only a "wholesome education" can liberate us completely. A wholesome education is an approach to education that focuses on the five essential foundations of a student's development, religious, moral, social, intellectual, and physical.

1624)   Five foundations of educational enlightenment must have measurable outcomes that are similar to academic information literacy and numeracy measures (Reference: *Five Foundations of Human Development* (FFHD) —Figure 22: Five Foundations of Educational Enlightenment).

1625)   A school curriculum that excludes any one the five foundations depicted below will fail to fully actualize student learning in a wholesome way.

FIVE FOUNDATIONS
OF EDUCATIONAL ENLIGHTENMENT

1626)   **Foundation 1: Religious education** provides students with an understanding of the origins of religions, their belief systems, and their cultures. It should not be an opportunity to teach dogma, but to enhance religious understanding in a world polarized by religious misunderstanding. This understanding helps students to function in a multi–religious world and to better understand the moral codes that underpin religion.

1627)   **Foundation 2: Moral education** helps students to exercise moral courage in making unpopular decisions, as they use moral persuasion to influence the behavior of their peers. It provides students with an opportunity to examine different styles of world leadership and authority, past and present, and the impact of decisions made within those styles on respective nations and the world.

1628) **Foundation 3: Social education** provides students with the capacity to develop social relationships not only within their families, but also with other races, cultures, religions, and nationalities. Social education helps students to see every human being as equal and deserving of universal social justice. Social education is the chief ingredient needed to understand the many forms of relationships at different stages throughout the student's lifetime.

1629) **Foundation 4: Intellectual education** provides students with the capacity to develop their mental faculties to take on intellectual and academic pursuits. Intellectual education helps students to understand the different concepts of intelligence and education. It increases their understanding of human limitations and capabilities. It helps students to better understand the role of intellectual leadership in the world, and it forms the basis for intelligent decision making.

1630) **Foundation 5: Physical education** provides students with an understanding of the sanctity of the human body and also with an awareness of both their physical and mental vulnerabilities. It helps students to develop their human physical abilities and their self–esteem, while cultivating a greater awareness of God's image, in which they are made. It helps students to regard their mortality and the care that is essential to a healthy body through proper sleep, nutrition, and exercise.

1631) Education begins with the student and the teacher, and learning is the critical component in the academic information exchange.

1632) Students' learning abilities, ages, maturity, and the emergencies, needs, and priorities of the nation ought to dictate the design of educational tools.

1633) Our materially driven life demands the fuel of academic information literacy and numeracy; however national stability prompts the demand for religious, moral, and social education of students as well.

1634) The academic prism from which we measure and record education outcomes, limits our full appreciation of the great potential of education to transform the lives of individuals and nations.

1635) The legacy of the modern educational journey is the pursuit of materialism as the ultimate objective, hence our materially oriented education. More to the point, how does modern education impact the religious, social, and economic dynamics of our existence?

1636) Educators recognize that students have different mental and physical capabilities and that some have limitations that need to be overcome.

1637) The development of the intellectual capacity of individuals is possible when education takes into consideration the whole person – body, mind, and soul (Reference: *Five Foundations of Human Development* (FFHD) —Figure 10: The Three Components of Human Beings).

1638) Over the past several decades, the Western world has witnessed both growth and collapse of mega corporations. Certainly some of the best and brightest university graduates manage corporations. Why did these corporations fail?

1639) Rather than education or lack of education, ethical management strengthens the viability of corporations, and the lack of it leads to collapse.

1640) Despite advancements in deterrent military technology and despite the creation of national and international peace organizations, nations face threats of terrorism, genocide, and wars.

1641) Despite decades of war against the use and trafficking of illicit drugs, drug abuse is still a problem in modern society. Concurrently, the demand for scientific intelligence and scientific education grows with each passing decade.

1642) Tension among nations grows in parallel with trillions of dollars in expenditures in scientific education.

1643) Our great humanitarian and peace organizations are unable to stem the tide of international unrest, leaving little hope for peace among nations.

1644) It is necessary that we shift to the new paradigm of education for the survival of future generations and to fulfill God's spiritual purpose for our existence.

1645) Underdeveloped and developing nations face economic challenges that might relegate their education spending to the lower end of the priority spectrum.

1646) Nations are not harvesting the benefits of adept leadership and authority in the world, despite mass education.

1647) Affluent Western nations spend billions of dollars to ensure the education of children. Boards of Education (BOE) strive to provide a meaningful learning experience for students; however, the main impetus is student achievement in terms of academic information literacy.

1648) Despite great efforts on the part of educators, some students fail to achieve the national learning standard that is required for graduation. Reports indicate that some students, particularly in some urban schools, do not graduate.

1649) As national education budgets grow, so does the storehouse of knowledge with each passing decade. World troubles grow exponentially as well.

1650) There must be empirical reasons why nations miss key opportunities to become truly inclusive, peaceful, and harmonious in light of increasing expenditures and costs in education (Reference: *Five Foundations of Human Development* (FFHD) —Table: 5 Domestic Spending on Research and Development (GERD).

1651) Education and material progress are at the roots of a nation's desire to build bigger and better-equipped colleges and universities and to fund necessary educational research with billions of dollars.

1652) Among the G8 nations, high schools, colleges, and universities graduate millions of students yearly. We have produced more educated generations, but have nations reaped the benefits of stable national and international economies and of peaceful relations?

1653) Advances in science and technology are not the cause of the troubles in the world, but they also are not leading us to permanent solutions for fundamental problems of living.

1654) Nations measure Gross National Product (GNP) and Gross Domestic Product (GDP) economic growth and outlook monthly, quarterly, and yearly as indicators of productivity and economic performance.

1655) GNP is described briefly as a measure of the value of goods and services that the country produces both nationally and abroad. GDP is described briefly as a measure of a nation's production both domestically and abroad.

1656) It would be a noteworthy statistical asset to nations to develop a third gross statistical measure, described as Gross Social Product

(GSP) (Reference: *Five Foundations of Human Development* (FFHD) —
Figure 17: Three Key National Progress Measures).

1657)   Gross Social Product (GSP) is an essential barometer of a nation's
social health, and it reflects the true progress of nations. GSP
provides measures concurrent with GNP and GDP statistics, which
reflect a nation's productivity.

1658)   Gross National Product (GNP) and Gross Domestic Product
(GDP) are indicators of the aggregate domestic and national
manufacturing and production capabilities.

1659)   Gross National Product (GNP) and Gross Domestic Product
(GDP) are more representative of machine capacity (artificial
intelligence) in the modern era of high technology production.

1660)   The Western world is at the forefront of the greatest expansion of
education and human knowledge in the history of civilization, but
we must recognize God as the great Educator.

1661)   To exclude God from our initiatives to reform education or any
other human endeavor is to deny the great opportunity for, and to
exclude the key ingredient of, success (Reference: *Five Foundations of
Human Development* (FFHD) —Figure 27: Five Key Principles of
Successful Living and Fulfillment).

1662) . The biblical view of education points nations in the right
direction. The success of every human endeavor hinges on a simple
biblical principle given to humanity over two thousand years ago. It
is our spiritual and moral guide: "But seek first the kingdom of God
and His righteousness, and all these things shall be added to you"
(Matthew 6:33 NKJV).

1663)   Educational school boards among the nations are constrained
within a framework of constitutional laws. They may not readily
contemplate God's knowledge, wisdom, and understanding as key
components of the educational reform equation, notwithstanding
the desire; faith, belief, and practice of the individual school board
member.

1664)   The world cries out for educational and scientific answers to
problems such as international peace and harmony, and the
eradication of world hunger and disease, but the solutions to these
problems also have roots in a wholesome education curriculum.

1665)   Education for the global village demands new approaches to
address new problems. It demands that we share some of the fruits

of production with our global neighbors, including technological know-how to enable them to gain some level of technological self-sufficiency. We must, of necessity, exercise "technological empathy" for our neighbors that are falling behind.

1666)   Intellectual observation indicates that there is a religious, social, cultural, and economic evolution taking place in Western nations and throughout the world. This evolution is neither positive nor negative; it simply reflects a new pattern in the evolution of Western civilization and the world.

1667)   The current diversity in races, cultures, and religions has been unprecedented in recent Western world history. The Western classroom is no longer a domain of Christian religious instructions. God, in the context of Western Christianity, is no longer prominent in our public schools and public places.

1668)   Western nations are experiencing a "cultural evolution" for which we are unprepared, even though we have been in a state of evolution for more than a century.

1669)   The need for equity-based education reaches beyond academic information literacy, to addressing major issues that enable ethnic, cultural, and religious unity (Reference: *Five Foundations of Human Development* (FFHD) —Table 7: Statistics Canada (Statistique Canada) Population by Selected Ethnic origins, by Provinces and territories).

1670)   There is a need for new evolutionary approaches to management in a racially, culturally, and religiously diverse marketplace.

1671)   Can the highly automated job market parallel the growth in a diverse student population and support students with non-traditional needs and values?

1672)   Western nations are capable of building their physical infrastructure (roads, bridges and buildings) regardless of their population demographics.

1673)   The challenge for Western nations is to use their moral capacity to educate and build their religious, social, and intellectual infrastructures concurrent with our physical infrastructure.

1674)   Observation demonstrates that there is great vitality in Western economies. Concurrent with great advancements in corporate management, the past decade has seen the collapse of many great Western corporations, including those that have filed for bankruptcy protection, or that have experienced decline from positions of great prominence.

1675) As an aggregate, corporations spend millions of dollars annually on corporate education, yet corporate collapse and excess resonate in some sectors of the economy, shattering lives and careers.

1676) Deployment of educational tools and augmenting our capacity to learn are the pathways to human knowledge, and they establish human progress.

1677) When nations deliver education equitably, it produces better societies. As well, it produces nations that have a balanced growth of knowledge in all of the critical areas of human development.

1678) Education also involves the learning of family heritage and national history. Knowing these things promotes a sense of self and self–worth.

1679) Learning about others' country, race, culture, history, and religion provides a knowledge platform upon which to build lasting and peaceful relationships.

1680) It is only a new educational perspective through a *wholesome education* can bring about solutions to our past, present, and emerging challenges of the future.

FOUNDATION 4
INTELLECTUAL FOUNDATION
—4.3. KNOWLEDGE
(UNDERSTANDING)

"Instruct a wise man and he will be wiser still; teach a righteous man and he will add to his learning. 'The fear of the LORD is the beginning of wisdom, and knowledge of the Holy One is understanding. For through me your days will be many, and years will be added to your life. If you are wise, your wisdom will reward you.' "

Proverbs 9:9–12 (NIV)

1681) **What is knowledge?** Where does knowledge come from? Is human knowledge the ultimate source of all knowledge? The Word of God is the foundation of all knowledge.

1682) Some twenty–five hundred years ago, the Hebrew prophet, Daniel, clearly foresaw an unprecedented knowledge explosion. He wrote: "Many shall run to and fro, and knowledge shall increase" (Daniel 12:4 NKJV) (circa 537 BCE).

1683) We live in an age of mass information and mass communications enabled by the revolution in digital electronics. As stated by Price Pritchett (1998): "There has been more information produced in the last 30 years than during the previous 5,000." Is our age of mass information the same as an age of knowledge? Price Pritchett (1998), *New Work Habits for a Radically Changing World* – 13 Ground Rules for Job Success in the Information Age – 3rd Edition, (Dallas, Texas).

1684) There are three sources of knowledge. *(1)* Spiritual knowledge, discerned from the Word of God, *(2)* material knowledge, gained through education, and *(3)* intuitive knowledge, innate, instinctive or sort of a six–sense (Reference: *Five Foundations of Human Development* (FFHD) —Figure 30: God's Threefold Gift to Humanity for Managing His Creation and —Figure 31: Three Sources of Knowledge).

1685) One who is educated has knowledge, and the more education one receives, the more knowledgeable one becomes as he or she retains knowledge.

1686) Knowledge is a product of learning, and our primary source of knowledge is human education.

1687) Without some form of national education of citizens, it would be impossible to build a stable knowledge base to build stable societies.

1688) When education is a *wholesome experience*, the knowledge gained enables religious, social, and economic growth and helps to bring about national and international peace and stability.

1689) Over twenty–five hundred years ago, the prophet Hosea lamented: "My people are destroyed for lack of knowledge" (Hosea 4:6 NKJV) (circa 762 BCE).

1690) Basic knowledge, fundamental to survival of the human species, seems to elude us in our highly developed multi–media societies. Solomon wrote in the book of Ecclesiastes: "For in much wisdom is much grief, And he who increases knowledge increases sorrow" (Ecclesiastes 1:18 NKJV) (circa 947 BCE).

1691) An observation of human conditions in our twenty–first century calls to mind the deep spiritual insights of the prophetic writers, Hosea, Daniel, and Solomon.

1692) Hosea writes regarding humanity's lack of God's divine knowledge. Daniel writes regarding human knowledge, and likewise, Solomon writes regarding human wisdom and human knowledge.

1693) A knowledge gap is attributable to human knowledge and human understanding as opposed to God–inspired knowledge, which guides us to understanding, truth, and righteousness.

1694) An interesting paradox of modern times is the constant wave of information sweeping across the landscape of nations. Clearly, information is not knowledge, and human knowledge may not always come from the primary source of God's knowledge.

1695) Despite the vast amounts of information that come to us in many forms, it is still quite difficult to reach definitive conclusions on life–saving issues and to make life–saving decisions.

1696) National and international world events dominate the airwaves as the primary source of information for individuals throughout the world. Our reactions have been a mixed blessing, from great humanitarian responses to natural disasters, to violent responses to wars, assassinations, and social and economic conditions, as we search for answers to the human condition.

1697) We can describe the past several generations and the present generation as *the searching generations*. We seek answers to problems that perplex us in the twenty–first century and to unresolved problems of past centuries.

1698) Ancient civilizations did not have an intellectual understanding of the vast universe. The great universe and the constellation of stars perplexed ancient astronomers.

1699) Pagans considered themselves helpless and at the mercy of their gods. Understandably, pagan gods were credited with everything from rainfall, sunshine, thunder, lightning, and volcanoes to the birth and death of villagers.

1700) Mythology, to a large extent, was the basis of ancient religions. Their gods represented everything from the sun and the moon to love, war, and even jealousy.

1701) Modern civilization makes great expenditures in scientific research and experimentation in search of scientific answers to the origin of the universe.

1702) Can we say that the search for answers to the universe is strictly a scientific search? Why has the scientific search been set-apart form the search by religions?

1703) If we deny God in our search, would we not face the challenge of finding a superior intelligence of similar credentials to answer our questions?

1704) Astronomers provide us with images of the vast universe beyond the Milky Way Galaxy, and they also provide us with scientific theories, such as the beginning of the universe with a "big bang" some ten to twenty billion years ago.

1705) Are human beings merely on a meaningless journey? If human life is meaningless then everything we do lacks meaning, yet there cannot be motivation without meaning, nor meaning without purpose. What then is the purpose of our existence?

1706) The answer to these questions should derive *all* intellectual, scientific and religious enquiries. It should bring evolutionists and creationists together in a sober repose to discuss whether there is conformity or conflict on so great an enquiry.

1707) The sum total of human intelligence teaches that behind everything there is a design, and behind every design there is a Designer. Try to imagine, if possible, the scale of the universe in comparison to these manmade entities; one wonders about the design and the Designer.

1708) Can anyone imagine that our universe came about by an accident, or that the intelligence of human beings was not derived from a higher source of intelligence?

1709) Could artificial intelligence in machines have come about without a higher source of human intelligence? Are we to conclude that human intelligence is the highest form of intelligence?

1710) The awesomeness of the universe led English historian and Member of Parliament, **Edward Gibbon (1737–1794)** to conclude: "The great and incomprehensible secret of the universe eludes the inquiry of man."

1711) With every passing decade, and with great scientific intelligence, space vehicles penetrate deeper into the infinite universe with the eternal hope that human beings will finally have scientific answers to the universe and to their existence.

1712) Despite our vast storehouse of human knowledge in the twenty–first century, human knowledge is relatively minimal, compared to the evolutionary cycle of civilizations.

1713) Some two thousand years ago, the world entered the Christian Era (CE), followed by many ages, such as the Dark Ages (Middle Ages), the Age of Enlightenment, the Age of Industrialization, the Electronic Age, the Space Age, and our current Information Age, which some refer to as the new knowledge economy.

1714) Will human knowledge and the genius of science produce definitive answers to the universe or will the search be a never–ending quest, always falling short of real understanding?

1715) We have entered a new age of "new knowledge" in the twenty–first century. The only word to describe advancements in human knowledge in our twenty–first century is *phenomenal!*

1716) The accelerating pace of change is creating great anxiety among individuals, societies, and nations. With mastery of mass production techniques, and with the design of new high–speed machinery, fewer workers are required at the wheels of production (Reference: *Five Foundations of Human Development* (FFHD) —Figure 33: Deflation in Labor Requirements versus Growth in World Population and Human Knowledge).

1717) **Price Pritchett (1998)** informs: "In the 1900's more than ninety–five percent of the people in every country around the world did manual work. Today in the U.S. only twenty percent still do manual work."

1718) Modern medicines have stemmed, (if not cured) the tide of many diseases that once crippled past civilizations; but do these achievements infer that human civilization is at the apex of human knowledge in the twenty–first century?

1719) Medical news reports warn that we might lose the war against new diseases, and some scientific productions might pose a risk for the emergence of new drug–resistant strains of dangerous microbes.

1720) When we consider the infinite knowledge of God, human knowledge is infinitesimal in its reach, and this awareness should humble us.

1721) There is no doubt that human knowledge has benefited us scientifically and materially, but we are losing out on great benefits of valued communication that engenders the best qualities in human beings.

1722) With the advent of mass education, the world has made awesome progress in human knowledge of the universe. Paradoxically, human knowledge has set apart religion and science as generally distinct and separate schools of thought regarding the origin of the universe, evolution *versus* creation.

1723) Schools, colleges, and universities have become the manufacturing centers of human knowledge. The knowledge base of our modern era is testimony to our vast progress in the understanding of physical matter.

1724) Despite the great diversity of world religions, scientific knowledge seems to surpass religious knowledge, with physical evidence of scientific progress represented in every aspect of daily life.

1725) In terms of conclusive answers to evolution and the purpose of our existence as a scientific construct, our search is a never–ending pursuit for answers.

1726) Scientific and religious education divide school board members and their constituents, as opposed to bringing them together intellectually in a knowledge–sharing environment.

1727) From scientific and religious perspectives, the nature of God, the origin of life, and the purpose of human existence will continue to perplex humanity in the twenty–first century, as we change our perspectives with the evolution of human knowledge.

1728) A recurring message is that history repeats itself. Our past is full of practical demonstrations of the futility of self–reliance to the exclusion of God.

1729) War is inevitable, misery is persistent, and our human condition is always in need of improvement.

1730) Every nation and every society in history has known that its knowledge was incomplete, as we also know, today.

1731) If the ancient prophets were to suddenly appear on our twenty–first century stage, they would be better able to comprehend the God they worshipped in a way only they could understand. They would understand why Jesus Christ gave the two great commandments during His ministry and time on earth (Matthew 22:37–40).

1732) Jesus *pleaded* with human beings to be reconciled to Him, for His suffering and death for the mission to reconcile humanity to peace, through the grace of God rather than human will.

1733) The present world conditions would allow ancient prophets to understand the significance and authenticity of the God–inspired writings they penned in the Holy Scriptures.

1734) The enormous violence, unhappiness, discontent, genocide, wars, and human suffering in parallel with the vast human knowledge would be sobering to the prophets.

1735) Although the prophets wrote more than two thousand years ago, the continuing accuracy and relevance of their vision would overwhelm them.

1736) The correlation between prophecies that other prophets wrote in a different time of religious history would probably astonish them even more.

1737) The prophets warned us that as human knowledge increased so, too, the suffering of humanity would increase (Ecclesiastes 1:18).

1738) How could knowledge bring suffering? The prophets are telling us (empathically) that apart from God's knowledge, human knowledge brings sorrow.

1739) The knowledge referred to in the prophetic writings is human knowledge. Hence, nations in the modern world should be mindful of the warnings of the ancient biblical writers.

1740) The rejection of God's knowledge, wisdom, and understanding would become clear in the observation of the pursuit for the philosophies and ideologies of human beings.

1741) Many throughout the world have rejected God's knowledge, wisdom, and understanding in light of great human achievements, earlier thought impossible by the great thinkers of history.

1742) Human knowledge has blinded us, to a great extent, to the spiritual knowledge that God made available to us through the teachings of His Son Jesus Christ.

1743) The full storehouse of human knowledge over the past centuries is infinitesimal in comparison to God's storehouse of His spiritual knowledge.

1744) We have attained great levels of scientific intelligence that have caused some of us to abandon the pursuit of God's knowledge to guide us and to not place God's knowledge visibly at the forefront of every human endeavor.

1745) The chronicle of the past century is our legacy of unresolved human problems and international conflict as we enter the new millennium.

1746) The overwhelming weight of unresolved human problems is a drain on the religious, moral, social, human, intellectual, and financial capital of developed, developing, and underdeveloped nations.

1747) Hunger, poverty, wars, and militia wars have become permanent fixtures on the human landscape as millions go to bed hungry, and many are homeless in the shadows of great national and international wealth.

1748) The drug epidemic is a sign of emptiness without God's knowledge and wisdom. What can human beings do to stem the rising tide of drug addiction?

1749) Millions throughout God's creation continue to experience mental and physical suffering as a result of their use of legal and illegal drugs.

1750) Problems within nations grow exponentially, despite billions of dollars in expenditures on scientific research and massive programs to feed hungry individuals worldwide.

1751) God's knowledge transforms. This knowledge, through the Spirit of God, awakens the spiritual law of God, and it enables a way of life that brings about peace, happiness, and every good result.

1752) God's knowledge can preserve humanity from a world beset by war, insecurity and human suffering.

1753) Obedience to God allows His Spirit to enable the mind, from which He enables us to comprehend spiritual knowledge.

1754) The human condition after thousands of years of human guidance provides irrefutable evidence of the need for God's providential intervention in the affairs of human beings.

1755) Many of us do not realize that our actions are often hostile against God and the things of God (Romans 8:7). Our academic, scientific, and technological advancements, if not ably guided, can act as barriers between human knowledge and God's knowledge.

1756) We are capable of building national and international groups, unions, leagues, organizations, and coalitions to promote good and to address major world problems. We desperately need to form a coalition with God against the unseen enemy, which is the greatest threat to our survival (Ephesians 6:10–17).

1757) Human guidance is failing us in a monumental way, because we have not fully acknowledged the words of the Psalmist: "Your word is a lamp to my feet And a light to my path" (Psalm 119:105 NKJV) (circa 444 BCE).

1758) When we fail to accept God's guidance and fail to seek His knowledge, our knowledge is limited to that which enters the human brain through the five senses. This knowledge is natural, physical, and materialistic.

1759) We are born with carnal minds limited to materialistic knowledge; therefore, we must seek God's knowledge to enable the true potential of human knowledge.

1760) World nations have not fully demonstrated the capacity to permanently curtail violations of human rights in developed, developing, and underdeveloped nations.

1761)   Despite many pledges and laws formulated to prevent slavery, some human rights organizations estimate that millions of individuals work under forced conditions that amount to abject slavery.

1762)   Child labor exists in various parts of the developing and underdeveloped world. The world community rightfully condemns these actions, but our religious practices should compel us to go further and to strive to avoid any act that would violate the love of God for His creation (Romans 12:9–11).

1763)   Despite this knowledge from God, we often struggle to reach a state of inner tranquility without some form of physical and material compulsion.

1764)   What is it that compels us to take for granted that we cannot positively alter current trends in society?

1765)   Enabled by God's knowledge, we have the capacity to alter conditions often taken for granted, conditions which permeate and impair friendships, families, homes, neighborhoods, communities, nations, and the international community.

1766)   A life of fulfillment requires two distinct kinds of knowledge: *(1) Spiritual Knowledge* and *(2) Material Knowledge.*

1767)   *Spiritual knowledge* is used to relate with our Father (God) in our vertical relationship. It is also used to elevate us to acts of righteousness behavior to relate to human beings, our horizontal relationship.

1768)   *Material Knowledge* is used to be creative, to make things out of physical matter, and to have dominion over creation. Spiritual knowledge can only be imparted through the Spirit of God.

1769)   The scriptures teach that this good news is not earthly wisdom; therefore it is foolishness to the unwise, because the foolishness of God is wiser than men, and the weakness of God is stronger than men.

1770)   God has chosen the foolish things of the world to put to shame the wise, and God has chosen the weak things of the world to put to shame the things which are mighty" (1 Corinthians 1:25–27 NKJV).

1771)   The natural man, with the natural knowledge of this world, cannot comprehend the things of the Spirit, which are most important for our survival.

1772) Gains in human knowledge in the twenty–first century have only brought more complex unresolved problems of living (Daniel 12:4).

1773) Every great material invention will become obsolete as time passes and will be buried in the dust of tomorrow's knowledge, as human beings embark on new frontiers in search of new knowledge.

1774) New knowledge will once again become obsolete, as history repeats itself, but God's knowledge is infinite, purposeful, lifesaving, and is the same yesterday, today, tomorrow, and forever (Jude 1:25).

FOUNDATION 4
INTELLECTUAL FOUNDATION
—4.4. CAPABILITY (ABILITY)

"Stand firm then, with the belt of truth buckled around your waist, with the breastplate of righteousness in place, and with your feet fitted with the readiness that comes from the gospel of peace. In addition to all this, take up the shield of faith, with which you can extinguish all the flaming arrows of the evil one."

Ephesians 6:14–16 (NIV)

1775) **What is capability?** How do we develop the ability to form better societies and nations? Capability is the ability to complete a mission or a task, meet all of the stated objectives, and achieve the desired result.

1776) The word "capability" is commonly used, but the power it implies is important to understand. For instance, why do we seem to lack the capability to build great societies and nations with peace, happiness, and security?

1777) Capability may be latent and may need external stimulus to aspire us to a high level of achievement. Moreover, who or what is our "capable" guide?

1778) No individual, society, or nation can achieve a state of capability based purely on his, her, or its sole efforts, human intellect, or acting without God's guidance.

1779) Capability requires a capable guide to help individuals develop their abilities, whether they are spiritual, moral, social, intellectual, or physical.

1780) We are blessed to have a capable guide in God through His Son Jesus Christ: "For this *is* God, Our God forever and ever; He will be our guide Even to death" (Psalm 48:14 NKJV). This is a most incredibly comforting statement that comes from our most capable guide on high.

1781) Some ancient rulers — dictators, monarchs, emperors, pharaohs, and kings — ruled autocratically. They produced unstable societies with demands that their subjects worship them and their gods, or themselves as gods.

1782)   Ancient rulers did not understand that they needed a capable guide. They assumed *all* power. Unenlightened as some authorities were in moral authority, their ego was their guide, which often led to catastrophic failure.

1783)   Ancient rulers, blinded by their ego, they did not know the way to create peace and harmony or how to secure their kingdoms. Students of history might argue that knowing how to create peace and harmony was not a requisite trait of ancient leadership.

1784)   Ancient rulers relied upon brute force to dominate and conquer other nations. Fostered by their egos, the pain and misery they inflicted was merely a natural consequence of their triumph over nations.

1785)   Some two thousand years ago, Jesus Christ came to redeem mankind to a righteous relationship with God, to build His church, to establish a new perspective on human leadership, and to set up a relationship between God and man and between man and his neighbors.

1786)   Despite many trials, persecutions of the church, and religious wars, the church (with Jesus Christ as its "capable guide") flourished and still does today.

1787)   A capable guide is necessary for any individual, system, or nation to exist and progress in any meaningful capacity. Observe the current social and economic challenges of our twenty–first century, evidence that human beings need capable guidance.

1788)   Jeremiah affirms: "O LORD, I know the way of man is not in himself; It is not in man who walks to direct his own steps" (Jeremiah 10:23 NKJV) (circa 622 BCE).

1789)   Would anyone disagree that children, parents, students, surgeons, and religious and political leaders need capable guides?

1790)   The Psalmist reveals an account of God's guidance. "Yea though I walk through the valley of the shadow of death, I will fear no evil; For You *are* with me; Your rod and Your staff, they comfort me" (Psalm 23:4 NKJV) (circa 1029 BCE).

1791)   Throughout the book of Psalms, the Psalmist points the modern world to the need to be dependent on God's capable guidance. The Psalmist finds delight in God's Word, seeking always to please God;

206

petitioning for deliverance; thanking for deliverance; trusting in His Word; praying in the midst of peril; and declaring the glory of God without ceasing (1 Thessalonians 5:15–22).

1792)   Every person and entity, every condition of human existence, requires a capable guide to provide leadership and direction. The most important aspect of having a capable guide is the positive outcome the guidance produces.

1793)   The word *capable* has inherent positive characteristics measured by positive outcomes. Likewise, the word *incapable* has inherent negative characteristics measured by other negative outcomes.

1794)   The Father sent His son Jesus Christ to earth to be our capable guide. He took upon Himself every wrongdoing of the world. He suffered on the cross and died in the ultimate sacrifice for our transgressions.

1795)   Jesus Christ became the perfect example and capable guide to humanity through His persecution, death, burial, and resurrection from the dead.

1796)   When Jesus Christ ascended to His heavenly Father, there would be a need to maintain their contact with Him. For this reason, Jesus Christ assured His disciples and the world that His capable guidance would always be available to humanity (Luke 1:79; John 15:26).

1797)   The Old Testament (OT) provides humanity with great lessons of humanity's disobedience and trials when living apart from God's capable guidance. It gives humanity a comprehensive picture of a nation's weakness when it tries to exist without God.

1798)   The Old Testament (OT) lessons of biblical history provide us in the modern era with a wealth of knowledge, which we can apply to our time. The student of the Bible can draw many parallels to our current times.

1799)   The New Testament (NT) ushered in a new dispensation with Jesus Christ as Savior and authority for the earth and as our capable guide through God the Father and by the leading of the Holy Spirit.

1800)   The New Testament (NT) pivots around Jesus, the living Word, who lives His life in and through us as we walk in dependence on His capable guidance. God manifested His spiritual guidance of the Old Testament (OT) in human flesh in the New Testament (NT) (John 12:44–48).

1801) God, knowing human nature, the nature of man, recognized the need to present Himself in the flesh to physically guide us to a better understanding of His spiritual nature.

1802) Human beings acting on their own free will have chosen to reject God's guidance; hence our twenty–first century world conditions.

1803) When we fail to accept and follow God's capable guidance and act in accordance to His will for our lives, we imperil our lives and the lives of those who we guide.

1804) History has recorded monumental achievements by human beings, such as the building of the great pyramids of Egypt, the discovery of penicillin, the invention of the electric light bulb, and the moon landing.

1805) Despite these great achievements, the ability to eradicate evil in the world eludes all of the great minds. Why do we seem to lack the capacity to permanently solve the world's troubles and to bring about peaceful coexistence among neighbors?

1806) The more we become awestruck by the achievements of the human mind, the more we drift away from God's guidance, and the less we recognize the need for God's capable guidance.

1807) What is it that inspires our imagination today? Is it the awesomeness of God's creation or the greatness of human inventions?

1808) How often do we take time away from our busy schedules to contemplate the greatness of God's creation?

1809) When was the last time we stopped for a moment to ponder the finite nature of our capability in the context of God's infinite capability? Have we simply taken for granted that we are capable of anything that we can imagine?

1810) God's spiritual purpose for our existence is superior to any purpose that we can formulate through the human intellect. His wisdom and intelligence are superior.

1811) Our hidden vulnerability and inability are the primary sources of our weaknesses and helplessness, and they create fear in us. Fear incapacitates us, and sets us apart from each other, against each other, and against God.

1812) Fear overpowers us. With fear as our guide, we are led along paths of distrust, misunderstanding, miscommunication, apprehension, and aggression against other human beings, because of race, color, culture, or religion.

1813) Our response to fear is aggression between individuals, within families, between and among neighbors, communities, and nations.

1814) Fear is our greatest distraction and preoccupation, and it leads us away from the pursuit of our spiritual purpose.

1815) Fear distracts us from realizing our God–given capabilities and exaggerates human weakness, fuelled by fear itself.

1816) Fear takes us away from our focus on God, who is our capable guide, and puts our focus on man. Fear distracts, it disables, it incapacitates, and it often diminishes our faith in God.

1817) Fearlessness is the first imperative of spiritual and moral bravery, and of spiritual and moral capabilities.

1818) Fearlessness has nothing to do with our intellectual, physical, or military capabilities. It is a fearlessness that comes from knowing that God is our capable guide.

1819) Our egos get in the way, inspiring pride, which acts as a barrier to God's divine love, protection, and guidance. Pride then becomes our convenient guide. Solomon in the Proverbs warns: "Pride goes before destruction, a haughty spirit before a fall.

1820) Are we capable of advancing modern civilization beyond our fatalistic outlook? Many in our modern era believe that human life is helpless and hopeless and that we can do nothing to change our hopeless state.

1821) Why are we not capable of developing a universal love of humanity? Is it simply because society consists of different racial groups that it constitutes a catalyst for conflict?

1822) James the Scriptural writer asks: "Where do wars and fights *come* from among you? Do *they* not *come* from your *desires for* pleasure that war in your members? You lust and do not have. You murder and covet and cannot obtain (James 4:1–3 NKJV) (circa CE 45).

1823) We have the capacity to improve our conditions and, as a consequence, to change our habits and shape our destiny as ordered by God.

1824) God has made us the highest form of His creation with great mental abilities, unlike animals that possess limited or no ability beyond the instinctive.

1825) The very nature of our capacity to think and to be creative demonstrates that the human brain is free of fixed programs, and that God has created us with great mental capacity. We can apply reason and responsibility; make educated judgments regarding right and wrong actions; and make timely life–saving decisions.

1826) Human beings have a choice of order rather than chaos; love rather than hate; sharing rather than hoarding; tolerance rather than intolerance; racial harmony rather than strife; peace rather than unrest; religion rather than retaliation, and mercy and justice rather than revenge.

1827) God's endowment of our great mental capacity of free will enables us to make intelligent decisions and to display superior qualities. These qualities include love, hope, peace charity, fairness, justice, compassion, patience, and wisdom, which lead to peaceful co-existence among individuals and nations.

1828) Is it sufficient to display godlike qualities to our friends and family or toward those whom we love? Is it sufficient to display such qualities to those who belong to our race, culture, class, or religion when it is convenient to us, but then to try and find a moral defense for our ungodly behavior toward others who are not like ourselves?

1829) The irony of the spiritual dilemma is that in our relentless pursuit of material wealth, power, and human authority, we have inadvertently dismissed the powerful spiritual nature of our existence.

1830) The Western world is made up of developed nations with great capacity for growth in many dimensions of human endeavor.

1831) The astonishing material progress of the West is testimony to our great physical and mental capabilities and creative faculties.

1832) Some developing and underdeveloped nations fail to make progress due to totalitarian regimes that stifle the creative energies that God has placed within every human being.

1833) Human civilization would not be possible without great struggle against the forces of holocaust, genocide, slavery, apartheid, and political and ideological wars. All humanity must, in the interest of our survival, marshal the spiritual forces of good against such regimes.

1834) The twenty–first century has emerged with many new and unfamiliar challenges and opportunities. We have the opportunity to look to God's Word for guidance, knowing that we have brought the world to its current state by relying upon human guidance, alone.

1835) We are confronted by six thousand years of recorded history as our jury in the twenty–first century. The world is threatened by more great challenges to human survival than ever before in the history of civilization.

1836) Do our leaders have the capacity to manage challenges such as: HIV/AIDS, world hunger, poverty, economic collapse, famine, water and environmental pollution, mass migration, new communicable diseases, earthquakes, volcanic eruptions, refugees of militia wars, scarcity, aging populations, religious divisions, genocide, wars, and human trafficking?

1837) The world is fast becoming a global village, but the present trends paint a picture of a village divided against itself. The Synoptic Gospel writer, Luke, points modern civilization to the primary problem: "But He, knowing their thoughts, said to them: "Every kingdom divided against itself is brought to desolation, and a house *divided* against a house falls" (Luke 11:17 NKJV).

1838) No individual, society, or nation can progress if it attempts to be exclusive.

1839) There is a need for some level of racial, cultural, social, economic, and religious synthesis for civilization to advance, and this advancement can only come from sharing with less capable individuals, societies, and nations.

1840) Sharing does not simply entail giving money, but sharing knowledge of science, technology, and practical know–how to develop a technical infrastructure in order to make progress.

1841) Developed nations can liberate themselves when they share with weaker nations to help build their capacity. The converse is also true; if developed nations fail to liberate developing nations, all nations weaken themselves.

1842) Developed nations must aim to engage in every political, social, educational, and humanitarian effort directed at elevating developing and underdeveloped nations.

1843) The existence of civilization lies in moral and religious living, which incorporates love, joy, peace, patience, kindness, goodness, faithfulness, gentleness, and self–control.

1844) Leaders of developing and underdeveloped nations must exercise greater confidence in the creative energies, creative powers, and in the inherent capabilities of their citizens, as developed Western nations do.

1845) Developing and underdeveloped nations can then benefit from the same nationalism that inspires love for one's country and that leads to hopefulness and a sense of duty toward fellow citizens.

1846) The word *nationalism* is often perceived in a negative context when, in fact, nationalism can be both positive and negative. One can make an intellectual argument in favor of positive nationalism over its negative connotations.

1847) One might argue that nationalism is a personal stake that one must have in one's nation or adopted nation.

1848) Nationalism is a state of being, not a state of having. Nationalism can be a force for good. The nationalism that we refer to extends to all aspects of a nation's endeavors.

1849) Although developed nations respond positively to catastrophes that afflict poor nations, they often, even daily, fail to make a spiritual connection between God's compassion for the poor in national and international commercial affairs.

1850) These nations must recognize that there are reasons for God's compassion for the poor, though it demands great moral courage, moral persuasion, and moral capacity to love the unlovable.

1851) The more we distrust human beings in private, public, social, or political life, the more we degrade ourselves and others and the more we diminish our capacity for peaceful co-existence.

1852) We often forget that the trust that is fundamental to basic human goodness (righteousness) can surface with the application of love and reason. We cannot improve human relationships while mistrusting others.

1853) These attributes of God are essential for humanity to realize the fruits of the long hard journey ahead. To do otherwise would consign humanity to its carnal nature and to the hatred and violence it perpetuates.

1854) Without God's capability, rather than the progress of civilization, modern civilization will plunge forward into a new and sophisticated, yet nevertheless hopeless, Dark Age.

1855) There are certain pitfalls in the use of might for might, and in the bad reactions that it creates, but the scientific world that we live in does not adequately prepare us for unconditional love in our modern era.

1856) The formidable force of God's love, as a companion to our faith and which alone is the only hope of the survival of civilization, needs to be our capable guide.

THOUGHTS
TO ENLIGHTEN
AND EMPOWER
THE MIND

*2001 QUESTIONS AND PHILOSOPHICAL THOUGHTS
TO INSPIRE, ENLIGHTEN, AND EMPOWER OUR WORLD
TO LIMITLESS HEIGHTS*

—FOUNDATION 5
PHYSICAL FOUNDATION

*5.1. HEALTH, FAITH AND SUFFERING
5.2. CATASTROPHIC DISEASES
5.3. PHYSICAL HEALTH*

FOUNDATION 5
PHYSICAL FOUNDATION
—5.1. HEALTH, FAITH AND SUFFERING

"Your hands shaped me and made me. Will you now turn and destroy me? Remember that you molded me like clay. Will you now turn me to dust again? Did you not pour me out like milk and curdle me like cheese, clothe me with skin and flesh and knit me together with bones and sinews? You gave me life and showed me kindness, and in your providence watched over my spirit."

Job 10:8–12 (NIV)

Authors' Remarks: This discourse is intended as a means of offering another perspective regarding human health. It is not intended as a diagnostic tool or offering health advice. Always seek the advice of your physician or other registered health professional with any questions regarding your health. Furthermore, with each passing year, medical research provides us with additional information that enhances our understanding of symptoms, diagnosis, treatment, and cures of diseases. Therefore, you should contact the appropriate agency or organization for their latest research and publication of any article cited in this text, for general information only.

1857) What is health? The authors' non–scientific definition of health is a general good feeling of spiritual, mental and physical well–being (Reference: *Five Foundations of Human Development* (FFHD) —Figure 37: Three Attributes of Human Health).

1858) Although we have general control of our health, every aspect of our health is impacted by our nutrition, our nurturing, our knowledge of health matters, our personal behavior, and our environmental circumstances.

1859) Maintenance of health requires nutrition, which is the appropriate quantity and quality of foods and fuel (air, water, and sunlight) that is necessary to sustain our physical bodies.

1860) Nurturing is the spiritual and mental stimulation that helps us to maintain our emotional balance. Likewise physical activities contribute to our physical health.

1861) When we think of health, the absence of disease comes to mind, but although we might feel well, our health entails more than the absence of the conditions that cause diseases.

1862) A healthy and productive nation is merely the sum of healthy individuals. Medical science also teaches that our health is a function of a healthy environment.

1863) With every passing decade, scientists are detecting new chemicals that are present in the air, in water, and in foods. Some researchers indicate that pregnant women and young children are most susceptible to a chemical invasion through the fetus.

1864) We should applaud our scientific minds for their great efforts to help us to understand and manage health issues and to better comprehend the magnitude of catastrophic diseases that confront us.

1865) Unfortunately, some of the great efforts of medical science are negated by the incalculable harm that some of us cause to our bodies by not exercising regularly, by neglecting sleep and proper nutrition, or by working excessively, often pushing the limits of our mental and physical capabilities.

1866) We also need to examine biblical perspectives and non-medical ways to positively influence health care behavior.

1867) Health is, first and foremost, a gift from God. Longevity, by virtue of a healthy environment, is a birthright that we have denied ourselves.

1868) We need to return to botanical garden of Eden. Yes, this is where the power of nature (God) is at work in the original garden, full of all that we need to sustain life.

1869) The earth has been poisoned by man and is now sick. If the earth is sick, we become sick; hence the reason for the alarming rate of cancers and other degenerative diseases.

1870) Can our Doctors and pharmaceutical drugs truly cure us, or do so without other health consequences? Doctors have the capacity to provide support and suppression but should we expect permanent cures from them?

1871) What should we expect from nature? Can nature heal us after our health has degenerated beyond the limits of even the capacity of nature?

1872) We have been programmed to cure ourselves when we are given the right ingredients from nature.

1873) Everyday, medical researchers are determining the important value of certain herbs, grains, fruits, and vegetables in our health regime.

1874) We need wholesome, whole foods that are allowed to come to full maturity on the trees or in the ground. These foods provide live enzymes which our bodies lack.

1875) Most articles that speak about using fruits and vegetables for curing diseases emphasize that these must be from organic sources (free from hormones, pesticides, herbicides, and all other chemicals); this is the key to healing.

1876) We must also be aware that we are all biochemically different and we all have our own individual chemical sensitivities.

1877) What is different between Person A and Person B? The difference may lie in factors such as, unique biological makeup, personal diet, exercise, detoxification, and emotional and spiritual well–being.

1878) We cannot return to botanical Eden, because the purity of Eden has been destroyed by the drive for over–abundance.

1879) We are immersed in a world in which chemicals in food, air, and water all contain some level of pollutants that are harmful to our bodies.

1880) One might postulate that one of the keys to human health is regular detoxification of our bodies to get rid of malignant substances and to radically change our lifestyles.

1881) God has given us the ultimate "medical guide," along with all the ingredients necessary for a healthy life already planted in His garden.

1882) We cannot live forever, but the quality of our life is what matters while God grants us the privilege of a brief visit upon the planet earth.

1883) Is there any wonder why the forest is green? Perhaps God is sending humans a message. We have finally understood it with our "Green Revolution."

1884) We cannot, and should not engage in a discussion regarding human health without bringing God and the environment into the equation.

1885) From the medical scientist to the layperson, *all* will agree that the human body is complex but marvelously made (Psalm 139:14–16).

1886) We are also, as living beings, an integral biological component of the living and breathing universe. Even the living trees exchange matter with us human beings.

1887) Why are Botanists not given a prominent seat at the boardroom table when health care decisions are being formulated? Perhaps we need to consider this most important study of botany as a component of the health care equation.

1888) Botanists should chair national and international conferences on healthcare. Their research has brought us advancements in new and improved medicines, foods, fibers, and other plant–based products are attributable to the research by Botanists.

1889) The human body is God's masterpiece of His creation. God has not relegated His highest creation to a purposeless existence, devoid of guidance and incapable of maintaining the integrity of the body and of our spiritual, mental, and physical health.

1890) We take care of our material inventions and often neglect God's creation until it is broken down, sometimes beyond repair. Is it because our material inventions fuel our materially driven life with material things from which we derive pleasure?

1891) Over the centuries, as societies advanced through the Industrial Revolution (1800s–1900s), environmental pollution through mass manufacturing began to impact the quality of our environment and our health.

1892) Medical practitioners tell us that we are predisposed to inherit family diseases. They also tell us that an unhealthy environment has negative effects on human health. One might hypothesize that these genetic links are both generational and environmental in origin.

1893) We must be mindful that we are all immersed in our environment no different from fish submerged in water. The body of air that encapsulates the earth links every human being intrinsically.

1894) The ultimate goal of healthcare, therefore, is to strive to recreate (to the most practical extent) God's health plan for humanity through a healthy environment, relatively free of harmful chemical agents.

1895) One might postulate that every life–saving breadth of air that we inhale makes us less healthy. We can all agree that the air that encapsulates the earth is impaired.

1896) The capacity to maintain the purity of the atmosphere that encapsulates the earth is a monumental task, perhaps even impossible, challenge to nations because every action we take, it seems that we counteract our own actions by our demands for a life of abundance.

1897) The triumph of human beings over the earth and the sea confirms that God also provided us with the intellectual capacity to have some control over our environment for our benefit.

1898) The human brain, a creation of God, is even more complex. Despite our creations, our potential falls short because we are less than our Creator, though human beings possess the capacity for spiritual intelligence.

1899) Health care awareness is not restricted to the concerns of the individual, but of the community, the corporation, the national economy, and the international community.

1900) Environmentalists tell us that airborne microscopic particles can travel great distances. They also tell us that mass travel can bring communicable diseases to parts of the world within hours.

1901) Diseases can be communicated through humans, animals, or food sources. HIV/AIDS is the most alarming recent example of a disease that has established global transmission patterns through human interactions.

1902) Disease containment in the modern era has taken on global proportions. As human beings traverse the globe and settle in various parts of the world, nations will become less homogeneous.

1903) The scientific community is at an important crossroads in terms of understanding human health from geographic, cultural, environmental, and demographic differentiation.

1904) One can hypothesize that as nations in the global village become less homogeneous, the capacity to analyze demographic patterns of human health in the global village will likewise diminish for medical scientists.

1905) Developed nations are very cautious of the emerging health burden that looms in the future. The national scope of this financial and medical burden, if it remains unmanaged, will soon become a significant funding crisis.

1906) The medical crisis stage will bring greater significance to the oneness of humanity, as the cost of disease prevention, containment, and treatment place a burden on the world's financial and human resources, including the emotional cost to individuals and families.

1907) God's health perspective begins with His marvelous gift of free will. Our desire for freedom is part of our natural inclination. This freedom, however, is a double–edged sword.

1908) We are free to make choices that produce healthy and wholesome lives; conversely, we can make unhealthy choices that diminish the value of life, health, peace, happiness, beauty, and vitality.

1909) When we become ill, suddenly or progressively, we become vulnerable, because of spiritual, mental, and physical weaknesses that often overcome us. When we lose our physical health, it can have either a positive or negative impact on our spiritual health.

1910) Many who have been stricken with catastrophic illnesses will agree that there are intrinsic links among spiritual, mental, and physical health states.

1911) When our spiritual health fails, there is likelihood that all other aspects of our being will be affected.

1912) Many Christians testify to their miraculous healing because of their faith in God. They rely on His Word to comfort them through sickness and despair (James 5:13–15 NKJV) (circa CE 45).

1913) Despite our faith in modern medicines, and in the capacity of surgeons to perform mind–boggling surgical procedures, some medical practitioners are becoming interested in the healing power of prayer as an adjunct to the healing process.

1914) Some hospitals have Bibles for those who desire to meditate on God's Word. However, lack of healing does not mean lack of faith or lack of God's intervention. Ultimately, it is God's will that we must accept for our lives.

1915) Suffering often jolts us into a search for God. This search includes faith in God and hope in our surgeons. For some, faith in surgeons comes before faith in God, but God guides the hands of surgeons.

1916) Many of us, especially in our youth, perceive ourselves as invulnerable. We disregard the advice of parents, family members, elders, and perhaps even of doctors.

1917) We abuse our bodies, oblivious to the realities of aging and of the long–term effects of smoking, excessive drinking, poor diet and general stressful living.

1918) Often we blame God for our suffering; we may also blame others, and some of us blame ourselves for our uncontrolled compulsions.

1919) Evidently, some human beings have strong immune systems that can withstand the bombardment of some chemicals in the environment and of the harmful effects of smoking cigarettes and other carcinogenic substances, but these are not reasons to abuse our bodies.

1920) Medical scientists have made great progress in cancer research, detection, treatment, and prevention, but once the disease strikes, fear reverberates through the family, while on the national level, the disease continues to have an aggregate impact on the economy (Reference: *Five Foundations of Human Development* (FFHD) —Figure 36: Five Aggregate Health Care Impacts).

1921) Despite treatment regimens, the physical, psychological, and financial burdens and suffering become real. This leads us to one conclusion: prevention and early detection.

1922) Prevention measures are twofold. First, we must prevent degradation of the integrity of the environment, and second, we must take proactive care of our health. It seems simple enough, but to practice such measures requires both personal discipline underpinned by national healthcare policies.

1923) Nations can derive significant health–care medical and economic benefits when they initiate health care education at an early stage, beginning in kindergarten and continuing from there.

1924) Health–care is proactive and ought to have a different set of directives than sick–care, which is re–active care.

1925) A focus on health care education from five to eighteen years of age will establish patterns of behavior in our young adults that will lessen the need for great healthcare expenditures in later years.

1926) General healthcare and nutrition education should be made mandatory, at a suitable level of sophistication to engage students intellectually.

1927) The cumulative impacts of health care cost to the economy should heighten our resolve to declare health care an individual, national, and international priority and emergency.

1928) Boards of Education (BOE) should elevate health care education to the top of the education "pyramid of priorities" along with English, mathematics, and science.

1929) The extension of healthcare education from kindergarten to high–school graduation could result in future savings to nations—potentially billions of dollars in future savings that governments could redirect to more productive pursuits in medical care research.

1930) Nations should consider national and international competitions in healthcare and knowledge of the environment, similar to yearly national and international spelling bee competitions.

1931) A graduating student should be required to earn a mandatory credit in healthcare and environmental studies.

1932) Western nations have, arguably, one of the best general healthcare systems in the world for the medical protection for their citizens, and we should be thankful that Western governments place the healthcare of its citizens at a high priority.

1933) Notwithstanding, medical news reports tell us that we are not immune to emerging medical crises or to the potential for a major pandemic reminiscent of worldwide pandemics of past centuries.

1934) Our twenty–first century is one of medical and scientific breakthroughs. The medical community also alerts us to rising costs of treatment of illnesses, incidences of common diseases, and maintenance of various forms of universal healthcare provisions.

1935) Many in the nations are fearful of medical care crises and of national financial burdens of aging populations. Modern societies should be healthier with a diminishing healthcare burden.

1936) With great expenditures of billions of dollars in medical research, in longevity through modern technology, in new medical discoveries, and in new drugs for common illnesses, can we avert a health care crisis by adopting additional approaches?

1937) Could there be a point of diminishing healthcare return for our expenditures of health care dollars? In every human endeavor there is a point of diminishing returns.

1938) Is there a need for a major "conscription" of pre–teens, teen–agers, youths, adults, and the aged in the war on healthcare expenditures? Most would agree with the value of such a proactive response to rising health care expenditures.

1939) Despite new drug research and the constant stream of new drugs for every ailment, talks of losing the war on national and international health care resonate in the air waves.

1940) The elderly and those approaching middle age are becoming increasingly fearful about their health care future, even if they exercise regularly and take care of their health.

1941) Our multigenerational society differs greatly from the past, in which family members shared a more interdependent lifestyle and cared for older parents.

1942) The proliferation of homes for the elderly in every major city and town helps to facilitate the independent lifestyles of children who seek greater freedom from responsibility for their elderly parents.

1943) The aged in nations throughout the world face different degrees of abandonment as the young struggle for their own survival in our fast–paced societies.

1944) The world could face a catastrophic healthcare crisis as the world population increases and as the health care vulnerability index increases among the aged.

1945) With world population projected to be approximately 9.0 billion in the next fifty–five years, it is only by our immediate national and international policy interventions that nations can hope to prevent a collapse of our health care economies.

1946) We are thankful for the genius of biomedical solutions, but our modern lifestyles are counteracting the great benefits of modern medicine by inflicting incalculable harm to our bodies.

1947) Can our pharmaceutical industries, with our great genius in the production of modern medicines, bio–medically win the battle over human illness?

1948) National and International health organizations warn us of the catastrophic impacts of communicable diseases, such as HIV/AIDS and flu pandemics.

1949)   Medical practitioners also warn us about the health effects of some nutrient–deficient foods and about the need to meet daily intake levels of nutritious foods to sustain our health.

1950)   Future generations will ask: Why did they mortgage our future with such enormous medical care debt? Why did they not preserve the integrity of basic foods, clean air, and life–giving waters?

1951)   Can we continue to look to science and faith healing for miraculous spiritual and medical solutions (though they are actual aids) to human–inspired medical catastrophes in light of the foregoing arguments?

1952)   We must begin immediately to reverse the trend toward a monumental health care burden and toward global health deterioration, but we must first recognize that the source of our health goes beyond bio–medical cures.

1953)   Our healthcare visionaries could stress the need for personal healthcare accountability. Governments could enlist every citizen in the war against rising healthcare costs.

1954)   Governments should mobilize the youngest students and move along a path through high schools, colleges, universities, corporations, and private and public organizations and institutions.

1955)   Governments should establish a broad health care mandate that takes into consideration, spiritual, social, economic, and environmental health, as well as biological, mental, and physical health, as well.

FOUNDATION 5
PHYSICAL FOUNDATION
—5.2. CATASTROPHIC DISEASES

"I know that my Redeemer lives, and that in the
end He will stand upon the earth. And after my
skin has been destroyed, yet in my flesh I will see
God; I myself will see Him with my own eyes — I,
and not another. How my heart yearns within me!"

Job 19:25–27 (NIV)

Authors' Remarks: This discourse is intended as a means of offering
another perspective regarding human health. It is not intended as a
diagnostic tool or offering health advice. Always seek the advice of your
physician or other registered health professional with any questions
regarding your health. Furthermore, with each passing year, medical
research provides us with additional information that enhances our
understanding of symptoms, diagnosis, treatment, and cures of
diseases. Therefore, you should contact the appropriate agency or
organization for their latest research and publication of any article
cited in this text, for general information only.

1956) **What is disease?** The authors' non–medical definition is this: a
condition that affects the human body and impairs the regular
normal functioning of the body.

1957) It might be said that the physical foundation is the least of the five
foundations of human development in terms of glorifying our
Creator.

1958) Its importance arises when one considers that ill health or critical
illness can have a significant impact on one's spiritual, social,
emotional, and physical well being.

1959) We might contemplate ill health, especially when we interact
with someone who is critically ill, but can we anticipate how we
will respond if we are struck by critical illness?

1960) Medical research provides us with information to enhance our
understanding of symptoms, diagnoses, treatments, and cures of
diseases. Can nations eradicate disease?

1961)   Modern medicines have all but eradicated and brought under control smallpox, the bubonic plague, yellow fever, and even polio (poliomyelitis).

1962)   Unquestionably, medical scientists and doctors have made remarkable progress in the fight against disease, but new diseases such as HIV/AIDS have emerged on the human landscape to take their toll in human suffering and death. This emerging health care dilemma poses a threat to the cost of healthcare in developed, developing, and developed nations.

1963)   Common diseases, such as cancer in its many varieties, heart disease, and diabetes continue to strike fear in many who are afflicted or who have a family history of the disease.

1964)   Unquestionably, medical scientists and doctors have made remarkable progress in the fight against disease.

1965)   The developments of X-ray techniques, new surgical techniques, and wonder drugs have given modern medicine mastery over diseases that have afflicted human beings for centuries.

1966)   Some nations have eradicated *some* diseases, but the same diseases appear on the scene in other nations that are ill-equipped to deal with them.

1967)   The more important question might be whether nations can eradicate the *causes* of disease. This is the monumental challenge to healthcare organizations throughout the world.

1968)   Diseases have fundamentally shaped the fate of humanity, but the goal of eradicating disease has always been unreachable by human intervention.

1969)   Modern physicians have had great success with the aid of modern science and lessons learned from the study of diseases of past decades.

1970)   Eradication of common diseases and sickness and increasing longevity through modern medicine gives great hope to humanity.

1971)   Scientists hold out hope for mastery over diseases through research such as the Genome Project, which will allow them to identify the defective genes responsible for perhaps four thousand known human genetic diseases that scientists have identified. Scientists claim that someday we will have access to our own genome. (http://www.ncbi.nlm.nih.gov/sites/entrez?db=genomeprj)

1972) Scientific understanding, intellectual observation, and personal experience teach us that our environment has an impact on our health.

1973) The ultimate battle is to gain mastery of the environment in order to regain control of our health, and to create a relatively disease–free world. Is it possible?

1974) With scientific knowledge expanding with each passing decade, scientific research organizations spend billions of dollars in research with the confidence that they are getting ever closer to a solution to many of our common diseases.

1975) Despite great medical efforts, human beings are incapable of creating a disease–free human body, because the human body is the effect, and not the cause or the source of the disease.

1976) Impairment of the human body is a symptom of something greater that is causing human illnesses. Our physical and biological environments, our social environment, and our natural vulnerability to illness act in opposition to all of our great medical genius.

1977) Centuries of scientific research demonstrate that we are capable of eradicating some diseases. Medical scientists tell us that over the centuries, as they have deployed the tools of scientific research to achieve control over one disease, another more formidable disease has surfaced, even a mutant variety.

1978) The past century has seen great medical discoveries, such as penicillin (1929), which was the magic bullet against pneumonia, syphilis, gonorrhea, diphtheria and scarlet fever, but will not stop the HIV/AIDS virus that presently threatens continents.

1979) The indiscriminating nature of the HIV/AIDS epidemic challenges our national and international will and medical resolve.

FOUNDATION 5
PHYSICAL FOUNDATION
— 5.3. PHYSICAL HEALTH

"Then your light will break forth like the dawn,
and your healing will quickly appear; then your
righteousness will go before you, and the glory of
the Lord will be your rear guard. Then you will
call, and the Lord will answer; you will cry for
help and he wills: Here am I."

Isaiah 58:8–9 (NIV)

Authors' Remarks: This discourse is intended as a means of offering another perspective regarding human health. It is not intended as a diagnostic tool or offering health advice. Always seek the advice of your physician or other registered health professional with any questions regarding your health. Furthermore, with each passing year, medical research provides us with additional information that enhances our understanding of symptoms, diagnosis, treatment, and cures of diseases. Therefore, you should contact the appropriate agency or organization for their latest research and publication of any article cited in this text, for general information only.

1980) **What is physical health?** Nations' healthcare expenditures equate to billions of dollars spent in an effort to find cures for illness.

1981) Health watch organizations tell us that physical neglect, poor food choices, and insufficient rest, relaxation, and exercise can have negative effects on human health.

1982) The medical community advises us that regular physical exercise can lower the incidence of heart disease, stress, diabetes, and arthritis and contribute to our general well–being.

1983) Medical advisors encourage us to eat balanced meals that include all of the four requisite food groups. Medical reports tell us that smoking impairs good health. They warn the public about alcohol use and health.

1984) Medical advisors tell us to be active, walk, jog, swim, lift weights, and do aerobics. Television commercials and infomercials bombard us with diet programs and weight reduction programs, exercise books and exercise equipment, from full body workout machines to equipment that targets specific body parts.

1985)   Today there is great awareness of the need for physical health. All of the major television news programs have a health advisory as an integral component of their news reporting, and they provide the vital service of informing us of trends in health matters.

1986)   Despite all of the scientific benefits of physical exercise, generally gaps still remain between our understanding of the need for physical exercise and its great benefits for our physical well–being.

1987)   Despite the great benefits of exercise, we have still added to our health legacy many diseases that physical exercise, among other health regimens, can help to reduce.

1988)   We have added to our list of advanced societal maladies significant incidences of ills such as high blood pressure, diabetes, high cholesterol, heart diseases, and emotional concerns.

1989)   Interestingly, the health and beauty industry seem to work very closely with the fitness industry. The demand for beautiful and healthy looking bodies seems to permeate every aspect of our lives.

1990)   While on one end of the human health spectrum, billions of dollars fuel wellness and physical beauty, on the other end, medical reports tell us that there is a growing problem with overweight children.

1991)   From grocery store magazine racks to Internet websites, beauty and healthcare articles offer us volumes of information on beauty, weight loss, and wellness.

1992)   The public and private sectors have done a remarkable job promoting physical and nutritional health education through medical research, food processing, packaging, labeling, and product marketing.

1993)   The twenty–first century has ushered in great opportunities for individuals and families to educate themselves on health and nutrition. Food information is available to us from libraries, doctors' offices, local pharmacies, and the Internet.

1994)   Several generations ago, families rarely ever thought of their food as being harmful to their health. Food consumption was generally close to the source of production.

1995) In many cases, families produced some of their foods on the family farm, in the backyard garden, and even in kitchen gardens. More importantly, the production of food was generally free of the chemicals that are presently applied to fruits, vegetables and even animal sources of food.

1996) Today food can be transported thousands of miles before it gets to our tables. A primary benefit of foods of past generations was that they were generally unrefined and rarely processed.

1997) The family bought and consumed many foods daily. The family focus was on fresh foods. Meat sources came from animals that grazed in open fields. Families were generally healthier, and rarely questioned the nutritional value of the foods they ate.

1998) Parents' intuitive knowledge of what was good for the family preceded the vast knowledge of food science, labeling, and calorie counting of today.

1999) Babies generally benefited from the most important source of natural food the Creator provided for their early physical development. Our mothers' rich incomparable source of nutrition promoted healthy growth and development.

2000) Health advisors tell us that mothers' rich milk is essential for childhood development in the early stages of a child's life. Today we have supplanted and supplemented God's source of basic nutrients with *our* plan for the essential early growth of the child.

2001) When we make the right choices and care for ourselves, our minds, and our bodies, we can begin relationships from a position of strength — the strength of righteous living and self-direction. Only then do we bring with us the tools to improve our relationships with others and with God.

APPENDIXES

SELECT BIBLIOGRAPHY

The authors' bibliography sets out a sampling of books read as stimulants to thought over several years. The nature of their discourse obliges them to recognize those who have made contributions in many specialized areas that they have merely touched upon. The list includes many diverse works in the fields of religion, philosophy, psychology, business, management, and other academic theses. Despite this diversity of opinions, the authors respect the contributors to the vast pool of human knowledge.

A

Adler, Mortimer J. *Six Great Ideas.* New York, New York: A Touchstone Book Published by Simon & Schuster, 1981.

Anderson, Greg. *The 22 {Non-Negotiable} Laws of Wellness (Feel, Think, and Live Better Than You Ever Thought Possible).* New York, New York: HarperCollins Publishers, 1995.

Anderson, Ken. *Bible-Based Prayer Power (Using Relevant Scriptures to Pray with Confidence for All Your Needs).* Nashville, Tennessee: Thomas Nelson Publishers, 2000.

Angelo, Maya. *Even The Stars Look Lonesome.* New York, New York: Random House, 1997.

Ankerberg, John & Weldon, John. *The Facts on World Religions.* Eugene Oregon: Harvest House Publishers, 2004.

Arrington French L. *Christian Doctrine: A Pentecostal Perspective,* Volume One. Cleveland, Tennessee: Pathway Press, 1992.

Aultman, Donald S. (Editor), Contributors: Conn, Paul; Fisher, Robert W.; Goff, Doyle and Hammond, Jerome. *Understanding Yourself and Others.* Cleveland, Tennessee: Pathway Press 2001.

B

Bachrach, Peter & Baratz, Morton S. *Power & Poverty – Theory & Practice.* New York · London · Toronto: Oxford University Press, 1970.

Barna, George. *Leaders On Leadership (Wisdom, Advice and Encouragement on the Art of Leading God's People).* Ventura, California: Regal Books – A Division of Gospel Light, 1997.

Barna, George. *A Fish Out of Water (9 Strategies to Maximize your God –Given Leadership Potential).* Brentwood, Tennessee: Integrity Publishers, A Division of Integrity Media, Inc., 2002.

Billson, Mancini Janet. *Keepers of the Culture (The Power of Tradition in Women's Lives).* New York, New York: Lexington Books, 1995.

Böckle, Franz. *Moral Theology – War Poverty Freedom (The Christian Response)*. New York, New York/Glen Rock, N.J.: Paulist Press, 1966.

Brooks, Keith L. *Ephesians – The Epistle of Christian Maturity*. Printed in the USA: The Moody Bible Institute of Chicago, 1964. *[One in a series of Bible Study Course Books]*

Buxton, Clyne., W. *END TIMES (A Biblical Study of Current and Future Events)*, Cleveland Tennessee, Pathway Press, 1993.

C

Chambers, Oswald. *The Highest Good (The Born–Again Christian Sees Things From An Entirely New Perspective)*. London, England: Oswald Chambers Publications Association, 1976.

Collins, Gary R. Ph.D., *Christian Counseling (A Comprehensive Guide)*. Waco, Texas: Word Books Publisher, 1980.

Colson, Charles *Who Speaks for God? (Confronting the World With Real Christianity)*. Westchester, Illinois, Crossway Books, a division of Good News Publishers. 1985.

Conn, Charles W. *The Living Book (A Disciple's Guide to understanding the Bible)*, Cleveland, Tennessee: Pathway Press, 1989.

Covey, Stephen R. *The Seven Habits of Highly Effective People (Powerful Lessons in Personal Change)*. New York, New York: Simon & Schuster, 1989.

Cummings, Milton C. Jr. and Wise, David. *Democracy Under Pressure (An Introduction to the American Political System)* (Seventh Edition). Orlando, Florida: Harcourt Brace Jovanovich, Inc., 1993.

D

Datta, Dhirendra Mohan. *The Philosophy of Mahatma Gandhi*. Madison, Wisconsin: The University of Wisconsin Press, 1953.

Dawood, N. J. *The KORAN*. Middlesex, England: Penguin Books, 1956.

Desai, Mahadev. *M. K. Gandhi An Autobiography or The Story of My Experiments with Truth*. New York, New York: Penguin Books, 1927.

Dillenberger, John (Editor). *Martin Luther: Selections from His Writings*. New York, New York: Doubleday, 1961.

Diop, Cheikh Anta. *The African Origin of Civilization (Myth or Reality)*. Westport, Connecticut: Lawrence Hill & Co., Publishers, Inc., 1974.

Dobson, James Dr., and Bauer, Garry L. *Children at Risk (The Battle for the Heart and Minds of Our Kids)*. Dallas · London ·Vancouver · Melbourne: Word Publishing, 1990.

Dobson, James Dr., *The New Dare To Discipline.* Wheaton, Illinois: Tyndale House Publishers, Inc., 1870, 1992.

Dockery, David S. *The Challenge of Postmodernism* (Second Edition). Grand Rapids, Michigan: Baker Academic a division of Baker House Company, 1995, 2001.

E

Earhart, Byron. *Religious Traditions of the World,* New York, New York: HarperSanFranciso, 1993.

Eichler, Margrit. *Families in Canada Today (Recent Changes and Their Policy Consequences).* Toronto, Ontario, Canada: Gage Publishing Limited, 1983.

Epp, Theodore H. *The Times of the Gentiles.* Lincoln, Nebraska: Back to the Bible, 1968.

Every, George. *Christian Mythology.* Middlesex, England: The Hamyln Publishing Group Limited, 1970, 1987.

F

Foner, Philip S. and Du Bois, Shirley Graham. *W.E.B. Speaks Speeches and Addresses 1920–1963.* New York · London · Sydney · Toronto: Pathfinder, 1970.

Ford, Leighton. *Transforming Leadership (Jesus' Way of Creating Vision, Shaping Values & Empowering Change).* Downers Grove, Illinois: InterVarsity Press, 1991.

Fox, Emmet. *Find and Use Your Inner Power.* New York, New York: HarperSanFrancisco, 1937.

Fox, Emmet. *The Sermon on the Mount.* New York, New York: HarperSanFrancisco, 1934.

Freud, Sigmund. *Civilization and its Discontents.* New York, New York: W. W. Norton & Company, Inc., 1961.

G

George, Bill. *What God Expects of Me (First Steps for New Christians).* Cleveland, Tennessee: Pathway Press, 1982.

Getz, Gene A. *The Measure of A Church.* Glendale, California: Regal Books Division, G/L Publications, 1975.

Gilbert, Elizabeth, Eat, Pray, Love (A Woman's Search for Everything Penguin Books 2008 Italy, India and Indonesia). New York, New York:

Goodman, S.F. *The European Community.* London, England: MacMillian Education Ltd, 1990.

H

Haywood, Dale M. ; Nash, Timothy G. and Amin, R. John. *When We Are Free* (Third Edition). Midland, Michigan: Northwood Institute Press 1981.

Hendricks, Howard G. *Teaching to Change Lives.* Portland, Oregon: Multnomah Press, 1987.

Hill, V.E (Edward Victor). *A Savior Worth Having* (Foreword by Joseph M. Stowell). Moody Bible Institute of Chicago, 1962.

Hughes, Ray H. *Church of God Distinctives.* Cleveland, Tennessee: Pathway Press, 1968. Revised Edition, 1989.

Hüng, Hans. *Does God Exist (An Answer for Today).* Garden City, New York: Doubleday & Company, 1980.

Hunter III, George. G. *Church for the Unchurched.* Nashville, Tennessee: Abingdon Press, 1996.

I

Inch, Morris, A. *My Servant Job (A Discussion Guide on the Wisdom of Job).* Grand Rapids, Michigan: Baker Book House, 1979.

J

Jakes, T.D. *Woman Thou Art Loosed! (Healing the Wounds of the Past).* Shhippensburg, PA: Destiny Image Publishers. 1993

Johnstone, Patrick. *Operation World (The Day–to–Day Guide To Praying For the World).* Cleveland, Tennessee: Zondervan Publishing House, 1983.

K

King, Martin Luther Jr., *Why We Can't Wait.* New York, New York: Signet, Signet Classics, Signette, Mentor and Plume Books, 1963, 1964.

Kinney, Charles. *Living for God.* New Kensington, PA: Whitaker House, 1985.

Krishnamurti, R. J. *Talks and Dialogues* (The Intelligence That Transcends Thought). New York, New York: Avon Books, 1968.

L

LaHaye, Tim. *The Battle for the Public Schools (Humanism's Threat to our Children).* Old Tappan, New Jersey: Fleming H. Revell Company, 1983.

Lane, Tony P. *Changing Ministry in Changing Times.* Cleveland, Tennessee: Pathway Press, 2000.

Lewis, C. S. *Mere Christianity.* New York, New York: Macmillan Publishing Company, 1943.

Lotz, Anne Graham. *God's Story (Finding Meaning for Your Life through Knowing God).* Nashville Tennessee: WORD PUBLISHING, 1997, 1999.

Lucado, Max. *Give it All to Him (A Story of New Beginnings)*. Nashville, Tennessee: W Publishing Group, A Division of Thomas Nelson, Inc., 2004.

M

Maxwell, John C. *Developing The Leader Within You*. Nashville, Tennessee: Thomas Nelson, Inc., 1993.

Maxwell, John C. and Dornan, Jim. *Becoming A Person of Influence (How to Positively Impact the Lives of Others)*. Nashville, Tennessee: Thomas Nelson, Inc., 1997.

McCann, Richard V. *The Churches and Mental Health (Monograph Series No. 8. Joint Commission on Mental Illness and Health)*. New York, New York: Basic Books, Inc., 1962.

Macpherson, Crawford B. *The Real World of Democracy (The Massey, Lectures Fourth Series)*. Toronto, Ontario: CBC Merchandizing, 1965.

McDowell, Josh & Hostetler, Bob. *Right from Wrong. (What you need to know to help youths make right choices)*, USA: WORD PUBLISHING, 1994.

McDowell, Josh. *Reasons Skeptics should Consider Christianity*. Wheaton Illinois: Living Books – Tyndale House Publishers, Inc., 1981.

Mears, Henrietta C. *What the BIBLE is All About* (Foreword by Billy Graham). Ventura, California: Regal Books, A division of Gospel Light, 1983.

Mitchell, Roger & Sue. *Target Europe (Interpreting the Times and Seasons of God's Kingdom in the Lands and Islands of Europe and the Challenge for Today!)*. Kent, England: Sovereign World Ltd, 2001.

Moore, Thomas. *Care of the Soul (A Guide for Cultivating Depth and Sacredness in Everyday Life)*. New York, New York: HarperPerennial –A division of HarperCollins Publishers, 1992.

Morris, Charles G. and Maisto, Albert A. *Psychology An Introduction* Tenth Edition (Study Guide Joyce Bishop), Upper Saddle River, New Jersey: Prentice–Hall Inc., 1999.

Murray, Andrew. *Humility*. New Kensington, PA: Whitaker House, 1982.

N

Nehil, Thomas E. *A Cultural Guide to the Global Village*. Midland, Michigan: Simon & Schuster Custom Publishing, 1997.

P

Parrinder, Geoffrey. *World Religions (From Ancient History to the Present)*. New York, New York: The Hamlyn Publishing Group Limited, 1971.

Paul, John II. *Crossing The Threshold of Hope.* Toronto, Ontario, Canada: Alfred A. Knopf Canada, 1994.

Peale, Stafford Ruth. *A Lifetime of Positive Thinking.* Pawling, New York: Guideposts, 2001.

Peters, Tom and Austin, Nancy. *A Passion For Excellence (The Leadership Difference).* New York, New York: Warner Books, 1985.

Phillips, Michael. *God A Good Father (On the Intimate Mysteries of God's Fatherhood).* Shippensburg, PA: Destiny Image ® Publishers, Inc., 2001.

Porter, John. *The Vertical Mosaic.* © University of Toronto Press 1965, Toronto and Buffalo, Thirteenth Printing. 1977.

Pritchett, Price. *New World Habits For A Radically Changing World (13 Ground Rules for Job Success in the Information Age).* Dallas, Texas: Pritchett, 2008.

Pritchett, Price. *During unrelenting High-pressure Change (Business as Unusual).* Dallas, Texas: Pritchett, 2009.

R

Rea, Homer G. (Editor), Contributors: Vest, Lamar; George, Bill; Byrd, Joe and Roebuck, David G. *Knowing Your Church.* Cleveland, Tennessee: Pathway Press, 2001.

Reese, Edward. *The Reese Chronological Bible.* (King James Version) Minneapolis, Minnesota: Bethany House Publishers, Copyright ©1977. Edward Reese, Dating System Copyright ©1975 Frank R. Klassen.

Rolls, Charles J. *The Indescribable Christ (Names and Titles of Jesus Christ A-G).* Neptune, New Jersey: Loizeaux Brothers, Inc., 1983.

Rose, Jerry D. *Introduction to Sociology* (Third Edition). Fredonia, New York: Rand Mc Nally College Publishing Company, 1976.

Rourke, John T. *Taking Sides (Clashing Views on Controversial Issues in World Politics* (Eight Edition). Guiford, Connecticut: Duskin/ McGraw-Hill A division of McGraw-Hill Companies, Inc., 1998.

S

Sheenan, James, *The Law of Second Chances.* New York, New York: St Martin's Press, 2008

Sherratt, Timothy R. & Mahurin, Ronald, P. *Saints as Citizens (A Guide to Public Responsibilities for Christians).* Grand Rapids, Michigan: Baker Books, 1995.

Smalley, Gary. *Hidden Keys of a Loving Lasting Marriage.* Grand Rapids, Michigan: Zondervan Publishing House, 1984, 1988.

Sproul, RC. *One Holy Passion (The Attributes of God)*, Nashville, Tennessee: Thomas Nelson Inc., 1987.

Strong, James, L.LD., S.T.D., *The New Strong's Exhaustive* Concordance of the Bible, Nashville, Tennessee: Thomas Nelson Publishers, 1990.

Sweeting, George. *How to Discover the Will of God*. Chicago, USA: The Moody Bible Institute of Chicago, 1975.

Swindoll, Charles R. *Strengthening Your Grip*. Waco, Texas: Word Books Publisher, 1982.

T

Taylor, Susan L. *(Author of In the Spirit)*. *Lessons in Living*. New York, New York: An Anchor Book – Published by Doubleday, 1995.

Thurman, L. Duane. *How to Think about Evolution & Other Biblical Science Controversies*. Downers Grove, Illinois: InterVarsity Press, 1977.

Trudeau, Kevin. *Natural Cures" They" Don't Want You to Know About*. Elk Groove Village, Illinois. Alliance Publishing Group, Inc. 2004Twenge, Jean M. *Generation Me*. New York, New York: FREE PRESS, a division of Simon & Shuster, Inc., 2006

Twenge, Jean M. *Generation Me*. New York, New York: FREE PRESS, a division of Simon & Shuster, Inc., 2006

U

Underwood, B.E. *Spiritual Gifts (Ministries and Manifestations)*. Franklin Springs, Georgia: Advocate Press, 1984.

V

Vanzant, Iyanla. *One Day My Soul Just Opened Up (40 Days and 40 Nights Toward Spiritual Strength and Personal Growth)*. New York, New York: Simon & Schuster Inc., 1998.

Vanzant, Iyanla (Author of in the Meantime). *Until Today (Daily Devotions for Spiritual Growth and Peace of Mind)*. New York, New York: Simon & Schuster, 2000.

W

Weaver, Grady Henry. *The Mainspring of Human Progress*. Irvington–on–Hudson, New York: The Foundation of Economic Education, Inc. 1997.

Warren, Rick. *The Purpose Driven Life (What on Earth I am doing here)*. Grand Rapids, Michigan: Zordervan, 2002

White, Ellen G. *The Great Controversy*. Pacific Press® Publishing Association. Nampa, Idaho; Oshawa, Ontario, Canada, 1990.

Wilkerson, David. *God's Plan (To Protect His People) in the Coming Depression.* Lindale, Texas: Wilkerson Trust Publications, 1998.

Williams, Eric. *Capitalism and Slavery* (Introduction by D. W. Brogan) London, England: Andre Deutsch Limited, 1944.

Williams, Eric. *From Columbus to Castro (The History of the Caribbean).* New York, New York: Vintage Books a Division of Random House. 1984. Originally Published by Andre Deutsch Limited, London, England in 1970.

Y

Yancey, Philip. *Disappointment With God (Three questions no one asks aloud),* Grand Rapids, Michigan: Zondervan Publishing House, 1988.

Yogananda, Paramahansa. *Where There Is Light.* Los Angeles, California: Self Realization Fellowship, 1988.

Z

Zacharias, Ravi. *Can Man Live Without God* (Foreword by Charles Colson). Dallas · London · Vancouver · Melborne: WORD PUBLISHING 1994.

Ziglar, Zig. *Confessions of a Happy Christian.* Gretna, Louisiana: Pelican Publishing Company, 1978.

EPILOGUE

We have chronicled *Thoughts to Enlighten and Empower the Mind* to present an alternate perspective from which to engage in discussions of human development in our modern era. In this innovative *"Reading by versus"* format of our main text *Five Foundations of Human Development* (FFHD), we present you with our deep concern for the plight of humanity in our modern age, and the stark evidence of greater challenges on the horizon. We put forward these 2001 questions and philosophical thoughts —a Biblical potion for the chronic ills assailing modern man. Though we may never meet in person, we can mutually agree in our spirits that there is a need for a revolution of our thoughts.

We recognize the challenges that many throughout the world face in their daily struggle for fulfilled living. The book resonates with a recurring message that history repeats itself. The threats of war, hunger, poverty, and natural and man-made disasters are ever present, and underpin our mortal fears. Our past is full of practical demonstrations of the futility of self–reliance to the exclusion of God. Every nation, every society in history, has known that its knowledge was incomplete, as we know today; despite the advancements of human knowledge, science and technology, and great material wealth built up over the centuries.

The scientist, the doctor, the nurse, the lawyer, the engineer, the professor, the politician, the philosopher, and the ordinary person, feel a dual sense of hopefulness and hopelessness. Whether the model is a rural farming village or the global village, the foundation of hope is crumbling. You have discovered that we wrote this book to offer a view of the world through a different set of lenses; not merely to pan the horizon with fear of emerging crisis informed by our observations and the mass media, but with hope for a better world through a revolution of our thoughts.

We urge you now, not to dismiss the power of these 2001 questions and philosophical thoughts as "mere idealism." The unquenchable light of idealism lives within and underpins our hope for survival in the twenty–first century and in the new millennium. You must now engage in the global struggle to create a better world. This struggle requires a new *blueprint of hope* for our survival. It begins with an understanding that only God knows all, and only through God can we hope to achieve our full potential for enlightenment and empowerment of the mind. These 2001 Thoughts only scratch the surface of the knowledge that is available to enlighten and empower the mind.

BIOGRAPHY OF ERROL A. GIBBS

Errol was born in the Republic of Trinidad and Tobago, West Indies, where he lived until his mid–20s. He also lived in the United States and Canada. He currently resides in Milton, Ontario, Canada, with his wife Marjorie. Errol was fourteen years old when his father died in a catastrophic accident. The preceding years instilled in him an understanding of the multiple dimensions of human suffering and the need for empathy on the journey from childhood to adulthood. He is a devout Christian who strives daily for congruity of faith, belief, and practice in every human endeavor. Errol made a commitment to the faith in 1982 and was baptized in May 1983. Thus began his journey from baptism (*an event*) to his transformation (*a process*).

In 2002, Errol was awakened to a higher calling than his career and material rewards it afforded him, not primarily due to impending surgery after a diagnosis of prostate cancer, but from the discovery of purpose — of filling emptiness. *Five Foundations of Human Development* (FFHD) was conceived during this awakening. Thus began extensive research and writing. Errol made an irreversible life–changing decision to relinquish his career in engineering project management, to commit his life to research for answers to human development. He believes that human beings are capable of making new history.

Errol is an intellectual observer of the phenomenon of life, with its myriad of religious, racial, cultural, political, social, and economic challenges that have taken on global implications in the twenty–first century. He studied and researched the Holy Bible for several years, for its basic 'Spiritual truths' and not as a purely theological study. His discourse on human development is underpinned by other great works of the past century; international travel, experiential knowledge, and motivational speaking engagements. His work transcends any underlying belief that human beings are incapable of making new and positive history, but the impetus lies in a revolution that must begin from within the human heart, rather than the head.

Errol has an advanced polytechnic background, primarily in the energy industry. This background is augmented by extensive continuing education, corporate, and professional development training. Errol is a certified Project Management Professional (PMP); a Certified Engineering Technologist (CET); and the holder of a Full Technological Certificate (Instrumentation Maintenance Technology). During his career, Errol has held positions such as: Sr. Engineering Technician, Scientific Technologist, Planning and Scheduling Engineer/Officer, Project Management Analyst, Sr. Process Designer, and Project Management and Business Consultant.

BIOGRAPHY OF PHILIP A. GREY

Philip Grey is an international evangelist, author, and motivational speaker. He was born in Leeds, Yorkshire, England (UK) where he lived until his mid-20s. Philip also lived in Liberia, West Africa for approximately three years, and in the United States of America for approximately nine years. Philip began ministerial work in the United States in 1976. He immigrated to Canada in 1992. He currently resides in Toronto, Ontario, Canada, with his wife Sandra and four children. In 1996, Philip embarked on global missions in an administrative capacity.

Philip has extensive travel, humanitarian, and missions experience in twenty-six countries, including the following: Belgium, Cameroon, Canada, China, England, Equatorial Guinea, France, Ghana, Holland, Hong Kong, India, Indonesia, Italy, Japan, Mexico, Singapore, Thailand, the United States of America, Wales, and West Germany. This extensive travel background has enabled him to observe, intellectually, and help to alleviate some of the myriad of challenges that millions face daily, throughout the globe. Philip's experiential background also enabled him to make a significant contribution to *Five Foundations of Human Development* (FFHD).

Philip has also observed, empirically, the challenges that confront leaders in politics and religion, and corporate, national, and international world leaders. From his vantage point, he endeavors to make a positive contribution to the vast pool of human knowledge for the management of God's creation and for the betterment of humanity. Philip currently serves with Christian Horizons, Ontario, Canada, a humanitarian organization whose focus is to improve living conditions, promote social awareness, provide education and training, and promotes greater opportunities for individuals with exceptional needs.

Philip has an extensive background in international ministerial research and practice. He has held positions from Youth Pastor to National World Missions Director with the Church of God. He has been a keynote speaker for national, international, and regional ecumenical and denominational conferences on several continents. He has served in various capacities, boards, and committees, which include Instructor for a Bible College and Educational Coordinator for an Ontario Pre-ministerial Training Program. Philip has served on an International Leadership Advance Conference Committee; a Regional Council for Ontario Churches, the Ontario Ministerial Development and Credentialing Board, and has been a member of the Board of Directors for the International Bible College (IBC), Moose Jaw, Saskatchewan, Western Canada.

CPSIA information can be obtained at www.ICGtesting.com
Printed in the USA
LVOW050658200612

286837LV00001B/13/P